Essentials
of
Public Speaking

Richard L. Weaver II
Bowling Green State University

GSP
Gorsuch Scarisbrick, Publishers
Scottsdale, Arizona

To Florence B. Weaver
With whom I first publicly communicated.

Publisher: Gay L. Pauley
Editor: A. Colette Kelly
Developmental Editor: Katie E. Bradford
Production Manager: Cynthia Lefton
Cover Design: Don Gianatti
Typesetting: ProType Graphics

Gorsuch Scarisbrick, Publishers
8233 Via Paseo del Norte, Suite F-400
Scottsdale, AZ 85258

10 9 8 7 6 5 4 3 2 1

ISBN 0-89787-358-0

Printed in the United States of America.

Brief Contents

Contents

Preface

Essentials of Public Speaking originated from a simple premise: the need for a brief public speaking textbook that would provide all the information students would need to prepare and present effective public speeches. I thought a short but complete book would allow students and instructors to focus on preparing and giving speeches rather than completing and discussing reading assignments. I also sought to write a book that students would enjoy reading and instructors would enjoy using—one that would be easy to read with interesting examples and strong visual appeal.

Essentials of Public Speaking is written for a course for those with no experience in public speaking. The book establishes a solid foundation for success, offers plenty of examples, and employs an informal and encouraging writing style. Divided into four parts, *Essentials of Public Speaking* covers "The Overall Perspective," "The Substance of the Speech," "Making the Presentation," and "Types of Presentations." I have included all the traditional public speaking chapters, but I have also emphasized areas where beginning speakers need special assistance: overcoming nervousness, finding originality and focus, and establishing credibility. I have encouraged readers to learn about their audience, to establish a solid knowledge base, to organize their presentations according to the type of speech they are developing, to use visual support when possible, and to deliver their speeches confidently and dynamically. *Essentials of Public Speaking* provides all the basics for public speakers to achieve effectiveness and success.

Each chapter begins with a list of chapter objectives. Within each chapter, a feature called *The Heart of the Matter* highlights information essential to the chapter. *The Heart of the Matter* can be used as a focal point for class discussion or as key organizing point for understanding. Chapters also include partial or complete student sample speeches, providing readers with opportunities to identify and critique the strengths and weaknesses of the various speeches. At the end of each chapter, an annotated list of suggested readings and review questions help the reader gain further understanding of the concepts discussed. Finally, *Words in Action* is a special feature that facilitates a case study approach to the videotape accompanying this textbook. By asking leading questions about the video segments for the chapters, this feature stimulates analysis and discussion of the content and delivery of the student and historic speeches presented. This process helps readers apply the concepts learned from the text to the video, reinforcing key chapter ideas. An added value of this feature is that it guides readers to see and understand how others struggle, succeed, or fail as they seek to put "Words in Action."

Finally, a personal note. After writing many books, being a public speaker for many years, and having a dozen of my speeches published, I wanted to return something to the profession I love and have learned from. I wanted to write the kind of book I wished I had when I began learning about public speaking. This is that book. And I hope that it brings you the same kind of challenge, interest, and inspiration that I have enjoyed in writing it.

ACKNOWLEDGMENTS

Although writing is a solitary act, I want to express appreciation to those who have had the greatest influence on the ideas in this book and thus were with me in spirit. First, the graduate teaching assistant at the University of Michigan who first introduced me to public speaking, Roger Sherman. I was fortunate to have Mr. Sherman in the Advanced Public Speaking class as well, and it was because of him that I pursued speech as a major, discipline, and profession. Although we have not maintained contact, I would like to take this opportunity to thank him for his knowledge and inspiration; this book would never have been written without his influence.

I want to thank William Norwood Brigance (who wrote the first public speaking textbook I read), Howard Martin, and Herb Hildebrandt, who built on the foundation at Michigan that Roger Sherman laid. I am indebted to J. Jeffery Auer, Robert Gunderson, and Raymond Smith at Indiana University for cementing my interest in the discipline and Karl Wallace, Ken Brown, Ron Reid, Jane Blankenship, Herm and Sara Stelzner, Malcolm Sillers, Vern Cronen, and Richard Conville at the University of Massachusetts for their knowledge and influence. Many thanks to Donald Klopf and Ron Cambra, University of Hawaii; Peter Putnis and Adam Shoemaker, Bond University in Australia; Bruce Molloy and Roslyn Petelin, Brisbane; Bill Ticehurst and Gael Walker, Rob Pascoe and Helen Borland, St. Albans (Melbourne); and Ray and Sheila Dallin, Western Australia University in Perth, Australia. I'd like to thank my colleagues at Bowling Green University: John Makay, Chair, Julie Burke, Donald Enholm, Al Gonzalez, Tina Harris, Ray Tucker, and Jim Wilcox for their understanding of my interest in writing textbooks. And thanks, too, to Howard Cotrell, who now has courtesy appointment at Bowling Green, for close to 20 years of sharing, writing, and solving the world's problems.

Thanks to my mother, Florence B. Weaver, who has been a continuing source of inspiration and motivation, as have my sisters, Margery F. Walker and Marilyn E. Hulett. Thanks also to Paull Walker. A special thanks to my wife, Andrea, to my supportive family—Scott, Jacquie, Anthony, and Joanna—and to my extended family members: David Smeltzer and Jeff Limes. You make it a joy to be alive.

I would like to thank the following reviewers for their pointed and meaningful comments: Timothy Sellnow, North Dakota State University; Stephen A. Bobek, Kirkwood Community College; Mary Hogg, Eastern Illinois University; and John Gregory, Pasadena City College. A special thanks to Denise Vrchota, Iowa State University, whose many constructive suggestions helped shape the final manuscript.

Finally, and perhaps most importantly, thank you to my good friends at Gorsuch Scarisbrick. A writer must write in tandem with knowledgeable and resourceful editors. Thank you to Gay Pauley, Publisher, Colette Kelly, Editor, Katie Bradford, Developmental Editor, and Cindy Lefton, Production Manager. You are professionals with whom I have had the pleasure of association. Thank you for your on-going assistance and encouragement.

Dick Weaver

PART 1

The Overall Perspective

Getting Started

After reading this chapter you will be able to:

- have both the motivation and interest to improve your public speaking skills
- understand the positive role that nervousness can play
- apply techniques for controlling your nervousness
- use the nine steps necessary for speech preparation

Learning how to speak effectively will equip you with *the* most effective success and leadership tool available. An effective public speaking book is not just about the techniques for preparing and presenting a good speech, however. It is also about making meetings more effective, creating stimulating after-dinner speeches, gaining success in the boardroom, preparing outstanding impromptu speeches, and writing clear reports, persuasive memoranda, and compelling letters. These skills are basic, essential, and, for the most part, directly related. In education, business, and society these are successful coping skills.

A study by Johnson[1] surveyed close to 1,000 public secondary school principals across the United States to determine the criteria they believed most important to teaching effectiveness. Communication skills were the most important criteria used by principals in hiring teachers. Included in these criteria were interpersonal communication, poise, oral communication, enthusiasm, listening skills, and writing skills.

Johnson based his study on one by Curtis, Winsor, and Stephens.[2] Like Johnson, these authors surveyed a random sample of 1,000 personnel managers across the United States. Their goal was to determine both the most important factors in obtaining postgraduation employment and the factors or skills most important for successful job performance. The top four essential factors in obtaining employment were oral communication, listening ability, enthusiasm, and written communication skills. The most important skills for successful job performance were interpersonal and human relations skills, speaking skills, and written communication skills.

These studies show the importance of speaking skills. The essential skills developed in the arena of public speaking are closely linked to all other communication skills—skills that can have a powerful and lasting effect on us all.

Effective speaking skills are not important just to those who want to be public leaders and speakers. They are part of *all* effective interpersonal communication, whether public or private, personal or professional. They are an integral part of effective personal skills; therefore, developing skill in public communication increases self-confidence, poise, and assertiveness.

Effective communication has to do with control, assertiveness, and helping others. It means expressing our ideas so well that others are touched, moved, and persuaded by them. Effective communication puts people in charge of their lives.

Think about it for a second. What makes people good at anything— parenting, painting, teaching, doctoring, managing, preaching? What makes people good is something in addition to skills and techniques: *attitude*. When people care about their sons and daughters, the subject they are painting, or their students, clients, employees, or parishioners, that care manifests itself as success.

Thus, a book on public speaking has to motivate and inspire you. When you *care* about your communication ability, you are more likely to *want* to increase your effectiveness. The creative use of words is a powerful tool but not one you can take for granted. Just like any tool, you must learn how to use it with precision, command, and expertise. As Thomas Mann (1875–1955) wrote, "Order and simplification are the first steps toward the mastery of a subject."[3] Indeed, order and simplification will lead you to mastery of the communication skills described in this book.

This chapter will get you started. It discusses nervousness or anxiety about public speaking and offers guidelines for overcoming nervousness. It also discusses the nine basic steps necessary for preparing a speech, each of which will be discussed in more detail in later chapters.

NERVOUSNESS IS NORMAL

It is normal to experience nervousness or anxiety when speaking in front of others. In fact, public speaking is a natural, normal stimulus for anxiety. Speech anxiety, stage fright, and fear of public speaking take many forms. People may give themselves negative messages such as "I am no good at this," "I can't speak before these people," or "I feel really stupid when I have to give a speech." Others experience physiological symptoms such as a faster heart rate, contracting blood vessels near the skin (a blanched appearance), feeling cold or clammy (wet palms), a dry mouth, difficulty standing still, or shaking and shivering. Speech anxiety may be revealed through behaviors such as shaking, stammering, stuttering, repeating words or ideas, avoiding eye contact, or appearing rigid.[4]

Although you may view anxiety as a threat to your speech-making success, it can play a positive role. It keeps you focused on the task at hand, making you less likely to be distracted. Anxiety also keeps you alert and sharp, concerned about the details that will make your speech unique. Because you are a bit anxious you are likely to practice more effectively, which in turn leads to greater confidence and a well-prepared speech. As you can see, some anxiety is healthy, and if you learn how to capitalize on it, your speech may be more effective because of your anxiety.

If people had to be free of fear, tension, stress, and nervousness to be successful speakers, no one would venture to speak. Speakers cope successfully with these problems all the time. They do this through attitude, preparation, and presentation.

Get your nervousness under control

Attitude matters. *Attitude* refers to your way of thinking and, consequently, your way of feeling and acting. For example, we all know people who approach life with a positive or a negative attitude. Before your speech, you can do things that contribute to a positive attitude. Getting enough sleep and eating sensibly make you feel your best and give you the vitality required for an enthusiastic speech. You should also use positive self-talk such as "I can do it," "I am prepared," and "I will succeed." Remember positive experiences where you felt strong and in control. Picturing oneself doing well, or using positive mental imagery, is a tactic many athletes employ right before executing a play; this will reinforce your positive attitude about your speech-making ability. Also, don't worry that there is only one right way to give your speech: There are as many ways to give speeches as there are people giving speeches, and each person develops his or her own style through experience.

Finally, keep in mind that mistakes are not fatal; you don't have to deliver a perfect speech to deliver a good speech. Although perfection is a nice ideal, when it is your overriding goal and you do not meet it, the frustration and disappointment can be devastating. Rather than striving for a perfect speech, do the best you can in the time you have. Think of listeners as people just like you, a cheering section rooting for your success. The best way to handle mistakes is to laugh them off and let listeners laugh with you. In this way mistakes enable you to develop rapport with your audience.

Prepare thoroughly. If you begin working on your speech as soon as the assignment is made and continue to work on it until it is delivered, you are sure to deliver a well-prepared speech. Little advice can salvage severe procrastination. Get a good topic, thoroughly investigate and precisely organize your ideas, and plan your introduction, transitions, and conclusion. Practice delivering your speech, including a few times in front of family or friends. If you use an audio- or videocassette recorder, you will be able to critique yourself.

Present your ideas with confidence. To feel your best during your presentation, dress in clothes that are comfortable yet make your audience take you seriously. Arriving early allows you to collect your thoughts, and if you can sit in the audience before your presentation, you may feel more comfortable with your listeners. As you walk to the front of the room to speak, take several deep breaths. Once again, use positive self-talk and visualize a successful speech.

During your presentation, concentrate on your message and focus on your listeners. To maintain confidence, make eye contact with receptive, encouraging audience members. Rather than standing in one place, try moving when you change to a different point or convey a personal example; this releases nervous energy and adds emphasis to your speech. Just be sure to avoid pacing!

A final key to establishing or creating confidence is *experience*. The more opportunities you have to give speeches, make reports, and offer presentations, the more confidence you will gain. With experience people learn how to deal with nervousness, think on their feet, be spontaneous, handle unexpected circumstances, and be successful.

To summarize, it is *how* one handles fear, tension, stress, or nervousness that counts, not whether it exists. The box entitled "Channel Your Nervous Energy" summarizes some of these suggestions for dealing with fear.

UNDERSTANDING THE PROCESS OF SPEECH PREPARATION

Because many of you will be called upon to prepare a speech before you have read many chapters of this book, this section summarizes the process so that preparation can begin at once. All of the nine steps presented here will be expanded upon in later chapters.

Select the topic

This is your first important job. In some situations the topic will be given to you. For example, when asked to be a presenter at a leadership conference with the theme "redefining leadership," Anne took the conference theme as her speech title and formulated three main ideas for the body of her speech: change norms, redefine power, and be sensitive to inequality. Sales presentations, speaker introductions, and award ceremonies all offer fairly specific ideas about what listeners expect. The classroom, however, usually offers speakers a chance to be creative. Sometimes this freedom is difficult for beginning speakers to handle.

> ## Channel Your Nervous Energy
>
> Speakers need to channel their nervous energy into constructive forms. The following techniques are often useful:
>
> - Use gestures.
> - Vary your volume, tone, and inflection.
> - Practice simple relaxation techniques.
> - Concentrate on your ideas, not on the delivery.
> - Slowly inhale and exhale deeply on the way to the lectern.
> - Use positive self-talk: "I am calm," "I am in control," "I am comfortable," "I am confident," "I am in charge."
> - Mentally rehearse all parts of the speech.
> - Make direct eye contact with supportive listeners.
> - Physically move in front of the audience when it is comfortable, at transitions, on important points, or to convey a personal example.

Selecting a topic is important for several reasons. First, a good topic will energize you. Second, that energy will make preparation easier to face and accomplish. Third, and perhaps most important, a well-chosen topic helps ensure that listeners will respond positively to the message.

In choosing a topic, first search your own background and history for possible speech subjects. To find current ideas, examine newspapers and news magazines. Ask friends, classmates, and family members for ideas. If these methods fail, try brainstorming—coming up with as many ideas as possible without judging, evaluating, or rejecting the ideas.

Test the topic

Ask yourself if the topic is appropriate for your speech. Just because you think of it and you know something about it does not mean it is appropriate for you or for your audience. Do you find it interesting? Will they? Can you and the audience get involved in it? Do you have any personal experiences that bear on the topic? (This certainly isn't a prerequisite for topic selection, but if you can find a topic with which you *do* have personal experience, it might be a good choice.)

When testing the topic, ask these questions: Is the topic appropriate for the occasion? Is it appropriate considering the resources that are available? Is it appropriate for the time you have available? Is the topic appropriate for your listeners? This last question moves us to the next step.

Analyze the audience

Remember that you will be giving your speech to listeners. The audience will probably determine the success or failure of the entire effort. For example, when I gave a speech in Australia, I talked about the qualities of dynamic teachers. A friend who was in the audience later told me that Australians resent being told *anything* by Americans because Americans always appear to think they are right, better, and more perfect. From that time on I was careful in the way I handled my Australian listeners.

A number of questions need to be asked during audience analysis. How much do audience members know about the topic? How much do they care about it? What attitudes and beliefs do they hold that relate to the topic? Whatever factual information you can obtain about your audience—age, gender, education, occupation, nationality, ethnic origin, geographic location, and group affiliations—will help you understand them better and aim your message precisely toward their attitudes, needs, and interests.

Rework the topic

Often your first topic choices will not be your best topic choices. Continue fine-tuning your topic; this process can and should continue right up to your final presentation. Along the way you are likely to discover information that helps to narrow, focus, and tune the topic. Good speakers accommodate and respond to such information by continually adjusting their messages.

Consider timing

One student gave a speech on hazing while the student newspaper was running a series of articles on the topic, yet the student did not refer to the series at all; she was unaware of it. Her audience noticed the oversight. A speaker addressing a high school audience forgot that the attention span of high school students tends to be short. His speech lasted over an hour and was unsuccessful. Another speaker giving an after-dinner speech in a hall ignored the unbearable heat, the uncomfortable chairs, and the kitchen noise, continuing on as if none of the problems existed. Her talk, too, was unsuccessful.

Timing means considering what else might be occurring at the same time as the speech. Be sensitive to how long the speech should last. Consider the physical setting and the comfort of audience members. You will gradually develop the command and control to respond to unexpected circumstances, unwanted intrusions, and unanticipated events.

Select information

In selecting information for your speech you should be guided by two interrelated questions: (1) How much information do I already have on the topic? and (2) Will the information I have, and the information I collect, interest my audience members? Decisions at this crucial stage of speech preparation must be governed by audience knowledge, needs, and interests. Why give a speech to an audience that has no interest in it? And why waste the valuable time of audience members?

You will probably collect more information than you will use in the speech itself. How much more? There is no universal answer. The more information you have, the easier it is to choose what to use. Of course, if you collect no more than you will use, there are no choices about what to use and what to leave out: You are going to use it all because it is all you have! It is always better to have more information than you need. Choices lead to both quality and effectiveness by allowing you to adapt, mold, and shape the material to the specific needs of the audience, yourself, and the speech occasion. Specific and detailed adaptation is what makes speeches great.

Test thought patterns

Often the thought pattern or organizational scheme that is best for a topic is clear when the topic is selected. For example, a speech on the benefits of volunteer work would probably be organized around the benefits. These might include the following: (1) It helps others; (2) it contributes to society; and (3) it contributes to our own sense of well-being.

On the other hand, the thought pattern may not be known in advance; you may need to discover it during research and investigation. Let's suppose, for example, that you chose the topic of travel but did not know what approach to take. You could talk about advantages, benefits, or destinations, any of which would require an organizational scheme much like the one just discussed for the benefits of volunteer work. If preparation or planning for travel were selected, you might use a step-by-step pattern describing how to get ready to travel. Problems in traveling and solutions for travel problems could be another approach. There are numerous possibilities: raising money for travel, traveling light, staying in inexpensive accommodations, or facing the problems of foreign travel. The speech could even discuss problems within the travel industry. But what if you wanted to explain to beginning travelers how to fully devour a location once they are there? Another kind of organizational scheme might be used for that, too, which would differ from the other travel-related topics mentioned.

To test a thought pattern, ask the following questions:

1. Does this thought pattern fit the topic?
2. Do the major points I want to talk about fit into this thought pattern?
3. Will this thought pattern help audience members understand the topic more easily?
4. Can I satisfy the demands of this situation by using this thought pattern?
5. Does this thought pattern add clarity to the entire effort?
6. Is this a thought pattern I can stick to throughout my speech?

After selecting the information and testing potential thought patterns, you are ready to examine the language you will use.

Examine the language

You should not wait until you are in front of an audience to decide what words you will use to frame your ideas. On the other hand, speech performances do not demand a formal, written style either. What tends to work best is a style of speaking that is slightly more formal than informal conversation but not as formal as the way you write. Strive for a comfortable speaking style.

Informal ◀———— Comfortable ————▶ Formal

Informal conversation   Speaking style   Written communication

The language tools you use will be influenced by your audience. For example, a college student was asked to speak to young children to motivate them to go to college. She kept her language and ideas simple and talked about their interest in reading, writing, and arithmetic and how important it was to remain interested in school, in learning, and in becoming a better person. She also talked about how much her early education had helped her.

When she was invited back to speak to her high school on the same topic, her whole approach changed. First she talked with her sister, who was still in high school, so she would be able to refer to some things that interest high schoolers. Although she adapted some of her language, she did not have to make as many changes as when she talked to the young children. Also, she talked about comprehension skills, computational skills, and computer skills. She found adapting her language to the high school audience much easier because she did not have to alter her vocabulary as much.

When choosing language you need to keep the desired effect in mind. For example, if you wanted to increase understanding about self-defense, there would be little need for strong, motivational words that would forge emotional connections with listeners. The words would instead be descriptive, seeking to increase understanding: about the different kinds of self-defense, where self-defense tools can be purchased, and the availability of classes in or lectures on self-defense. A persuasive speech imploring an audience to learn self-defense would require different language choices: defending yourself against "vicious attacks," "protecting your personal safety," or not being "helpless." Language cannot be separated from other aspects of presentation.

Some speech ideas need special language planning. For example, speakers may want to set ideas in parallel form: Read the book. Prepare an outline. Write the report. These three ideas are composed in parallel form. A speaker who wanted to show students how to write a book report might use these as main heads for a short explanatory speech. It is unlikely that such parallel construction could be done spontaneously as one stood before an audience.

There are other reasons for planning language in advance. Speakers may want to work on a special thought or idea to summarize a series of ideas. For example, a teacher trainer framed this alliteration (words that begin with the same first consonant sound) to summarize his speech to teachers: "That's why teachers need to 'take time to think training.'" The trainer probably could not have thought this up on the spur of the moment.

Also, speakers might want to phrase a complex idea to be clearly understood. If speakers want to strengthen or soften a point, words can be prepared to achieve this exact effect. Alliterations, metaphors, similes, and allusions are usually best thought out in advance. The point here is simply that language works best if it is not left to chance.

Practice the speech

Closely associated with selecting the language of the speech is practicing the speech. The following is a simple, easy, and straightforward plan for practice. First compose a complete outline of your ideas. Condense the complete outline to keywords, and put those on three-by-five cards, one side only. Begin giving the speech out loud from the keyword outline. Occasionally, if an idea needs to be written out, or certain words need to be remembered, or facts need to be exact, these can be placed in the keyword outline as well. Each time you practice, use different words to describe the ideas. Try not to memorize or say the ideas in exactly the same way over and over.

The Heart of the Matter

The key to practice is comfort. How long will it take for you to feel comfortable with all aspects of the presentation? In some cases, this may mean more time; in others, it may mean less. Some people want to know precisely how much time they should practice. Answer the following questions with a "yes" or "no":

1. Are you familiar with the topic?
2. Do you know the main points well?
3. Are you in full command of the supporting material?
4. Can you present your introduction and conclusion without using notes?
5. Do you feel at ease standing in front of the audience?
6. Do you know how long your speech will take (within 15 or 30 seconds)?
7. Have you anticipated any distractions that may occur during your speech?
8. Can you deliver the body of the speech without heavy reliance on your notes?
9. Are you at ease looking eye-to-eye with individuals in your potential audience?
10. Can you answer questions about your speech with poise and confidence?

If you have answered most of these questions with a "yes," you need little time for practice. If there are one or two "no" answers, then allow a day or two at least. If there are three or four "no" answers, allow three or four days as a minimum. If five, six, or more questions received "no" answers, then you may need more than four days—even a week or more—to become comfortable with your material.

By practicing like this you will find several different ways to express ideas. And when you get in front of the audience you will have choices as you share your ideas. When you memorize, on the other hand, you don't have choices. Rather, you have one exact way of saying everything. And when one word is lost or missed, every word that follows is gone until you can get back on track. Most people do not memorize well, nor do they give effective memorized speeches. What many people may not realize is that however strong their memories are, when they add the stress and nervousness of standing in front of a live audience, plus the possibility of distractions, often memory will play tricks. They will lose control. That is why you need several different ways to express your ideas: to give you choices.

How long should you practice? Until you feel totally comfortable with the ideas in your speech and until they flow smoothly and effortlessly; until you feel in charge of the material. There really is no specific answer; it is up to you. See "The Heart of the Matter" for some specific guidelines. For some people the practice time can be brief—going over the speech only four or five times. For others, ten times may not be enough. One thing is clear: Speakers should allow plenty of time for practice.

SUMMARY

Effective communication skills play a significant role in success in education, business, and, indeed, most of life. And although skills and techniques are important to speaking well, attitude is even more important. How much do you care about and want to improve your speech making?

This chapter discussed nervousness. It is natural, normal, and can take many forms. Although often viewed as a threat, nervousness can play a positive role. Speakers need to get their nervousness under control by maintaining a positive attitude, preparing thoroughly, and presenting their ideas with confidence.

The speech preparation process was summarized because you will probably be asked to make speeches before you read the rest of this textbook. Nine steps were outlined: selecting the topic, testing it, analyzing the audience, reworking the topic, considering timing, selecting information, testing thought patterns, examining language, and practicing your speech.

There is enough information in this chapter to get you started. The following chapters in Part I will address foundation elements, listening, and audience analysis to give you an overall perspective of public speaking.

The remaining parts in the book—including The Substance of the Speech, Making the Presentation, and Types of Presentations—provide the essentials you need to be an effective and successful public speaker.

Chapter Questions

1. What do you think most people who experience fear when speaking in public are afraid of?

2. What might you tell a friend who is frightened by a speech assignment?

3. Have you ever given a speech before? What was your subject? Who was your audience? Describe the organization pattern you used for your speech and the reactions of your audience.

4. Based on the information in this chapter, what specific adjustments might you make in the practice phase of speech preparation?

5. For your first speaking assignment, answer the questions raised in "The Heart of the Matter." From your answers, determine how long it will take to feel comfortable with all aspects of your presentation. Considering your overall speaking background and experience, is this amount of time likely to vary dramatically in the future? Why or why not?

6. Name some specific circumstances (not discussed in this chapter) in which good communication skills might be useful.

7. What are two potential speech topics that would require different patterns of organization? How would you organize these speeches? Why?

8. Using the speech topic, "Making A Public Presentation," what specific alterations in your language would you make if you were giving the speech to these audiences: elementary school students, high school students, your public speaking class, and a group of senior citizens at a local nursing home?

Further Reading

Gordon L. Dahnke and Glen W. Clatterbuck, *Human Communication Theory and Research* (Belmont, CA: Wadsworth Publishing Company, 1990).

The authors offer a broadly representative survey of current developments in the communication discipline. For the serious student who wants more depth on some of the ingredients of public speaking offered in this chapter, Dahnke and Clatterbuck discuss channels, contexts, persuasive functions, and methods of communication inquiry.

Em Griffin, *A First Look at Communication Theory* (New York: McGraw-Hill, 1991).

Griffin has written a theory book for those who have no previous background in communication. The author investigates 31 theories and makes them both interesting and understandable. Not only does this book explain a wide range of communication phenomena, but it draws together the various parts of the communication process into a unified whole.

Endnotes

1. Scott D. Johnson, "A National Assessment of Secondary-School Principals' Perceptions of Teaching-Effectiveness Criteria," *Communication Education* 43 (January 1994), pp. 1–16.

2. Dan B. Curtis, Jerry L. Winsor, and Ronald D. Stephens, "National Preferences in Business and Communication Education," *Communication Education* 38 (January 1989), pp. 6–14.

3. Thomas Mann, *The Magic Mountain* (New York: Knopf, 1924), p. 5.

4. Joe Ayres and Tim Hopf, *Coping With Speech Anxiety* (Norwood, NJ: Ablex, 1993), pp. 5–7.

Words in Action: VIDEO STUDY

Good communication skills are important to your success for many reasons; certainly they will give you a competitive edge in most job situations. The accompanying video provides a sampling of individuals who are successful leaders in part due to their public speaking abilities. After watching the video, consider the following question.

- How are public speaking skills critical to the success of each of the speakers on the videotape? Consider such factors as the time period, the individual's background, and the individual's accomplishments.

The Basics

After reading this chapter you will be able to:

- use a model of public speaking for analysis, anticipation, and evaluation

- appreciate the communication opportunities a free society provides

- understand some of the responsibilities imposed by freedom of speech

- be a responsible communicator

- know where standards of right and wrong come from

You expect to be scared. You may even expect to fail. Remember, each person who has prepared and delivered a public speech has experienced these common emotions. Having to prepare and deliver a public speech is difficult, but many things are difficult before they become easy, and the process of public speaking is no exception.

Most successful speakers will tell you that they initially saw the task as almost insurmountable and that they were frightened before the task became easier for them. Speakers will also tell you how satisfying and rewarding success in public speaking can be once those early feelings of fear have been faced and overcome. *Anyone* can be a successful speaker and enjoy the results. We must be willing to take small risks if we want to grow. Public speaking success requires only small risks if we proceed one step at a time.

The first chapter presented steps for preparing and presenting your first speech. This chapter moves you to a broader perspective. The first section discusses a model of the communication process and its components. The second section puts public speaking in the larger framework of a free society and describes the opportunities for growth, development, and change offered by U. S. culture. But with freedom comes responsibility; the final section will help you distinguish right from wrong as you make the decisions necessary to prepare and present your speeches.

Figure 2.1
A model of communication.

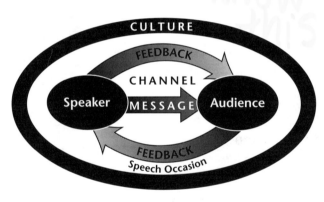

A MODEL OF COMMUNICATION

Figure 2.1 portrays a model of communication. This model distinguishes the components of the communication process, helps speakers anticipate and prepare for a great variety of speaking situations, and provides a framework for analyzing why things worked or did not work as they should have.

Consider any speech occasion. With that occasion in mind, next to each of the components in the model, list all the attributes or characteristics that you know about. This personalized revision of the model can be used as you prepare for your presentation, and it can be used again after the event to evaluate your strengths and weaknesses and to suggest areas for possible improvement.

Let's use a specific example to explain the components of the model. Brian is a college student in his thirties and a candidate for his state's house of representatives. To be on the ballot in November, he must first win the primary election. Let's examine the model with reference to Brian's speech to a local college audience. Part of his speech follows.

Let me begin by introducing myself. You might wonder, "What's an old man like you doing here?" Of course, you probably know the answer to that question already because two of my opponents for this position were here earlier this week—and both are quite a bit older than I am, although I'm also middle-aged. I am a political science major here with future plans of going into politics. After all, what else can you do with a political science background except teach or go into politics? When I graduated from high school, I went to work for my dad in his water treatment company. I was ready to accept any kind of handout at that time. So I began as a custodian until I learned the business. When I developed the appropriate computer skills I became an accounts recorder, which was essentially a secretarial position. Then I became a sales representative, and when the company expanded, I became manager of a new plant. But I always regretted not having gone to college, and as I traveled and saw more of this country, I wanted more out of life. So I trained someone to take my place, took a leave of absence, and began my college education at an older age.

I am a candidate for the state house of representatives, and I am running because I care and because I think I can make a difference. Although I have no political experience, I figure that I have to start somewhere. Also, I have seen how well other politicians have done, and I think I can do better.

Since I hope to represent this area, let me tell you what my major concerns are. First, I think there is little doubt that we need additional state spending to help us clean up the pollution in our air and in our surrounding waters. Second, I think we need additional state funding for improved roads and bridges in this area. Third, and this is the area that concerns all of us here, I think we need more concern at the state level for higher education. If I can just get more attention from our state government to the needs and interests of the people from this area of the state, I think I will have made a difference. Of course, I am here because I need your help.

Speaker

Although the topic of credibility will be discussed extensively in Chapter 9, it needs to be mentioned here in reference to Brian's speech. *Credibility* is the character of the speaker in the minds of the audience. When listeners respond to speakers they respond to a mental image they form of the speakers, not to the speakers themselves. Audience members don't really know the speakers; they know only the impression they have of them. With respect to classmates, for example, if we think they are friendly, intelligent, dynamic, poised, honest, and hardworking, we are likely to rate them highly with respect to their credibility. The important point is that this rating is a response to a mental image and not necessarily to reality.

Brian gave his campaign speech in one of the residence halls on campus. As a nontraditional student in his thirties, he was perceived by audience members as older and wiser. But that perception had a downside: Brian had to demonstrate to students—some half his age—that he was not out of touch, that he knew their problems and concerns, and that, despite his age, he could fairly represent them. In other words, Brian had to establish his credibility as a candidate and, in this case, as a speaker. Notice in the portion of Brian's speech reproduced above that he probably could have spent more time establishing his credibility with the students.

Message

The *message* is the idea or substance of the communication situation. Messages can be verbal and nonverbal. Two important ideas about messages need to be mentioned here. First, listeners may or may not receive or interpret speakers' specific intentions as speakers want them to. Second, every audience member is likely to receive a different message from a speaker; none of these messages will be exactly alike.

Brian's campaign speech illustrates both of these problems. Brian intended to convince his audience that he had ideas that related to them. At first Brian was unable to convey this; many audience members initially presumed his ideas were more relevant to community members than to college students. Further, audience members received a number of different messages near the beginning of his speech. Some of these were nonverbal messages. One listener said he was arrogant, another said he was too old, and a third said he was patronizing. Still another, responding to the ideas Brian mentioned, thought he had nothing new to offer. Only one thought he might be the best candidate, but this listener came from the same town as Brian and was a classmate of Brian's younger sister in high school. However, Brian's speech had just begun.

Channel

Messages must pass through the channel to get from speaker to listeners. The *channel* is the medium by which the message is carried. For most public speaking the channel is air. But a speech can be shown on television or from videotape. The channel can also be a telephone or a tape recorder. When a speaker's words are transcribed, the channel is the printed word.

When we see speeches live, we benefit from additional cues or stimuli. For example, Brian chose to dress informally. He wore blue jeans and a plaid shirt. He did not use the lectern that had been provided, instead leaning comfortably against a table that was in front of the audience. His voice was relaxed but projected clearly, and his gestures, although natural and easy, seemed larger and more expansive than necessary. While tangible stimuli such as voice and gestures may be conveyed through indirect channels, other qualities are conveyed to listeners only through a live performance. Some of these stimuli allow us to judge a speaker's trustworthiness, commitment to the topic, honesty, sincerity, and ethical sensitivity.

Many of these factors played a part in the positive and negative impressions conveyed by Brian. He had a terrific baritone voice, used meaningful gestures, and exhibited a comfortable and poised stage presence. However, in the informal setting with college students surrounding him, he was less effective. He seemed a bit awkward and out of place. His interpersonal skills were not as strong or as impressive as his public speaking skills.

Speech occasion

The *speech occasion* is when and where the speech actually occurs. It is a location in both time and space. A classroom speech has certain expectations attached to it, such as dress, time limits, and appropriate behavior, just as all speech occasions do. The place, event, and even the traditions surrounding the event help speakers define the moment. A speech occasion is located in time as well, aside from time limits. For example, one student speaking about the information highway referred to the then-current space shuttle flight that launched a satellite to assist in developing a worldwide communication network. Another student, talking about the expense of going to college, referred to the cost of a new building that had just opened on campus. In both cases the speakers drew recent events into their speeches and thus acknowledged the significance of time to their speech occasions.

Brian used both space and time in his campaign speech. He seated the group in a large semicircle and then leaned against the table in front of them so everyone could see him. He knew his speech was slated for 9:15 P.M.—after a long day—so he used humor, made an informal presentation, and allowed questions during his speech to help maintain a lively pace, active interaction, and audience involvement. In addition, he referred to the campus appearances of two of his rivals earlier in the week. Brian was sensitive and responsive to the occasion.

Culture

A *culture* represents a specific group of people's values, beliefs, artifacts, behaviors, and ways of communicating that are passed on from one generation to the next. Every speech occasion occurs within the broader context of a culture, and that culture determines, at least in part, the identification that occurs between speakers and listeners. When visiting countries where people do not speak English as a primary language, for example, U. S. presidents often learn phrases in the local language to encourage identification or a common bond.

But culture needn't be defined on such a broad scale. There are subcultures within cultures, and these subcultures may have their own values. College students, for instance, are a subculture. The beliefs, dating habits, language, and other behavior of college students are unlikely, in many cases, to reflect the beliefs or actions of the people in the towns from which the college students come. Students form their own subculture, especially at a residential college.

Brian, being a student, could identify with many of the beliefs, much of the language usage, and some of the other behaviors of college students—such as their preference for sitting around him in a large circle. Also, he was aware of their preferences for an informal speech permitting interruptions and for informal language rather than the slightly more formal speech of a planned presentation.

Audience

The *audience* members are those to whom the speaker is speaking. The problem here is that audience members may not operate as a group; that is, audience members bring their own specific frames of reference to a speech. Let's take an example. Say your speech instructor has just announced the next speaker, Roger, who will talk about the Study Skills Center (SSC). What frame of reference do *you* bring to Roger's speech? Perhaps you are a senior, and the SSC seems somewhat irrelevant to you right now. But for a freshman or sophomore in the audience, the SSC could have direct relevance.

Here are a number of speech topics. Think for a moment about your own attitudes, beliefs, values, experiences, religious convictions, and personal ways of thinking that might bear on each of them:

homosexuality	abortion	organized religion
pollution	gun control	crime
capital punishment	smoking	universal health care
welfare	poverty	taxes

Clearly, any person considering one of these speech topics might have impressions different from yours.

Brian tried to control audience attitudes toward himself as best he could. He was aware that as a nontraditional student in his thirties he had to win skeptical audience members to his side. In his presentation he clearly showed his listeners that he respected them by expressing his need for their help. In the speech segment that followed the printed sample, he gave them counsel, offered some wisdom, tried to inspire them, and gave them an inside look at what it means to be a candidate for public office. Many students left impressed, but only after Brian had won them over. He did two things well: First, he provided information that his listeners did not have or know, so they learned something. Second, he touched their lives by showing them respect, by revealing his need of their support, and by proving he had their interests at heart.

By the end of the speech, most of the students who attended, even the skeptical ones, thought Brian's speech was worthwhile. Would they vote for him? He had no way to know for sure. Brian hoped his audience would talk to their friends and parents because he needed the publicity.

Feedback

Feedback is the response speakers get from listeners and the adaptations they make in their message to compensate for or acknowledge that response. There are many different kinds of feedback; applause and cheers are two obvious kinds. But audience members boo, yawn, read the news-

immigration

paper, talk, move around, look bored, ask questions, and appear quizzical as well.

Brian did two things to encourage feedback. First, he seated his audience fairly close to him and stood near them. This closed the distance between himself and them and thus provided him greater feedback. Second, he allowed questions during his speech. This provided him ongoing feedback about how well audience members understood his ideas. Brian was also skillful in quickly adapting to the feedback he received. This showed listeners that he respected them, he was sensitive to their ideas, and they really mattered to him. Listeners appreciate respect, and often a responsive speaker will win listeners over.

The elements that all communication situations have in common are isolated and depicted in our model of communication. But remember that communication situations differ. Communication is a process, and this perspective views the model components as dynamic, ongoing, ever-changing, and continuous.[1] The process of communication has no beginning, no end, and no fixed sequence of events. "It is not static, at rest. It is moving. The ingredients within a process interact; each affects all others."[2]

You can learn all the elements of the model of communication and even put them together in an aesthetic way. You can say that if all of these ingredients are present, there is likely to be a communication event. But this misses the element of process; the dynamics of communication, the mixing and blending that make a good speech, are missing. The model ingredients are necessary, but they are not sufficient.[3]

Three additional components are not represented on the model but are important to capturing a complete picture of the communication process. Noise, effects, and social facilitation all strongly affect the communication event.

Noise

Noise is any disturbance or problem that comes between the speaker and the audience. Considering that a group of people is present and a speech occasion exists, you would expect noise. *Physical noise* interferes with the physical transmission of the message. Physical noise can consist of someone coming in late and walking toward the front of the class to find a seat; the sound of sirens or a lawn mower; or, as is common in large group lectures, loud talking among the audience.

Psychological noise, however, can be a more serious barrier or distraction because it is not as easily detected or controlled. *Psychological noise* is any psychological interference that distorts the reception or processing of the message. It occurs in people's minds. When Laurie gave the presidential address to her sorority, she was psychologically distracted by an ornery microphone. David gave a business report in a seminar room and was distracted by poor lighting. Shirley was worried about forgetting information. Audience members also experience psychological noise, and this is where detection and control become problems for speakers. Listeners may be distracted by what went on before the speech or what is going to happen afterward, or they may have a lot on their minds at the time of the

Semantic - language that is not appropriate.

speech. Lack of sleep can reduce the level of attention or concentration. These kinds of distractions in listeners' minds are difficult to detect, adapt to, or compensate for. But knowing that they are likely to exist can encourage greater efforts by speakers to hold audience attention.

Effects

Effects are the consequences that occur as a result of a speech. Many effects of public speeches are not measurable. For example, how can we know whether listeners have increased their knowledge, changed an attitude or belief, or taken an action if that action occurs in the future? Effects can be immediate or delayed. The important question to ask when considering effects is, Did the speaker achieve his or her goal? However, often this question cannot be answered.

A creative method of determining the immediate effects of a speech was used by Mike, who was trying to get additional lights installed in the central campus area. As part of the conclusion to his speech, Mike circulated a petition; every audience member signed it.

Kelly, at the conclusion of her speech, used a different tactic. She was promoting a health fair being put on at the student union. After talking about all the benefits and the quality of merchandise to be displayed, she asked her class for a show of hands: "How many of you plan to attend the health fair?" Everyone raised a hand. The show of hands probably did not predict actual attendance, but it revealed some involvement and perhaps a small degree of commitment.

Steven talked about donating blood. At the beginning of his speech he asked how many of his classmates already had donated blood. Fewer than 10 percent raised their hands. At the end of his speech he handed out a brochure published by the American Red Cross on the procedures for and the benefits of donating. But he did not ask for a second show of hands by those who intended to donate blood, because of what he felt to be the touchiness of his topic. Steven raised awareness about donating blood and may have provided the impetus for fellow classmates to do so.

Speech effects can also be negative. People in the United States have been exposed to many public speeches, and some of these have been negative or weak experiences. Thus, some audience members probably approach speech occasions with negative, self-fulfilling prophecies. That is, they expect negative effects and those negative effects occur, thereby fulfilling their expectations. Second, often in the United States we tend to be overly critical, looking for negative rather than positive traits and events. Thus, sometimes even when people succeed, in other people's minds they fail. For example, Kristine's speech called "Exercise Is Good for Everyone" may have failed in some listeners' minds because she dressed in sweats, or because she had a slight stutter, or because she lost her place at one point—even though her central thesis is accepted by most people.

Social facilitation

Social facilitation is the way audience members influence each other. Have you ever heard a speaker ask audience members to come toward the front and fill in all those front chairs? Speakers are more likely to get a response, whether humor, sorrow, applause, or appreciation, from audience members who are seated close together. This occurs simply because each audience member has a direct effect on the others nearby. An example of social facilitation can be seen when one or two audience members begin to clap and suddenly the whole audience follows suit.

All 10 of these components of a total speech event (the seven in the model plus the three additional factors just discussed) are tied together and affect each other. Think of them as strands of a web. When one strand of the web is plucked, all other strands are affected. For example, a speaker is giving a convocation address when suddenly a spirited audience member provides some overt, obvious, and disruptive feedback. Suddenly another member makes a (socially facilitated) comment. The speaker may shift the message slightly to accommodate the disruptions. New stimuli flood the channels as the speaker tries to adapt quickly and not lose control. The message is changed; other audience members may be embarrassed or concerned; the physical noise of the disruption may create psychological noise; and the feedback may cause other audience members to respond in some way. Effects are turning out different than intended now and the first disruption may cause other similar disruptions such as supportive responses ("Yes!") or maybe suppressive responses ("Shhhhh-h-h-h") from audience members. Certain cultural norms have been threatened or broken, and the entire event has been altered. The nature of social facilitation is clearly illustrated in this example, and one can see how difficult it is to anticipate or accommodate. How the communication model components can interact with each other is also illustrated in this example.

It should be clear by now that no two speech events can ever be the same. Even if the speaker is the same, the messages are exactly alike, the listeners are identical, and the location is duplicated, the time has changed; and because human beings are not constant from moment to moment, the speech occasion is different. Because of the complex interaction of the 10 factors, any two events are likely to be radically rather than just slightly different. But the fact that these differences occur is part of living in a free society.

COMMUNICATING IN A FREE SOCIETY

No society other than that of the United States so openly and completely recognizes, encourages, and protects freedom of expression. This freedom is important to everyday life. Our society leaves to its members the responsibility to use this freedom well. Freedom of expression is a guaranteed right, and this right poses opportunities to grow, develop, and change in meaningful ways. Expressing one's opinion is both a privilege and a skill that can be improved.

Communication dominates most U.S. citizens' lives. From the morning news anchor who reports on what politicians, businesspeople, sports personalities, and actors are saying, to the teachers, clergy, community leaders, and advertisers who daily compete for your attention, you are bombarded with messages. You add your own messages to this cacophony of communication. With the rehashing, responding, and replaying of the news that you hear, you may have wished at some point that there was an on–off button for it all.

Most of this communication serves useful purposes. It increases understanding, entertains, forms or changes beliefs, or moves people to action. These purposes are not a recent phenomenon. Theorizing about public speaking dates back to a 3,000 B.C.E. Egyptian essay that provided elementary advice on effective speaking to the son of a pharaoh.

No matter what your plans for the future, if you want to be influential, then you very likely will have to express yourself effectively to others in public settings. For example, a speech teacher received a call from a former student who wanted help in becoming a more effective speaker. He had recently been promoted to manage a small college's food service area, and now he had to address his staff, give speeches to the administration, offer feedback in meetings, and inspire his student help. With a sense of delight, the teacher said to him, "Now you will be able to put into practice all that you learned in my speech course." He replied, "I did not take your course seriously. I blew off the lectures, I never read the book, and I did just enough to get by."

Many students do not know what they will be doing even five years after they graduate; often what they think they will be doing in five years is not what they actually end up doing. Planning for an unknown future is difficult. But recognizing the importance of effective communication in a rapidly changing world will help you set your priorities and is likely to enrich every aspect of your life.

U. S. culture encourages free exchange of information, rewards effective communicators, and depends on those who can effectively and efficiently articulate ideas. But a free society also imposes responsibility on its citizens.

TAKING ETHICAL RESPONSIBILITY

All speakers must make a number of decisions, beginning with planning the speech. The most useful guiding principle for all the decisions that must be made is "Demonstrate a genuine regard for listeners." This means that facts and opinions must be presented fairly; no ideas should be intentionally distorted; and no materials necessary for the proper evaluation of ideas should be purposefully concealed. A free society, so dependent on communication, also depends on the integrity of its public speakers.

The need for integrity in public speaking is not a recent idea. The Roman teacher Quintilian said the ideal orator is "a good man skilled in speaking." Because eloquence serves the public welfare, Quintilian felt speakers must be infused with virtue. His concern is equally important today.

Where does a standard of what is right or virtuous come from? Much of it, of course, comes from our families and our culture. Ultimately, however, we ourselves are the decision makers. Each of us must define what is right. As speakers we must have a strong sense of responsibility to ourselves and to others. Why? Because this is what living in a free and open society demands. The Golden Rule, "Do unto others as you would have them do unto you," provides a solid base for most speech-making decisions. Perhaps, however, an even better guideline is the "Platinum Rule": "Do unto others as they want you to do unto them." Speakers must respond to others' needs rather than consider their speech making only in terms of the measurable benefit to themselves.

What does responsibility mean? It is related to trustworthiness, and if you want to be trusted as a public speaker, you must do things that engender trust:

- *Be true to yourself.* Accept accountability, and be aware of your own conscience and your feelings of right and wrong. Work at becoming secure in your values and beliefs, and resist conformity that does not represent your morals.

- *Act in a positive way.* Express yourself in such a way as to reveal your character. Can you be taken at your word? Can your behavior be counted on? If you act in a proper manner in all aspects of your life, you will be secure in knowing that your public presentation will match your private behavior. In this way, then, you will always be ready to act in a positive rather than a manipulative or exploitative manner.

- *Show concern for audience needs.* Do your homework. When you address listeners, accept responsibility toward that group of people. You owe these listeners your best thinking and your best performance. This means you must know as much as possible about your listeners. Audience analysis is considered in depth in Chapter 4.

- *Be emotionally aware and responsive.* It is easy to perceive trust as a logical outcome of logical thoughts and behaviors. But trust operates on an emotional plane as well. For example, if you are able to identify with listeners' feelings and emotions, you are more likely to be trusted. Politicians encounter difficulties in this area when they inadvertently offend a group of constituents by a careless comment, a thoughtless joke, or an ill-advised reference. When negative emotions are aroused, it is often difficult to reestablish the lost trust.

Aristotle (384–322 B.C.E.), among the greatest thinkers the world has known, cited three characteristics of credible speakers, and these are precisely the traits that we still tend to associate with the quality of trustworthiness. First, we trust those who are knowledgeable or well-informed. Second, we trust those of good character or people who are reliable and honest. Third, we trust those of good will or those who genuinely care about their listeners.

The benefits of developing trust are many. First, you will contribute to and support a free society. Second, you will experience personal, positive results. A certain peace and joy are connected with doing what is right; you will be free of the guilt or stress that surrounds manipulation, exploitation, and other unprincipled actions. Knowing that you are using all of your energy, all of your resources, and all of your abilities in communicating responsibly with others generates positive and uplifting feelings.

The third benefit of developing trust is that you will feel secure in attempting to achieve a positive, long-range outcome in your listeners. You will provide your listeners with sound, useful information on which they can base their decisions and grow in positive directions. You will connect with listeners and will demonstrate respect for them.

The Heart of the Matter

Two motives help us, as speakers, determine what is right and proper. First, speakers need to focus on assisting listeners in some way: adding to their knowledge, getting them to believe in better ways, or moving them to some beneficial action. Second, speakers must respect their listeners as active, involved thinkers and doers—people who care and whom we care about. If we assist audience members in selecting information, discovering good choices, and making sound decisions, then our focus will remain on what is right, proper, and correct.

SUMMARY

This chapter has offered a broader perspective of the basics of public speaking. A model illustrated the components of communication to help you anticipate circumstances and evaluate the process as well. The model included the components of speaker, audience, message, channel, speech occasion, culture, and feedback. Also discussed were the additional components of noise, effects, and social facilitation.

For a broader perspective, this chapter discussed what it means to live in a free society. Unfortunately, this opportunity does not encourage many people to polish their speech skills. People seldom think about how much they could accomplish, or how they could excel, if they just pursued their opportunities with enthusiasm, intensity, and readiness to communicate.

Finally, the chapter talked about the ethical responsibilities entailed by living in a free society and making speeches. These responsibilities have a direct bearing on every decision you make from the moment you begin planning your speech. To be trusted by listeners, you must be true to yourself, act in a positive way, show concern for audience needs, and be emotionally aware and responsive. These actions will help create trust.

Chapter Questions

1. Plan a speech with a specific topic and audience in mind. Then, for each of the components of the model of communication, list the attributes and characteristics that relate to the topic and audience you have selected.

2. How can effective communication skills improve your life right now?

3. Think about a speaker you have heard recently. Could he or she improve in communication skills? How?

4. What do you see as the benefits of following the suggestions regarding ethical responsibility?

5. Can you think of additional ways to gain the trust of listeners?

6. Is it necessary to use different methods for gaining trust with different audiences? What creates those differences?

Further Readings

Rob Anderson and Veronica Ross, *Questions of Communication: A Practical Introduction to Theory* (New York: St. Martin's Press, 1994).

> In this exceptionally readable book, Anderson and Ross describe all the major theories of communication and address common questions about the usefulness of communication theory. Chapters include concerns about ethical assumptions, theory building, the flow of communication, contexts of communication, personal experience, rules, communicative interdependence, changing minds, and the influence of the media. A good place to begin broad-context thinking.

Don Stacks, Mark Hickson III, and Sidney R. Hill, Jr., *Introduction to Communication Theory* (Fort Worth, TX: Holt, Rinehart & Winston, 1991).

> This comprehensive survey includes six sections: setting the bases, nonverbal and verbal codes, rhetorical perspectives, psychological approaches, sociological approaches, and integrating and living with the edifice. The authors provide readers with background information, results of theoretical approaches, and the different predictions that result from theories. Their goal is to help readers acquire better control over their communication.

Endnotes

1. David K. Berlo, *The Process of Communication: An Introduction to Theory and Practice* (New York: Holt, Rinehart & Winston, 1960), pp. 23–28. This book offers the best and one of the earliest descriptions of communication as a process.
2. Berlo, p. 24.
3. Berlo, p. 26.

Words in Action: Video Study

Your opportunity to establish credibility with an audience begins the moment you stand up to speak, and the message you convey is transmitted both verbally and nonverbally. These and other factors intertwine to create the speech event, and, as a result, every speech event is unique.

The accompanying video uses two versions of the speech example discussed in this chapter (Brian's speech) to demonstrate how a speech can differ in its effect even when the words spoken are the same. The same individual delivers both versions of the speech on this videotape to control for the possibility that you as an audience will perceive different speakers differently. After watching the two versions, answer the following question. You may want to review the different components of a speech event that are discussed in the chapter.

- Which presentation is more effective? Why?

3

Listening

After reading this chapter you will be able to:

- understand the prevalence and importance of listening in business, education, and life

- compare and contrast the six barriers to effective listening: laziness, a closed mind, opinionatedness, insincerity, boredom, and inattentiveness

- overcome the barriers to effective listening

- understand the difference between hearing and listening

- list and differentiate the five steps in the listening process: receiving, selecting, organizing, interpreting, and remembering

- distinguish between the two types of listening: listening for information and critical listening

- listen for information and listen critically

Dorian could not understand why he continued to get Cs on the examinations in one of his classes. He went to the lectures, took notes, and studied the notes and textbook, but he continued to get mediocre grades. When he went to see the instructor, she asked to see his lecture notes and was surprised by what Dorian showed her. Dorian's notes were confused, poorly organized, and in many cases undecipherable. There were no main heads, key supporting points, or details. When asked by the instructor, Dorian admitted he had difficulty concentrating during lectures.

Vicki sat in her public speaking class listening to her classmates giving speeches about breast cancer, the National Guard, racism, and caffeine. As she left class, her friend Julie asked her, "Can you believe those statistics on breast cancer?" Vicki asked her what she meant. Julie said, "I didn't know that for women breast cancer is the most common type of cancer and it's the second biggest cancer killer."[1] Vicki admitted she could not remember much about the speech and asked Julie, "How did you remember that?" Julie replied, "Oh, I was really interested in Becky's topic, so I listened closely."

Dorian and Vicki had direct experiences with ineffective listening. Dorian could probably improve his examination grades if he learned to listen better in lecture. This would result in better notes as well. Vicki would have been able to carry on a thoughtful conversation with Julie had she listened to Becky's speech; Vicki might also have learned some valuable information.

This chapter is about effective listening. Most people are not good listeners. Therefore, this chapter begins by discussing the barriers that interfere with effective listening and offering numerous suggestions for overcoming these barriers. A definition of listening is offered, and the different types of listening are explained.

Knowing about listening is important. Think of the amount of time you spend listening to others. Also, as a speaker you will need to structure your material so audience members will listen. (The chapters that follow this one will help you to grasp and hold audience attention.)

BARRIERS TO EFFECTIVE LISTENING

Steven Golen, a researcher on listening, has studied the barriers to effective listening.[2] Knowing about these barriers will help you control them. Golen lists six barriers: laziness, closed minds, opinionatedness, insincerity, boredom, and inattentiveness. According to Golen, these factors are important because they are real and because they can be controlled. All of Golen's factors are closely related to attitudes and habits.

Attitudes

An *attitude* is a predisposition to act in a certain way. For example, if someone tells you an instructor is hard, you are predisposed to believe that this instructor is hard whether she is or not. A predisposition to believe that a course is worthless or that an idea is too complicated can cause poor listening by turning off your attention. Attitudes, if you let them, can cut off or short-circuit your listening powers. But because the attitudes are your own, you can change them.

Habits

Habits, which are also predispositions, are acquired ways of acting that have become automatic. Like attitudes, they can affect how well you listen; but unlike attitudes, they are less easy to control. Typically, people do not habitually listen well because they are surrounded by constant and over-stimulating communication. As a result of this excess, for example, you have likely learned how to look attentive while your mind wanders, and probably try to get the general picture without having to listen for facts. These habits are how most people defend themselves against a continual barrage of information. Unfortunately, these habits also explain why many students have difficulty on objective tests, which require remembering facts. Many of Golen's barriers are entrenched habits that will take considerable effort on your part to change.

Laziness

Golen's list of the barriers to listening is in the order of importance; he believes that laziness is the biggest barrier to effective listening. Laziness occurs when you avoid listening because the subject is complex or difficult or takes what you consider to be too much time. For example, imagine an instructor explaining what the Hubble space telescope found using these words: "It was lurking about 50 million light-years away, at the core of galaxy M87—something with the mass of more than 2 billion stars the size of the sun crammed into a space no bigger than our solar system."[3] This instructor might help some listeners become lazy because of the complexity of this information. Some students might want the instructor to get along with the explanation and make the point.

Closed-mindedness

Closed-mindedness can be seen when listeners fail to maintain a relaxing and agreeable environment or refuse to relate to and benefit from a speaker's ideas. For example, a classroom speaker delivered a persuasive speech supporting the idea that homosexuals are suitable caregivers for raising children. The class discussion of this speech revealed some closed-mindedness and even homophobia among audience members. Many listeners thought that homosexuals could not be good parents; were afraid that homosexual modeling by parents or other adults could affect children or that homosexual parents might be sexually attracted to their children; feared that a homosexual household might be an unhealthy home environment or that the children of a homosexual couple would suffer ridicule from other children in the community. The speaker identified these concerns as misconceptions and offered considered and effective responses to many of them. However, in several cases those raising the issues did not hear the creative, thoughtful ideas the speaker proposed because their own concerns weighed so heavily on them throughout the speech. During the discussion, however, this closed-mindedness was pointed out and tied to the same problems some have listening to discussions of any controversial issue: abortion, federally supported erotic art, gun control, or universal health care, to name a few.

Opinionatedness

Closely related to closed-mindedness is Golen's third barrier, opinionatedness, which is evident when listeners disagree or argue outwardly or inwardly with a speaker. It also occurs if listeners become emotional or excited when a speaker's views differ from theirs. Any controversial topic is likely to provoke opinionated responses. For instance, a student giving a speech about legalizing drugs such as marijuana, cocaine, and heroin listed the proposed benefits of such a plan as the elimination of drug-related crime, drug dealers, and drug lords. The speaker inadvertently provoked an opinionated response from a listener who had used both marijuana and cocaine. From the outset of the speech this listener disagreed and argued with the speaker inwardly. During the question session following the speech, the listener spoke from personal experience. His point was simple: "Do you know what will happen to the youth of our nation if drugs are legalized? Do you know where I'd be if drugs were legalized? I'd be dead," he said, "along with a whole lot of other members of our society. No matter what the laws are, how harsh they are, or how well they are enforced, legalization will permit drugs to get into the hands of our youth just like guns have." This listener was opinionated—in his viewpoint, rightfully so.

Insincerity

Another barrier to effective listening is insincerity, which is evident when listeners avoid eye contact with a speaker or pay attention only to the speaker's words rather than also noticing the speaker's feelings. A painful example of insincerity occurred after a speech on rape, when one young man who had not been listening well and who had little interest in the topic asked the speaker, "Have you ever been raped?" Had this listener looked into the eyes of the speaker, or sensed the speaker's sensitivity on this issue, he would have known that the question should never have been asked. Unfortunately, the question caused the speaker to become emotional and leave the room.

Boredom

The fifth barrier to listening, boredom, is caused by the listener's lack of interest in the speaker's subject or impatience with the speaker. Boredom is likely to occur in speech classes because of the sheer number of speeches that are given. Many topics just don't interest everyone.

Boredom becomes even more of a barrier when speakers choose well-worn or irrelevant topics. Although an effective speaker can make almost any topic come alive, most listeners might become bored with a topic that holds little relevance for them. For example, a group of men may find little of interest in a speech on selecting the proper cosmetics, just as many women may have little interest in hair replacement techniques. In most cases speakers should accept the responsibility for listener boredom because it is probably caused by the speaker's lack of audience analysis.

Inattentiveness

Golen's final barrier to effective listening is inattentiveness. This can result when listeners concentrate on the speaker's mannerisms or delivery rather than on the message, or when listeners attend to noise rather than the message. Speakers can control some inattentiveness by eliminating mannerisms (if possible), strengthening weak delivery skills, and eliminating as many distractions or competing stimuli as possible.

OVERCOMING BARRIERS

How can you overcome barriers that prevent effective listening? It may be impossible to overcome strong negative attitudes or deeply entrenched habits, but neither of these problems should prevent you from trying.

Some specific methods for removing barriers have already been discussed. For example, as you select and test your topic, keep in mind appropriateness for you and your audience. In selecting information, think of the interests of your listeners. You will have a far better chance of having audience members listen to you when the topic of and the information in your speech relate to them.

In organizing a speech, remember that listeners must be carefully led. Use your introduction to get listeners' attention, establish rapport, and guide listeners into your speech. Use transitions to tell your listeners where you have been, where you are, and where you are going. You need to plan your conclusion, too; this is your last opportunity to make an impression on your listeners.

Here are some additional ways to overcome the barriers to effective listening. Select those that are likely to work for you. Any number can be chosen, and all will work as long as they are appropriate for you, your listeners, your topic, and the occasion.

- Prepare thoroughly.
- Use interesting examples and illustrations.
- Involve your listeners in your speech.
- Organize your ideas thoughtfully.
- Use dynamic and vivid language.
- Vary your inflection.
- Maintain a comfortable but energetic pace.
- Move in front of your listeners.
- Use visual aids.

- Listen to yourself selfishly; ask "What's in this for me?"
- Keep motivated.

More ideas for surmounting barriers to effective listening through effective delivery will be discussed in Chapter 11. For now, remember that increasing listening effectiveness is partly your responsibility as you speak. And as you listen to other people, you can do so more effectively if you keep in mind the difference between mere hearing and true listening.

HEARING VERSUS LISTENING

Hearing is the physical process of taking in sounds with your ears. *Listening* is the process of joining sounds with emotional and intellectual information in a search for meaning and understanding.[4] Thus, listening includes hearing, but hearing does not include listening, because hearing does not include emotional or intellectual processes.

Here is an example of this distinction: Trevor was sitting in class as the instructor clarified a point. To make sure members of the class grasped her meaning, she asked Trevor whether he understood. A bit ruffled by the instructor's intrusion into his daydreams, Trevor replied, "Yes."

The instructor, sensing his lack of sincerity, said, "Good. Could you cite an example of the point I just made?" Trevor was caught; he paused, collected himself, and then said, "Sure. But my example will be better if you could just restate the point in very simple terms."

The instructor smiled, restated the point, and then recognized Trevor for his example. Everyone benefited. The instructor had a chance to clarify her point for everyone in the class; Trevor had a chance to think of an appropriate example; everyone was more awake and alert; and in the end, nobody was embarrassed.

Before the instructor challenged Trevor, he had been hearing but not listening. He heard the words the instructor was saying but was not emotionally or intellectually engaged in the explanation. Had the instructor asked Trevor whether he was listening, he probably would have said he was, but that response would have been incorrect. Trevor listened closely after he was called on and as the instructor repeated her point.

THE IMPORTANCE OF EFFECTIVE LISTENING

Effective listening ability is essential for success in any occupation or profession. Moreover, becoming an effective listener can create "an interesting job, enjoyable relationships, numerous promotions, a higher-quality product, worthwhile contributions to a better world, and a competitive edge in a world marketplace."[5]

The study of a random sample of 1,000 personnel managers by Curtis, Winsor, and Stephens[6] (cited in Chapter 1) found that listening ability was the second most important factor (after oral communication) in helping graduating college students obtain employment. The personnel managers who were interviewed thought that the two factors most important for successful job performance included interpersonal and human relations skills (which would include listening ability) and oral communication skills. The courses these personnel managers thought most important for entry-level management included interpersonal communication (which would include training in listening skills), and public speaking. Finally, this study by Curtis, Winsor, and Stephens found that the ability to listen effectively and give counsel was ranked fourth in an ideal management profile.

The Curtis, Winsor, and Stephens study shows that personnel managers place great importance on effective listening skills in the business world. Excellent listening skills are likely to have a substantial payoff.

In another study, conducted by Johnson[7] (also cited in Chapter 1), similar results were produced in the field of education. Johnson found that high school principals rate communication-related skills, factors, and preparatory courses as most important when they assess candidates for teaching positions and when they rate teachers' in-class performance. Johnson's category of communication skills included listening skills as well as interpersonal communication, poise, oral communication, and enthusiasm.[8]

Figure 3.1
A breakdown of how a person in the United States communicates.

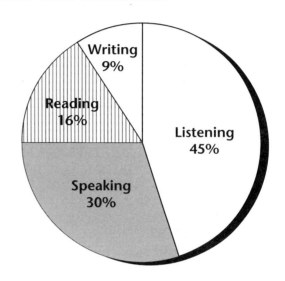

From Curt Bechler and Richard L. Weaver II, *Listen to Win: A Guide to Effective Listening* (New York: Master Media Limited, 1994) p. 26.

On average, people in the United States communicate during 80 percent of their waking time.[9] This communication consists of 45 percent listening, 30 percent speaking, 16 percent reading, and 9 percent writing[10] (see Figure 3.1).

THE NATURE OF LISTENING

When we define listening and analyze its steps, we are better able to describe what occurs, evaluate the process, and correct problems. The steps are difficult to clearly distinguish during listening, so this discussion will analyze the process by separating the process of listening into its component parts.[11] The process of listening includes five steps: receiving, selecting, organizing, interpreting, and remembering.

Receiving the information

To *receive* is to take into one's possession. Let's say that Dan gave a speech on planning a healthy lifestyle. If you were interested in the topic, or if you were partly responsible for evaluating his effort, you might give particular attention to his speech. Because of this you would be more likely to receive the information Dan shared.

Listening is a holistic process. You do not listen just with your ears; rather, reception occurs through all your senses. For example, during Dan's speech, let's say you are sitting in the front row. You see that he is neatly dressed and athletic in build, which makes him look like a model for the healthy lifestyle he is talking about. During the speech, he enters the seating area and puts a hand on your shoulder when he is talking humorously about people who need to be concerned about their health. These stimuli plus Dan's strong speaking voice help to counteract the tempting smells coming from the dining room next door, which might otherwise have acted as distractions. As you can see, a number of factors affect what you receive from Dan's speech. All your senses are taking in information and contributing to effective listening—not just your ears.

Selecting particular stimuli

To *select* is to pick out for special attention. Even when you are tuned in and involved, you may not receive every word a speaker says. That is, you select particular stimuli for special attention. For example, Dan has divided his speech into proper vitamin intake, proper diet, and proper exercise. Since you already know about exercise, you may pay more attention to what Dan has to say about vitamins or diet. When you listen you select the cues you need or want to hear about.

Organizing the information

To *organize* is to provide with a structure or system. Once you have selected information, the next step in the listening process is organizing it. You assign meaning to what you have selected by identifying, registering, and analyzing it. You also may enlarge, close, or simplify the information. For example, you might expand Dan's information on vitamins with information you learned in a health class by thinking, "I've heard that taking antioxidants daily can help." You might close the information (or complete a thought) he provided on adding vitamin supplements by thinking to yourself, "because the average diet is poor." You might simplify or summarize his information with the thought, "Basically, people are unhealthy."

You can now begin to see how complicated the process of organization is and in how many different ways organization can occur. Your way of organizing ideas is unlikely to match someone else's.

Interpreting information

To *interpret* is to explain or make understandable. Interpreting relates the information received, selected, and organized to your experiences or expectations. Let's say that your information on vitamin supplements is old; you don't remember it very well. In his speech Dan reminds you of what you have forgotten; and because you are interested in the possibility of using supplements, his ideas fit conveniently into your expectations as well. When he discusses specific vitamins and minerals and explains exactly how each one contributes to your health, growth, and protection, it is information that interests you. Mentally, you add to his explanations the information you already have, thus making it all more understandable to yourself.

Remembering information

To *remember* is to recollect, recall, or bring something back to mind again. This is the final step in the listening process. Most people remember only part of what they listen to; learning–forgetting curves indicate that 90 percent of information that is heard will not be remembered.[12] Usually you remember most easily the material that is important to you. You remember vitamins A, B, C, and E, for example, as well as calcium and iron, but you are unable to remember how each contributes to your health. You remember that vitamin A helps improve immunity because Dan talked about that one first. You remember that vitamin C could lengthen life by six years because that information really stood out. And you remember that calcium builds strong bones and teeth because you have heard that so many times. What you might do if you really want to remember which vitamins are important is jot down a few notes. Just the process of taking notes will help you remember.

But even if ideas are important to you, you may not remember them. This can happen for a variety of reasons:

1. The sounds were transmitted poorly.
2. You were not sitting where you could hear the sounds well.
3. You could attach no meaning to the actual sounds you heard (even though you knew by other indicators that they were important).
4. Too much physical or psychological noise interfered with the sounds.
5. You were too tired, hurried, aggravated, or annoyed to take the time to make sense of the sounds.
6. You were trying to remember too many other things at the same time.

As important as listening is, often you probably do not listen as well as you should. You may have instructors who do not speak clearly; some seats are too close to a door, window, or radiator to allow clear hearing; excessive jargon or technical terms may be confusing; classmates may distract you just as an instructor is giving an assignment; or perhaps you have too much on your mind at certain times or are too sleepy to pay attention. You may have just received a grade on a report that is lower than you expected; you might be told too much information at one time; or maybe the instructor speaks too quickly for you. To remember well you must first obtain the information to be remembered.

Even more important, though, is the fact that we think faster than we speak: People think at about 600 words per minute but speak at only about 150 to 200 words per minute.[13] In other words, your thoughts run well beyond the words that you hear. This is why it is so easy to daydream while others are talking. Letting your attention drift is especially easy when you listen to speakers because there is so little interchange in the sharing of ideas; often you are talked at rather than with. To combat this problem, you need to do things that will keep you focused while others are talking. Some ideas are provided in the "Listening for Information" section of this chapter.

TYPES OF LISTENING

We listen differently in different circumstances. To a lecturer, you may listen for information. To a politician, you may listen critically. To a friend in need of your support, you may listen empathically. To a comedian, you probably listen for enjoyment. This section discusses listening for information and critical listening.[14] Empathic listening and listening for enjoyment are less pertinent to our subject; empathic listening tends to be more interpersonally related, and listening for enjoyment is not something in which most people need training.[15] Listening for information and critical listening, on the other hand, are the types most closely related to public speaking.

Listening for information

When listening for information, strive to discover the *central thesis*. Once you discover this central thesis, many other things will become clear. Let's say you are listening to a lecture about Wolfgang Amadeus Mozart. Discovering the lecturer's central thesis—that Mozart was a musical genius—will make the lecturer's other points clear: Why did the lecturer define genius? Why did she talk about his youth in terms of his being a child prodigy? Why did she discuss his music in terms of its complexity? Why did she mention his amazing way of composing music? Why was his photographic memory important to his completing musical scores? The answers to all of these questions are oriented around the speaker's central thesis: that Mozart was a musical genius. The central thesis, then, becomes a hook onto which her other ideas can be hung.

Once you determine the central thesis, search for the main heads and then, finally, for the supporting points. It helps when listening to speakers to try to form a mental outline of the material. A mental outline makes it easier to predict what will come next in the speech. It will also aid in relating points to each other and to your own experience.

Finding a speaker's central thesis and outlining the speaker's material are two techniques that can help listeners stay focused. Because of the difference between thought speed and speech speed already mentioned, listeners often need to work at maintaining their focus on the message. Here are some suggestions:

1. *Keep motivated.* Depend only on yourself for maintaining interest in the message.
2. *Search the message for relevance.* Look for different ways to relate the information to yourself and your experiences.
3. *Avoid distractions.* Practice blocking out anything that draws your attention from the message.

4. *Stay active.* Question and paraphrase what you hear. Look for similarities and differences. Predict what will come next. Form a mental outline.

5. *Avoid arguing.* Argument is likely to take your mind away from the message.

6. *Take notes.* Taking notes can increase listening ability because it keeps the mind focused.

The Heart of the Matter

The key to effective listening is pure selfishness. Most of human nature is governed by selfishness (or, in other words, an ego orientation). The key, then, is to ask, "What's in this for me?" Although you may not like this orientation, the base of listening effectiveness is to discover why this message is important to you. When an agnostic young man was once asked, "Why do you, a non-religious person, attend church every Sunday without fail?" he replied, "There is something in every message, in every context, from every person, that is relevant to everyone, if he or she is just willing to search for it and apply it to his or her life." This young man not only discovered what was in the sermons for himself, but he found the messages relevant enough to continue to attend church regularly. The key to listening effectiveness is selfishness; when you listen, search for meaning from a personal perspective.

Critical listening

Critical listening goes a step beyond listening for information because it adds evaluation and challenge to the listening process. Let's say that a local politician, Maggie, has promised during her campaign to wipe out pornography in the local community. You have attended one of her campaign speeches, and you become concerned about her ideas. You begin to listen critically because she has linked pornography to crime, and you are not certain the link is correct. Maggie has stated, "Pornography promotes rape, pain, humiliation, and inferiority of women to men."

Critical listening means evaluating and challenging the messages you hear. In listening to Maggie's statement, one might come up with questions like these: Who defines pornography? Who says pornography promotes such behavior? Are there statistics to prove that pornography promotes crime? Will credible sources make this cause–effect link? Is this true of all pornography? Is this true in both large cities and smaller towns such as yours? This woman is a politician; but how credible is she in talking about pornography or crime? How has she gained knowledge about this issue?

Just as in listening for information, there are certain things that you can do to assist yourself as a critical listener. Here are some specific suggestions:

1. *Determine the speaker's motives.* Just because people are public speakers, politicians, or otherwise well known does not make them believable. Maggie

wants to be elected to office; that is an obvious motive. But does she have other motives as well? Does she own a shop that competes with a popular store that sells pornography? Could she have a personal agenda against a childhood antagonist? Is she influenced by strong religious beliefs?

2. *Challenge and question the speaker's ideas.* From where did the speaker get information? Are the sources of information identified and credible? Is information being taken out of context? Is important information being omitted? In persuasive situations, opportunities for asking questions are often provided. By asking questions, sometimes you can determine whether ideas are sound and believable.

3. *Distinguish fact from opinion.* Facts can be verified. That is, whoever applies the same test to the information should get the same results. For example, Maggie said, "In a survey of police chiefs, 58 percent believed that 'obscene' books and materials played a significant role in causing juvenile delinquency." If other researchers were to conduct similar surveys, would they get similar results? That is what distinguishes fact from opinion. If Maggie had instead said, "Police chief Jake Arnold says that the obscene books and materials sold in this community are responsible for our juvenile delinquency problem," not only would this clearly be opinion, but it would be difficult to prove. Common sense tells us that juvenile delinquency has other causes besides the availability of obscene books and materials.

In general, facts can be trusted more than opinions—if the facts are valid. But some opinions are more reliable than others, and some facts are better than others. And some people spout "facts" that are not really facts at all. Thus, sometimes one is left to one's own best judgment about what to believe.

4. *Recognize your own biases.* We hear what we want to hear. Let's say, for example, that Maggie cites a survey done in New York. She says, "Research shows that there has been an increase in addiction to violent pornography. The same survey," she says, "shows leveling in the rates of sexual assault and rape."

Let's say you do not believe in the pornography–crime link, and you do not believe that pornography is a problem in your area. You also don't believe there is a significant crime problem at all, so you might latch onto two items Maggie has said here: (1) The survey was done in New York, which is irrelevant to your area; and (2) the rates of assault and rape have leveled (not increased). Your own biases may cause you to listen selectively, but sensitivity to your biases may allow you to hear more complete information.

5. *Assess the message.* If you can suspend judgment long enough to weigh ideas, get more information, and seek answers and opinions from others, you are likely to base your decisions on better information, make certain that your actions are well grounded, and formulate your own attitudes and opinions with some certainty. After listening to Maggie's ideas, it may be time to find out the real story for yourself. Is pornography or crime a problem in your area? Does anyone else think there is a link? Are others besides yourself concerned about protecting free speech?

Listening effectively can protect against deception. It can help you guard against hasty decisions, solving problems on the spur of the moment, or being taken in by the effective manipulator.[16] Whenever you are told, "You must make your decision now," or "This is your last opportunity," such statements should warn you something is wrong.

SUMMARY

Effective listening may not get Dorian better than Cs on class examinations, but it is likely to help. Effective listening will help Vicki discuss issues with her classmates, and she will become a better conversationalist. When you become sensitive to your listening ability, you will probably be able to improve it.

Listening means drawing together physical, emotional, and intellectual information in a search for meaning and understanding. Because of its prevalence as an active force in business and education success and because of the amount of time we engage in it, listening requires our concern and attention.

The chapter began by discussing six listening barriers: laziness, closed-mindedness, opinionatedness, insincerity, boredom, and inattentiveness. All of these are affected by attitudes and habits. A number of remedies for overcoming these barriers were offered. The process of listening was considered next. The chapter ended by considering two types of listening: listening for information and critical listening. Because you need to be able to command listener attention in order to succeed as a public speaker, it is crucial that you understand how listening works as well as improve your own listening skills.

Chapter Questions

1. What problems in your life may have resulted from ineffective listening?

2. How much of a normal day do you spend listening? Name some of your typical listening activities.

3. Which of your own attitudes and habits promote effective listening behaviors? Which allow ineffective listening behaviors?

4. Which of Golen's six listening barriers is likely to affect you the most? In what circumstances does it affect you?

5. Can you think of other ways to overcome barriers to effective listening?

6. What situations have you experienced in which it was impossible for a speaker to overcome barriers to effective listening? What were the specific barriers? Did the speaker try to surmount them? How?

7. When you listen, are you able to detect the five parts of the process: receiving, selecting, organizing, interpreting, and remembering? Describe specifically how you have followed this sequence of activities for a recent act of listening.

8. Which area gives you greater difficulty—listening for information or

critical listening? What difficulty do you experience? How might you improve your use of this type of listening?

Further Reading

Robert N. Bostrom, *Listening Behavior* (New York: Guilford Press, 1990).
This is a fairly sophisticated book on listening and a useful resource for those who want to know more about how listening works. The author reviews most of the studies done on listening and provides some recent research as well.

Curt Bechler and Richard L. Weaver II, *Listen to Win: A Guide to Effective Listening* (New York: Master Media, 1994).
Although this book is aimed at managers, the examples, explanations, and suggestions are relevant to all readers interested in establishing good listening habits. Besides creating an awareness of the process, the authors offer specific methods for changing attitudes and habits in the workplace, in conflict situations, in meetings, and for personal growth.

Endnotes

1. These statistics came from a speech by Rebecca Shade given in a basic speech communication course on November 9, 1993. According to Shade's notes, the statistics came from three sources: Paula M. Siegel, "Breast Assured," *Harper's Bazaar* 124 (November 1991), p. 120; Claudia Bowe, "Breast Cancer: A Cosmo Checkup," *Cosmopolitan* 210 (February 1991), pp. 148–154; and Susan Rennie, "Breast Cancer Prevention: Diet and Drugs," *Ms. Magazine* 3 (May 1993), pp. 38–46.
2. Steven Golen, "A Factor Analysis of Barriers to Effective Listening," *The Journal of Business Communication* 27 (Winter 1990), p. 32.
3. Michael D. Lemonick, "A Real Space Monster," *Time* 143 (June 6, 1994), p. 60.
4. Richard L. Weaver II, *Understanding Interpersonal Communication*, 6th ed. (New York: Harper Collins, 1993).
5. Curt Bechler and Richard L. Weaver II, *Listen to Win: A Guide to Effective Listening* (New York: Master Media, 1994), p. xiv.
6. Dan B. Curtis, Jerry L. Winsor, and Ronald D. Stephens, "National Preferences in Business and Communication Education," *Communication Education* 38 (January 1989), pp. 6–14.
7. Scott D. Johnson, "A National Assessment of Secondary-School Principals' Perceptions of Teaching-Effectiveness Criteria," *Communication Education* 43 (January 1994), pp. 1–16.
8. Johnson, pp. 1, 13.
9. P. Morgan and K. H. Baker, "Building a Professional Image: Improving Listening Behavior," *Supervisory Management* 30 (1985), pp. 34–38.
10. See Bechler and Weaver (1994), pp. 25–26.
11. This section is drawn partly from Richard L. Weaver II, *Understanding*

Interpersonal Communication, 6th ed. (New York: Harper Collins, 1993), pp. 173–74.

12. See Robert R. Bostrom and Carol L. Bryant, "Factors in the Retention of Information Presented Orally: The Role of Short-Term Listening," *Western Journal of Speech Communication* 44 (Spring 1980), pp. 137–45.
13. Bechler and Weaver (1994), p. 179.
14. This information on the four types of listening is drawn partly from Saundra Hybels and Richard L. Weaver II, *Communicating Effectively*, 4th ed. (New York: McGraw-Hill, 1995), pp. 65–78.
15. See Hybels and Weaver (1995), pp. 72–78, for more information on empathic listening and listening for enjoyment.
16. See Everett L. Shostrom's *Man, The Manipulator* (Nashville, TN: Abingdon Press, 1967). Although dated, this book on manipulation is still valuable. Shostrom's examples of manipulation between lovers, children and parents, teachers and students, and husbands and wives, along with his discussion of profit versus people, are as relevant today as when they were written.

Words in Action: VIDEO STUDY

To keep an audience listening, a speaker selects a topic relevant and of interest to the audience, develops a dynamic introduction, and uses transitions as a road map—all strategies for overcoming listening barriers. Additional strategies are listed on p. 33.

In the accompanying video, a student discusses how smokers dispose of cigarette butts on her college campus. As you watch the video, consider which strategies the speaker employs to overcome barriers to listening. Then answer the following assessment questions to test both your skills as a listener and the speaker's skills for capturing and holding listeners' attention.

1. What is the speaker's central thesis?
2. What does the speaker claim increases the number of cigarette butts outside a building?
3. How does she support the contention that smokers are careless?
4. Does the speaker create confusion about her thesis?
5. How does she use humor to help the audience remember her message?
6. What visual aids does the speaker use to support her speech?
7. How does she help guarantee the audience will remember her main point?

Audience Analysis

After reading this chapter you will be able to:

- select a target audience
- adapt to the needs, interests, and desires of audience members
- ask the essential questions for audience analysis
- use several methods to get information about an audience
- gain listener's physical and psychological involvement
- maintain mutual respect with your audience
- use audience feedback as continuing audience analysis

L ori, the university's outstanding female basketball player, designed her speech to inform her audience about the forthcoming basketball season—the teams involved, where the games would be played, and the chances for a winning season. But the speech missed its mark entirely. Lori did not realize that she was talking to students who had no interest in athletics and had not attended a single athletic event during college. Lori's audience found her speech boring and irrelevant.

What could Lori have done to better address her immediate audience? I am going to save the answer to this question until a bit later in this chapter, but had Lori done some audience analysis, she probably could have selected a topic on which she had expertise to share that would have been of greater interest to her listeners.

The Heart of the Matter

In effective speech making *all* decisions regarding the planning and preparation of a speech are driven by audience-related questions and answers. Will this topic appeal to this audience? Will this evidence interest them? Will these examples hold their attention? Will this organizational scheme help them follow these ideas and add clarity to this speech? Will a transition here help listeners follow the ideas better? Will this introduction grab their attention and cement it to my central thesis? Will this conclusion best summarize these ideas and leave this audience with a positive impression and a clear sense of this speech? Audience-driven answers to these questions become the very heart of effective public speaking. Often when a speech falls flat it is because a speaker has not made the audience the determining factor in all speech-making decisions. Rather than "Know thyself," the guiding principle in speech making should be "Know your audience."

Tom's father is an investment broker, so Tom talked to his classmates about how best to invest their money. His topic, too, missed its mark because students usually have little or no money to invest. On the other hand, Jackson spoke about sources of financial aid: how to qualify, where to apply, and how to find out about deadlines. Do you think students were interested in his talk? Alicia talked about buying clothes at local used clothing stores and even Goodwill outlets. Students wrote down store names as she talked. As you can see, accurate audience analysis allows you to target your listeners directly and specifically and is likely to make your speeches more significant, relevant, and interesting.

This chapter discusses how you can select your target audience; adapt to the needs, interests, and desires of that audience; hold audience attention and get listeners involved; maintain mutual respect with your audience; and use audience feedback to your advantage.

IDENTIFYING THE TARGET AUDIENCE

The *target audience* is composed of the people capable of responding to the speaker's ideas. Because you can't affect everyone in an audience, your goal should be to inform or persuade those members of the audience who can respond to your ideas. Selecting a target audience will help you narrow and focus your ideas. In most audiences some people will be interested and some will not; some will be able to take action on the ideas shared, and some will not. In a heterogeneous audience everyone will be affected differently by a speech. If your goal is to satisfy everyone you are likely to be disappointed; it seldom happens. That is why it is better to select a target audience toward whom the message can specifically be directed. These are the people most likely to be affected by and gain from the ideas; and these are the people by whom success is likely to be best determined or judged—if, indeed, it can be judged by reactions of the target audience.

The speakers cited at the opening of this chapter had no members of their target audience present when they gave their speeches (if they had targeted anyone at all). To identify your target audience you need to ask several questions:

1. How important is my topic to these audience members?
2. What do my audience members already know about my topic?
3. How do my audience members feel about this topic?
4. To what extent can I identify with my audience members' interests, beliefs, attitudes, and values on this topic?
5. How can I build on the areas of commonality?

Had Lori, the basketball star, asked these questions about her audience, she might have redesigned her speech. Her topic—the basketball season—was unimportant to them. They did not know about the topic because they did not care about the topic and felt it was irrelevant. So if Lori wanted to identify with their interests, beliefs, attitudes, and values, she needed to begin differently.

ADAPTING TO AUDIENCE NEEDS, INTERESTS, AND DESIRES

It would be easy to determine a target audience and then stop there. But to do the discovery work and not use the information discovered would be like taking a trip to Europe and then coming back home once having stepped on European shores. The joy of traveling to Europe is taking advantage of all the opportunities Europe offers travelers. Similarly, how can speakers take advantage of all the information available in the process of selecting a target audience? Let's look at an example.

Nakisha wants to give a speech to encourage audience members to become involved in the Career Planning and Placement Service (CPPS) on campus. She knows from CPPS statistics that this service is not particularly important to her audience members; thus, she will have to make it important to them. From the same statistics she knows audience members have meager knowledge of the service, so she will have to add to that knowledge. How do they feel about the service? They probably like having it available, but in general their feelings are neutral. They just don't think about it much.

To what extent can Nakisha identify with her audience members' interests, beliefs, attitudes, and values regarding the CPPS? Closely. Until she investigated it, she was in exactly the same situation. Thus, this is the area where most of her effort can be focused—bringing audience knowledge on the topic up to the level of her own and then showing how the CPPS directly relates to their interests. For example:

1. The CPPS can provide counseling and feedback as students consider career decisions, especially if the decision process is lengthy because a student has many alternatives to consider.
2. The CPPS can supply solid supporting evidence for important career decisions.
3. The CPPS can help ensure that students' career choices are the right ones.
4. The CPPS is readily available and is already paid for out of student fees.

Nakisha can build on this information and identify with her audience members if she uses the many opportunities offered by the CPPS and then shows her listeners, by example, the benefits that can result. Taking them step-by-step through an actual visit may make her ideas more vivid and realistic. Further, if she can supply her audience with CPPS brochures at the conclusion of the speech, audience members will have something to take home with them after the speech as well as an exact location and telephone number for the CPPS.

Had Lori selected a target audience, she could have redirected her speech by analyzing that audience. Knowing that her audience had never attended a single athletic event and that they were not athletically inclined, Lori might have chosen one of these more appropriate topics:

1. How does basketball skill development relate to developing survival skills for life?
2. What does it take to become outstanding in any area of life?
3. What is life like for a student who has balanced athletic participation with academics?
4. Why are athletic events an important and integral part of any academic community?
5. How does developing the mind in athletics relate to developing the mind in being a successful college student?

The question is not "What do I want to speak on?"; rather, the question should be "How can I best connect what I know to my audience members' interests, beliefs, attitudes, and values?"

USING DEMOGRAPHICS TO UNDERSTAND YOUR AUDIENCE

The best way to know your audience is to find out everything you can about them. The more information you have about your audience, the better you will be able to understand them, adapt to them, react to them, and respond to unexpected circumstances during your speech. The term *demographics* refers to characteristics of a given group of people such as age, gender, level of education, and background knowledge. In this section you will see that audience characteristics affect both how you choose a speech topic and what approach you take in presenting that topic.

Age

Speakers can better tailor their presentations if they can determine the approximate average age of the people in the audience. The topics that interest audiences are likely to differ with their age. For example, 18- to 22-year-old college students might be interested in speeches on success, sex, grades, getting a job, adventure, education, getting ahead, and keeping a job. Although an audience of slightly older people might be interested in some of the topics above, they might better enjoy topics like succeeding in business, understanding our economy, raising children, keeping families together, using leisure time, and easing the tax bite. These topics of interest would likely change again if you considered topics that 50- and 60-year-olds would enjoy.

Once you have chosen your topic, you must decide on a *slant*—a way to approach and present the topic. Think about the differences between your ideas and those of your parents. Would you say your parents are more or less cautious than you are? More or less conservative? More pessimistic or more optimistic? Are their interests different? You should take these factors into consideration and adjust your approach to the topic accordingly. Without such adjustments your audience may not listen to, understand, or accept your ideas. For example, if you are presenting an informative speech about using a computer, you can assume an audience of college students knows the basics; in contrast, an audience of retirees, many of whom never have had to use a computer, may require you to begin from square one: how to turn a computer on and off. As another example, consider how you would speak about the environment to young children (say, 10-year-olds) as opposed to college students. When speaking to the 10-year-olds, you might discuss basic environmental protection topics such as preventing forest fires, not littering, and perhaps cleaning up a nearby stream. However, you would probably tackle more complex environmental issues when you speak to the college students: nuclear waste disposal, the greenhouse effect, agricultural runoff, or wetlands preservation. The average age of your audience, as you can see, makes a difference for your speech.

Gender

Although gender has long been recognized as an important variable in communication, an audience's interest in and understanding of any topic cannot be accurately predicted solely on the basis of gender. However, gender is still a factor to consider.

As a speaker, your goal should be to understand the interests, values, and language expectations of your audience, and this includes evaluating similarities and differences between males and females. On topics regarding sexual relations, education, and employment, males and females have grown closer together in their opinions. Although a speech on child rearing or resolving conflict within the family would make little sense for an audience of independent, single professionals of either gender, it should have equal interest to both male and female parents.

Education

Education can be an important factor in audience analysis. The more educated the audience, the more likely it becomes that speakers will need to use rational or logical appeals; recognize the stability and consistency of the audience's beliefs, values, and attitudes; and consider their knowledge. The higher the educational level, the more knowledge the audience will have of your topic—especially if the topic is oriented toward either current events or experiences that touch their lives. People with more education also tend to view issues in shades of gray, whereas people with less education tend to view issues as black and white. More educated people tend to be more pessimistic or fatalistic and are more active. They participate in community affairs, and they actively voice their opinions, interests, and reactions.

Background knowledge about the topic

Although the educational level of an audience may help determine how much background knowledge the audience has, you may want to find out how much they know specifically about your topic. For example, if you talk about a proposal such as a bond issue, it would be useful to know how many other speeches on the issue they have heard or how much information has been available in the local papers. Must you spend time with basics, or can you get right to the heart of the issue?

The audience's background knowledge may include prejudices and biases. If people feel strongly for or strongly against your topic, your speech will probably not change their attitudes. If might be better for you to take a different tack—perhaps trying to inform them about some new aspect of the problem—rather than trying to persuade them to change. However, your audience may contain members with varying views about your topic. A homogeneous group is sometimes easier to approach because you have a better idea of what kind of attitudes to expect. But even then, you need to evaluate factors such as these: How extreme is their position? How did they come by their information? How recently was it acquired? How strongly committed to it are they?

Knowing about the audience's background knowledge can also reveal its degree of involvement. You can estimate the level of audience involvement before a speech by judging how closely your topic matches audience members' needs and interests, how closely it relates to their self-image, how closely it reflects their central values, or how strongly committed they are to the topic. Estimating how involved listeners are *during* a speech may be easier because of obvious signs such as listener outbursts and reactions. Audience members may shake or nod their heads, clench their fists, tense their muscles, move nervously, or speak out.

The topics just discussed represent the major demographic variables. Depending on the circumstances and the nature of the topic, it might be helpful to ask, in addition, about the vocation, religion, geographical area, and lifestyle of your listeners. The purpose of your search is to find guides to audience members' values, attitudes, information, and even sense of humor.

Working with Audience Opinion

Here are some general suggestions that can help speakers handle preexisting audience opinions about a topic.

For audiences strongly in favor of the topic:
- Impress on them the truth. Encourage them to act when they can.
- Urge them to take a specific course of action.
- Encourage further, deeper commitment with more information and knowledge.

For audiences that are neutral or apathetic to the issue:
- Make your approach interesting. Combine emotion and information.
- Strive to avoid ideas that may alienate. Emphasize and reinforce any ideas with which audiences already sympathize.

For audiences that are strongly opposed or hostile to the topic:
- Establish your own credibility for speaking on this topic.
- Offer the audience preliminary explanatory material designed to minimize their opposition.
- Try to respond to the chief objections of the audience.
- Offer the audience new facts or new conditions.
- Strive to achieve identification with ideas and opinions that you and your audience share.
- Offer listeners as many options as possible, hoping to get some movement in your direction as opposed to none.

HOW DO YOU ANALYZE THE AUDIENCE?

How do you find out all this information? Basically, you discover it in the same way you find information that you need about anything: You ask a lot of questions.

If your audience is your class, you can question yourself as long as you can be objective about the answers. For example, what are my interests? What are my values? What is my income level? Are others in the class like me or different from me? If you are unsure of your responses, question your classmates as well.

If you will be speaking before an audience about which you need more information, your host or hostess or the program chairperson will be one of your best resources. Also consider any prior experience you may have had with this or another audience. Is this audience similar to one you know about?

If the audience belongs to or identifies with an organization or association, read the literature (pamphlets, newsletters, or journals) of the organization or association. What has been written in the newspaper about it? Libraries sometimes keep files on local organizations and associations. A call ahead might save you a trip, or it might help the librarian make the trip more profitable for you. Armed with enough information, the librarian will often help you with some of the initial searching. Other information sources may include the local chamber of commerce, local historical society, and other private agencies.

GAINING AUDIENCE INVOLVEMENT

There is, of course, a direct relationship between analyzing an audience and involving its members in your speech. The trick is being able to effectively use the information revealed in your audience analysis. Audience involvement can be either physical or psychological. For example, you could ask for a show of hands (physical involvement) or say, "Now I want you to picture this" (psychological involvement). When listeners are involved, the speech is more likely to have an impact on them—to increase understanding or change beliefs and attitudes.

The best way to involve audience members is to think "involvement" at all stages in speech preparation. In the questions that follow, notice how closely answers are tied to a thorough audience analysis:

1. Will listeners get involved with this topic?
2. Will they get involved with the information I am finding to support this topic?
3. Will this organizational scheme keep listeners involved throughout my speech?
4. Will this introduction, this conclusion, and these transitions help them stay involved?
5. Will my language choices help motivate them to be involved with my ideas?
6. Will my delivery style and approach help keep them involved?

Audience Analysis Checksheet

This checksheet will help you cover all the major items in your audience analysis. Such planning will add to the impact of your message and will increase your confidence; you will feel better about addressing the audience.

____ 1. What is the average age of your audience?

____ 2. Do you know the gender distribution?

____ 3. How much education do they have?

____ 4. How much knowledge do they have of your topic?

____ 5. How well informed are they generally?

____ 6. What else do you know about audience demographics?
    ____ a. Occupations?
    ____ b. Religions?
    ____ c. Socioeconomic status?
    ____ d. Cultural or ethnic composition?
    ____ e. Political affiliations?
    ____ f. Group memberships?

____ 7. Have you all the information you need on the logistics of the situation?
    ____ a. Size of the audience?
    ____ b. Seating?
    ____ c. Public address system? Microphone?
    ____ d. Type of hall (setting)?
    ____ e. Lighting?
    ____ f. Occasion?
    ____ g. Degree of formality or informality?
    ____ h. Time?
    ____ i. Other speakers?
    ____ j. Noise?
    ____ k. Lectern?
    ____ l. Visuals?

____ 8. What attitudes do audience members hold (favorable, neutral, or opposed)?
    ____ a. Toward you?
    ____ b. Toward your topic?
    ____ c. Toward the occasion?

____ 9. Have you made plans to gather information
    ____ a. Before the speech?
    ____ b. During the speech?
    ____ c. After the speech?

Involvement cannot be oversold. What is the point of talking to any audience, whether at a meeting, over dinner, or in a boardroom, if its members do not become involved with you? We imagine our audience members as involved with us, connected with our ideas, and responsive to us; then we make planning decisions that advance and promote this point of view. Why speak if no one listens?

MAINTAINING MUTUAL RESPECT WITH YOUR AUDIENCE

There are several ways to ensure that the impression you make on listeners is positive. One method is to respect your audience. When you maintain mutual respect with your audience, you are more likely to influence them. If you ask yourself what irritates you as an audience member about other speakers, you can probably come up with a number of additional points not mentioned here, but these will start you thinking in the right direction.

Use listener time productively. Audience members value their time. For example, let's assume you did no planning or preparation and you are speaking for five minutes to an audience of 25 people. This means you are wasting five minutes for each of the 25 audience members, which translates into 125 minutes or two hours and five minutes of wasted time!

Offer listeners valuable information. Audience members want information to further their thinking. Just providing common knowledge does little to advance the general human cause. People want new ideas, new thinking, and new perspectives. Old material will prompt listener boredom and frustration.

Be honest with your listeners. Audience members want honesty. If there is any possibility that ideas are being misrepresented, taken out of context, or in some way not provided completely, they should be avoided altogether. Audience members deserve the information necessary to make their own decisions, and they naturally resent being deceived, shortchanged, or misled in any way. A speaker who cheats an audience once, probably will not be given an opportunity to do so again with the same audience.

Stick to the time limit. Audience members do not like listening to lengthy speeches. One speaker who had prepared a half-hour speech for an organization was told when she showed up that the speech should be no longer than 15 minutes. She quickly went through her speech and deleted half the material. The speech turned out to be more powerful in its short form, and the speaker said she liked it better that way. Sometimes ruthless cutting strengthens speeches by removing distracting excess material. These are clear cases where less is more.

Show enthusiasm. Audience members want an enthusiastic presentation. Most people have experienced dreary monotonic speeches, and they do not like sitting through them. When asked whether they would rather have an enthusiastic teacher who does not know the material very well or a less enthusiastic teacher who really knows all the information, students usually prefer enthusiasm. This does not excuse poor preparation or a vacant speech delivered with high energy; it simply shows that audiences prefer some vigor and vitality in the way ideas are presented.

USING FEEDBACK

The goal of effective public speaking is to make an impression of some kind—to inform, to change beliefs or attitudes, to secure action, or to entertain. How do you know when this has been accomplished? Almost never will you know for certain because often you cannot see the changes. However, the best guideline available is the feedback audience members provide. *Feedback* is the ongoing response behavior of audience members that lets speakers know their message is being received. In one sense this is the ultimate in audience analysis because it is real, immediate, and important. If you cannot adapt to on-the-spot feedback, you miss your final opportunity to hone, polish, and perfect your performance as it occurs.

Feedback makes speaking a dynamic, transactional process in which you and your listeners participate in creating meaning. Feedback is part of the forming, shaping, and molding process that occurs as ideas take shape. To ignore feedback is a little like stepping outside the communication process and deciding not to participate. Feedback is essential if the process is to be more than one-way communication. Effective speakers notice and respond to the feedback they receive from listeners.

SUMMARY

This chapter examined the process of selecting a target audience and adapting your speech to their needs, interests, and desires. Sample questions were suggested to ask when you are analyzing an audience; such in-depth audience analysis will help increase audience involvement with your speech. Besides careful analysis of your audience, other ways to show them respect include using listener time productively, offering listeners valuable information, being honest with your listeners, sticking to the time limit, and speaking enthusiastically.

Finally, the importance of feedback in fine-tuning and adjusting ideas to fit audiences was discussed. If you spend the time necessary in thorough audience analysis, you will be proud and confident of your speech.

Chapter Questions

1. What is the overall value of audience analysis?

2. How does selecting a target audience improve your speech?

3. How would you get information regarding an audience about which you knew little?

4. Let's say that you are asked to speak to a group of local businesspeople about the need for a youth community center in the downtown area. About 35 businesspeople are expected to attend your presentation.

  a. How would you select your target audience from this group? What questions would you ask? What information would you want to discover?

  b. What needs, interests, and desires of your audience would you want to adapt your speech to?

  c. Do a brief audience analysis of the 35 businesspeople. (Guess at any information you do not have.) Would this information be helpful to know when you are preparing a speech for this group? How would it help?

  d. How might you hold the attention of 35 businesspeople?

  e. What things might you do in such a speech to help avoid annoying your audience?

  f. How would you adapt to the feedback that you might receive from audience members during your speech about the youth community center? (Be hypothetical here.) What kind of feedback can you expect to receive?

5. Can you think of additional ways to show respect for your audience?

6. Why is audience feedback important to a speaker?

Further Reading

Henry Ehrlich, *Writing Effective Speeches* (New York: Paragon House, 1992). The author has been a business and political speechwriter and is currently a senior writer for a major New York City corporation. He includes excellent chapters on knowing your audience and an entire section (five chapters) called "What the Audience Wants and Needs." This book is well written and has many examples.

Joan Detz, *How to Write & Give A Speech* (New York: St. Martin's Press, 1992). This is a practical book full of examples for executives, PR people, managers, fund-raisers, politicians, and educators. Detz's second chapter is on "Assessing Your Audience." She is a speechwriter and a speech coach.

Words in Action: VIDEO STUDY

As a speaker, your goal is to communicate a message to an audience. In almost all cases, achieving that goal requires that you adapt your speech to fit the audience. In the accompanying video, Senator Edward Kennedy adapts to his audience of Liberty Baptist University students. Notice the techniques he uses to engage this audience, and answer the following questions regarding his speech.

1. What potential problem does Kennedy face with this audience?
2. How do we know he recognizes this problem?
3. How does Kennedy attempt to gain audience acceptance?

PART II

The Substance of the Speech

Finding Originality and Focus

After reading this chapter you will be able to:

- illustrate how originality occurs

- pursue originality in your speeches

- discover appropriate topics for your speeches

- understand the nature and intent of the general purpose

- frame a specific purpose for your speeches

- demonstrate the importance of the central thesis in planning and focusing speeches

- explain the purposes and cautions of using visual support

Shane put a new twist on a common topic. Rather than talking about the benefits of exercise and a healthy diet, she talked about excessive exercise and dieting. Originally her interest was aroused by an article she read in *U.S. News & World Report* called "Buying the Perfect Body" (May 1, 1989, p. 69). She thought Americans had become obsessed with too much exercise and extreme dieting and that this might make an interesting and informative speech.

Shane began doing research. Because she exercised and carefully watched what she ate, she had an inherent interest in the topic. She also liked to read fitness magazines like *Runner's World* and *Crosstrainer*, and she had some recent issues with two articles that fit into her plan. In *Runner's World* she found Megan Othersen's article "My Body, Myself" (June 1993), and in *Crosstrainer* she found an article by Laura Dayton called "Are You an Exercise Addict?" (January 1994). Shane was on her way.

Although she was not sure what the title of her speech would be, she knew she wanted something similar to "The Price of Perfection." Her tentative purpose was to inform the class about the potential costs of striving to have a "perfect" body. Now she had an original approach to an interesting and relevant topic, and, even more important, she had some focus for her speech. Since it was still a week and a half away, she had time for further research and investigation. She also had time to get a better title and to polish her purpose statement.

This chapter discusses the process of choosing a speech topic and purpose. First originality and creativity are explained. Next the chapter explores speech purposes and central theses. Finally, the chapter provides information about using visual aids to support your presentation. This chapter enables you to put your own unique stamp on your speech. If you are concerned that your speech may bore your listeners or sound hackneyed, this chapter will help you make your presentation stand out.

ORIGINALITY

Authors, songwriters, painters, and others in the creative professions often are asked "From where do you get your ideas?" In the book *How to Be Funny on Purpose*,[1] author Willis mentions in Chapter 4 the renowned Canadian humorist Stephen Leacock. Leacock, who has authored numerous books, humorous essays, and lectures, was asked how he managed to produce all of his amusing material. He responded, "You just jot down ideas as they occur to you. The jotting presents no problem; it is the occurring that is difficult."

So how do creative people get this "occurring" to happen? As Willis points out, "'occurring' is not likely to happen at all in a mind whose cogitative [brain] machinery is idling. Some sort of organized thinking is needed to produce jokes."[2] The word "ideas" could be substituted for the word "jokes" in that sentence.

Notice, for example, the organized thinking that Shane used when she read that first *U.S. News & World Report* article:

1. How might this work for an informative speech?

2. How would my audience respond to this idea?
3. How much information can I bring to this topic from my own experience?
4. What additional ideas might I need to make this work?

When highly creative people are asked where they get their ideas, they often respond, "You know, I have so many ideas that I don't even have time to capture them all." Creative people's inspirations flow more or less constantly.

Originality is important because your speech topic can be a motivating force in the whole process of speech making. When you have an original perspective or point of view to share, it will make you more interested in speaking clearly and persuasively. So when you read, listen, and observe, record your impressions. When new ideas occur, if they are not written down, they may not return, at least not in the same form. Now comes only

The Heart of the Matter

From where does originality come? First, try to forget the idea that you need to come up with something entirely new—this is unlikely to happen. However, if you have ever been told that you are not an "original thinker," it's not true. You are; everyone is. Originality comes from a unique combination of ideas, and everyone is capable of seeing things in new ways. The key is to have the ingredients with which to work. The more you read, listen, observe, and experience, the more likely it is that your originality will be an ongoing stream rather than a stagnant pond. Openness, responsiveness, playfulness, and willingness to internalize new ideas prompt originality.

once and never waits, so record those ideas when you get them, no matter what they are. This is why diaries and journals can be valuable—especially to those who must often be original.

CHOOSING A TOPIC AND PURPOSE

Let's say that you have an open-ended speech assignment coming up, and you have not chosen a topic yet. Open-ended here means simply that the choice of a topic is left up to you. This is common in public speaking classes, and right now you stand at perhaps the most important point in the entire process of speech making.

Your choice of topic will make much of the difference in whether your speech will be successful. Most important, it will provide motivation for you as the speaker. With a great topic, you'll *want* to research and investigate the topic: to get just the right or the best information; to find the best organizing pattern to appropriately showcase your ideas; to rehearse your speech to get it just right; and to present your ideas to your listeners. You have something to say, and you are compelled to say it—all because of a great topic.

So where do speakers without great topics begin to find them? Let me list a number of possibilities here, any of which might work for you. As you read this list, let your mind wander freely over the images, perceptions, feelings, and ideas that are stimulated. Brainstorming to generate potential topics requires that you keep an open mind at first; try not to stem the flow with criticism. After you have several ideas jotted down, you can begin to narrow the list.

1. Search your own experience and background for areas of interest. Many of the things you have seen, heard, or done would also interest others. View yourself as a first source for ideas. Remember, the goal here is to come up with a good topic; at this point you are not trying to find supporting material to inform, convince, move, or change listeners. That will follow.

2. Pick up a daily newspaper, a weekly news magazine, or a weekly or monthly magazine that appeals to your interests. Read it. Does anything catch your eye? Editors, of course, must be in touch with the major issues of interest to the public if they want to sell copies. Shane found her topic in an issue of *U.S. News & World Report*.

3. Talk to roommates, friends, other students, or teachers about possible topics. Listen closely. Try to avoid commonplace topics that many people are tired of hearing about. If you are alert, and if you listen for a speech topic, then a normal day of exposure to the ordinary flow of events around you will probably produce some appealing ideas.

4. Go to the library and skim through a variety of magazines and journals. Does anything intrigue you? Don't just pick up magazines and journals with familiar names; try to find some unfamiliar sources that might offer you a unique topic, a different point of view, or a new lens through which to view the world. Often this difference will entice, lure, or provoke curiosity.

5. In the library, find the *Reader's Guide to Periodical Literature*. Sit down with the latest issue and run through the subject headings listed. Many of these are likely to merit closer consideration. This convenient source can lead you to your first set of readings on any topic.

6. Pick up several issues of *Reader's Digest* and skim some of the articles. Do any of these subjects look interesting? Two things about *Reader's Digest* articles make them an appropriate model for speeches. First, the articles are usually written in a simple manner with ordinary words—in almost, but not quite, an oral style. Also, the articles often begin with an example, illustration, or fact that reaches out and grasps the reader's attention—just as speeches need to do. Whether or not you get an idea for your speech from this magazine, many of the articles are good examples of effective writing.

When you speak, you speak for a reason. In public speaking this is called a *purpose. A speaker's purpose is what he or she expects to attain;* it is his or her intention. For example, Shane's purpose was to increase her audience's understanding. This is called a *general purpose*. A purpose grows out of the nature of the assignment, occasion, topic, information, or speaker's intent; it could be any one of these or all of them combined.

You may already have a purpose. A purpose helps you select your material for a speech because it serves as an overall guide, helping you decide which material is the most informative, persuasive, convincing, or entertaining. A well-defined purpose can cut your preparation time by limiting your reading to the most appropriate or specific material. Purposes provide focus and direction.

The general purpose

A *general purpose* is a broad, overriding goal for a speech. Such a goal might be to inform, to persuade, to convince, or to entertain. In many cases the general purpose is set for speakers. For example, asked to give an after-dinner speech, most speakers will recognize that the general purpose is to entertain. For a sales report the general purpose is to inform. For a report on a new product the general purpose may be to inform *and* to persuade: One intent of the report may be to try to get company officials to produce the product, and another may be to give them details about it.

Often it is difficult to distinguish between informative and persuasive speeches. You may engage in many of the same activities for each of these general purposes: gathering sound evidence, supporting ideas with necessary strength and clarity, grasping audience attention, and presenting ideas with conviction.

There are, however, several differences between informative and persuasive speeches. First there is your intent. Do you want to increase understanding (inform), or do you want to change beliefs, attitudes, or values or move your audience to action (persuade)? Second, your purpose may affect the kind of appeals you make. (This will become clear in Chapter 14, which discusses persuasive speaking.) Persuasive appeals are rare in informative speeches. Third, the outcome of a speech depends on the speech's purpose. Persuasive speeches are designed to change listeners or make them act. Informative speeches, on the other hand, explain their topic but do not solicit action.

Informative and persuasive speeches can be confused if you do not have a clear intent in the first place. Although you may begin by informing, you may end by persuading. A strong, convincing style of delivery may also blur the differences between the types of speeches.

The best way to clarify your own general purpose is to answer some specific questions. First, what is the end state that you want your listeners to experience when your speech is complete? You can answer this question by considering the following:

1. Do you want your listeners to have different or more information on a subject than they do now?
2. Do you want them to feel differently about a social, political, or economic issue?
3. Do you want them to take some specific action as a result of your speech?

If your answer to number one is yes and you find questions two and three irrelevant, then your general purpose is to inform. If you answer yes to questions two or three, even if you also say yes to number one, then your general purpose is to persuade. Of course, your general purpose could also include entertainment, or you may be speaking only to entertain your audience.

The specific purpose

From choosing a topic to selecting a purpose, and from the general purpose to the specific purpose, the goal is refinement, precision, and a more accurate goal. One frequent complaint about speeches is that the speaker had no focus, the speech went off in all directions, or there was no way to follow what the speaker was saying. Following the steps in this chapter will help prevent this from happening to you.

The *specific purpose* is a summary of what you want from your audience as a result of your speech. Thus, the specific purpose includes three parts: (1) you (the speaker), (2) your topic, and (3) your audience. Shane's specific purpose was to explain to her classmates the high cost of trying to attain a perfect body. Douglas's specific purpose, after he lost one of his best friends in a car accident, was to help his listeners learn to accept death and cope with it in a healthy way. Rebecca's specific purpose, after her mother had just undergone a mastectomy, was to make her listeners aware of the dangers of breast cancer. In each case these speakers stated exactly what they hoped to achieve with their topics.

Notice something else about the specific purposes just mentioned. They all use the infinitive form of a verb: to explain, to help, to make. Other such phrases might be to show, to motivate, to prove, to indicate, to convince, or to have. The *general* purpose determines what verb will be used in its infinitive form at the beginning of the specific purpose, as is shown in the following examples:

Informative	*Persuasive*
To explain	To prove
To indicate	To convince
To show	To motivate
To increase understanding	To have the audience believe or act

The infinitive part of the specific purpose indicates the intent of the speaker and reveals the general purpose. The rest of the specific purpose describes how the speaker will treat the topic itself and who the audience will be for the speech. An example will demonstrate how this narrowing and focusing can occur:

General purpose: To inform
Topic area: Marriage
Narrowed topic: Need for marriage
Possible specific purposes:
- Value of marriage
  This is incomplete; the direction is unclear.
- Criteria for determining the need for marriage

This is better, but it stil lacks specifics.

- To explain to the class the three major criteria to determine whether you should get married
  This is a strong specific purpose.
- To indicate to the class how backgrounds, interests, and life goals can bear on a marriage decision
  This is a further refinement of the specific purpose; it is more complete and more specific.

Now let's look at the process Shane went through as she selected her specific purpose:

Topic area: Exercise and diet

Narrowed topic: Perfecting our bodies

Further narrowing: The price of perfection

Possible specific purposes:
- Dangers of the goal of perfection
  This is too broad; it is incomplete; the direction is unclear.
- Criteria for determining when the price of perfection becomes too high
  This is better, but it lacks specifics.
- To show the class how trying to gain a perfect 10 through plastic surgery, excessive exercise, and extreme diets can be too high a price to pay for perfection
  This is a strong specific purpose because it is complete and focused.

Shane realized a couple of direct benefits when she developed her final specific purpose. First, she thought of a title for her speech: "The Perfect 10." Second, she realized she wanted to develop three main heads in her speech, for which she needed to find statistics, examples, and further information: (1) plastic surgery, (2) exercise, and (3) diet.

When you have developed your specific purpose to the degree of focus shown in these examples, you can put it to this test:

1. Is it a complete sentence? (not a fragment, phrase, or even a question)
2. Does it express a single idea?
3. Is it a simple (not a compound) sentence?

THE CENTRAL THESIS

You would think that by having a topic, a general purpose, and a specific purpose, you would have a central thesis as well. This is not necessarily true. The *central thesis* is the rallying point for speech material. It is the position speakers advance and are willing to support in their speeches. Shane's central thesis is that the price of a perfect body can be high and is often too high. She is not asking her listeners to take action for or against extreme diets or excessive exercise; she is simply increasing their understanding about the subject.

The speaker about marriage described earlier had a central thesis saying that "backgrounds, interests, and life goals can have a direct bearing on one's decision to get married." Douglas, in his speech about death, stated his central thesis in this way: "Learning to accept death as inevitable and understanding the process of coping with it in a healthy way are the two ways we have for dealing with it realistically." Rebecca, in her speech on breast cancer, decided to frame her central thesis like this: "Caution, prevention, and early detection are the ways women have to survive this threatening disease."

Discovering a specific purpose and then a central thesis are important processes that should be neither neglected nor eliminated. Time taken here will result in a clear and definite speech. Be sure to write out your purpose and thesis because seeing them written out will help you decide whether you like the way they are worded. If you are not satisfied with them, change them. Do not hold firm to the way you worded them the first time; at this point in the process, nothing is sacred! Even if you change the wording several times during the development of your speech, that is all right.

USING VISUAL SUPPORT

You may wonder why a section about using visual support appears here. The reason is that you should start thinking about visual support early in speech preparation because any visual support you use during your speech should be directly linked to your general and specific purposes as well as to your central idea.

Finding appropriate visual support for your speech is as related to discovering and organizing information as it is to originality. The considerations regarding the incorporation of visual support are often just as important as the facts, examples, and illustrations of a speech. Just as you may find a particular application for a statistic or example, you may find a particular use for visual support. Visual support should not be an afterthought; it is part of what you need to consider when you are building your speech.

Incorporating visual support into a speech may present special delivery challenges, and so Chapter 12 is devoted exclusively to this subject. Here I explain the purposes of visual support and several cautions about using it. You can improve listener perception of your presentation with well-designed, effective visual aids. Although most listeners will remember only about 10 percent of what you say, they will remember 50 percent of what you show them *and* tell them together.

There are numerous purposes for using visual material, and although some are relevant only to specific goals, others are general and apply to all speeches.

- Visuals enhance listener recall of speech content.
- Visuals improve the clarity of listener understanding.
- Visuals can motivate listeners.
- Visuals help hold listener attention.

- Visuals reinforce and magnify ideas.
- Visuals present an idea more quickly than is possible with words alone.

Here are some of the special purposes that visual aids can serve:

- Visual aids can clarify numbers and statistics or can show relationships between numbers and statistics.
- Visual aids have the power to sell a product or idea. (For example, color in advertising increases the response rate by 25 percent or more.)
- Visuals can simplify a complex presentation.

You should take note of several possible pitfalls if you plan to use visual support. First, if you use visual aids poorly or overuse them, they can obscure your ideas and slow your pace. Second, if the visuals are poorly prepared (too small, too complex, or vague), they will distract from your message. And finally, if visuals are not covered or put away after they are used, they will compete with you for your listeners' attention throughout the rest of the speech.

SUMMARY

This chapter has highlighted the need for originality and demonstrated how to lay a solid foundation for a speech. Many speakers want to move the process along to the kind of procedures that have easily perceived immediate results, such as research and organization, without going through the sometimes tedious processes discussed in this chapter. The result can be abstract, confusing speeches that were never carefully crafted or specifically focused. To avoid this problem, it is necessary to choose a topic and then narrow it, selecting a general purpose, refining a specific purpose, and then carefully shaping a central thesis. If you can find visual support that ties in with the specific purpose and central thesis, it will improve the potency of your speech.

Although the following speech is not perfect, it reflects the end product of Shane's thinking, as has been referred to throughout this chapter. It is presented here for further discussion.

Sample Speech

This speech was given by Shane Bateman in her basic speech communication class at Bowling Green State University. It is used here with her permission.

General purpose: To inform

Specific purpose: To show the class how trying to gain a perfect 10 through plastic surgery, excessive exercise, and extreme diets can be too high a price to pay for perfection

Central thesis: The price of perfection can be a high price to pay.

"The Perfect 10"

Introduction

I know most of you have walked by a girl or guy and wished that if only you had *their* hair, or *their* skin, or *their* body, life would be so perfect. Most people do it, and it is normal (thank heavens!) to compare ourselves with others. But usually, that is where the whole thing ends—at comparison.

Transition

But it doesn't end there for everyone. Some people take this too far, and they try to perfect their body and their lives into something that they are not—into something they were never intended to be. Some people, as a matter of fact, go so far as to use plastic surgery, excessive exercise, or extreme diets to perfect their bodies, and the price they pay for perfection may be too high a price to pay.

Body of the speech

I. Plastic surgery is a popular perfection procedure.
   A. In 1989, according to *U.S. News & World Report*, an estimated 1.5 million people had some type of plastic surgery.[1]
   B. Of the procedures done on men, 25 percent were nose jobs, 10 percent were face lifts, and 18 percent were done on the eyes.[2]
   C. As of April 1993, 87 percent of plastic surgery patients were women.[3]

Transition

All this plastic to change what is naturally ours. But exercise is another way people strive for perfection.

II. Excessive exercise is another attempt at perfection.
   A. In the sport of running, the thought is the thinner you are the better you perform.[4]
   B. Exercise becomes a problem when it interferes with one's family or one's career and when it becomes more important than one's health.[5]
      1. I have friends who run in every tournament and every meet available, no matter the cost and no matter the inconvenience to family, friends, and career. They are obsessed.

2. The January 1994 issue of *Crosstrainer* gives the example of an aerobics instructor who was so determined to do her workout every day that she would wrap her hurt ankle so tightly that it would bleed. Because of this, she now has a birthmark-type scar from the gangrene that had eaten away at her flesh under the bandage.[6]

Transition

But in addition to plastic surgery and exercise, people use diets to achieve perfection as well.

III. Diets are a third way to achieve perfection.
  A. According to the June 1993 issue of *Consumer Reports*, 50 million Americans are dieting at any given moment.[7]
    1. Of women with normal, healthy body weight, 50–60 percent think they are fat.[8]
    2. One in every six underweight women is on a diet.[9]
  B. In an article in *Seventeen* magazine, "Why Are Girls Obsessed with Their Weight," the writer says 7 million women have an eating disorder.[10]
  C. In this same November 1989 article in *Seventeen*, the writer claims that 10 to 15 percent of teenage girls have anorexia or bulimia.[11]
    1. Two of my own friends have had to undergo counseling to help them overcome anorexia.
    2. The *Seventeen* article discusses a 15-year-old slim girl who said, "I'd love to starve myself, but I get too hungry when I try. I'd like to be bulimic, but I cry whenever I throw up."[12]

Transition

And when you consider exercise and diet, who are the money-makers? Jenny Craig makes $400 million in annual revenues.[13] Soloflex had $100 million in annual sales.[14] The Amazing Micro Diet made $60 million.[15] And "Stop the Insanity" tapes made $50 million.[16]

Conclusion

Although I have barely touched the surface, I hope I have shown you that the price of perfection can be a high price to pay. Is the perfect hair, the perfect skin, or the perfect body worth the plastic surgery, the excessive exercise, or the extreme diet? Is it worth the price of your life? Rather than striving for perfection, perhaps it makes more sense to strive to make what we have better. After all, you know, nobody's perfect.

Speech Notes

1. Steven Findlay, "Buying the Perfect Body," *U.S. News & World Report*, May 1, 1989, p. 69.
2. Findlay, p. 69.
3. "New Face, New Body, New Self," *People Weekly*, April 26, 1993, p. 88.
4. Megan Othersen, "My Body, Myself," *Runner's World*, June 1993, p. 69.

5. Laura Dayton, "Are You an Exercise Addict," *Crosstrainer*, January 1994, p. 71.

6. Dayton, p. 123.

7. "Losing Weight, What Works, What Doesn't," *Consumer Reports*, June 1993, p. 347.

8. Marianne Walt, "Body Love, Body Hate," *Ladies Home Journal*, January 1992, p. 30.

9. Leslie Morgan, "Why Are Girls Obsessed with Their Weight?" *Seventeen*, November 1989, p. 118.

10. Morgan, p. 118.

11. Morgan, p. 118.

12. Morgan, p. 118.

13. Cynthia Sanz, "Fitness Tycoon Jenny Craig..." *People Weekly*, February 19, 1990, p. 91.

14. Ryan Murphy, "The Other Late Night Race," *US*, November 1993, p. 43.

15. Murphy, p. 43.

16. Murphy, p. 43.

Chapter Questions

1. From where does your originality spring? Write a speech about originality, coming up with an original title, an original specific purpose, and an original central thesis as well. Do original research for the speech, and then find an original way to organize the material. Make certain you make the actual presentation original, too. For this speech, you will be evaluated on your originality.

2. For the following topics, say what you think the general purpose would be:

   a. family life
   b. the death penalty
   c. campus humor
   d. happiness
   e. gun control
   f. oddities in nature
   g. success
   h. how to date
   i. plagiarism
   j. running a college or university

3. For the following topics, develop a specific purpose:

   a. materialism
   b. fads
   c. the information highway
   d. drug abuse
   e. divorce
   f. stress
   g. loneliness
   h. honesty in government
   i. two-career marriages
   j. universal health care

4. For the following speeches, frame a possible central thesis:

   a. interracial dating
   b. the career planning and placement office
   c. burnout and its warning signs
   d. booze and behavior

e. trust in relationships

f. how pollution
  affects people

g. food poisoning

h. the human memory

i. caffeine, the drug

j. the contribution of
  the National Guard to
  our country's needs

5. If you were giving a beginning speaker suggestions about choosing and using visual support, what would your suggestions be?

6. Critique Shane's speech. Based on the information provided in the outline, what were Shane's strengths and weaknesses? This was a three- to five-minute informative speech designed for a mixed group of sophomore students in a basic, required speech communication class. With respect to general purpose, specific purpose, and central thesis, how good do you think her speech was? What, specifically, could she have done better to make this effort stronger?

Further Reading

These books may help provide speech topics in wide potential areas of interest and concern.

Jack Canfield and Mark Victor Hansen, *Chicken Soup for the Soul: 101 Stories to Open the Heart and Rekindle the Spirit* (Deerfield Beach, FL: Health Communications, 1993); and Jack Canfield and Mark Victor Hansen, *A 2nd Helping of Chicken Soup for the Soul* (Deerfield Beach, FL: Health Communications, 1995).

The authors include sections on love, learning to love yourself, parenting, learning, living your dream, overcoming obstacles, and eclectic wisdom. The books are compilations of short entries that are both inspirational and motivational.

Gerald G. Jampolsky and Diane V. Cirincione, *Change Your Mind, Change Your Life* (New York: Bantam Books, 1993).

These authors help readers free themselves of grievances, blame, and condemnation so they can free their attitudes to think positively. They offer new methods of communication, changing beliefs, and discovering a more refined purpose for our lives. It is an uplifting, motivational book. Their book *Wake-Up Calls* (Carson, CA: Hay House, 1992) serves some of these same purposes.

John Roger and Peter McWilliams, *We Give to Love—Giving Is Such a Selfish Thing: Notes and Quotes on the Joys of Heartfelt Service* (New York: Prelude Press, 1993).

This book is described by its subtitle—it consists of notes and quotes. But it is inspirational and motivational and may well lead readers to topics of significance, relevance, and importance.

Endnotes

1. Edgar E. Willis, *How to Be Funny on Purpose*, (manuscript in production).
2. Willis.

Words in Action: VIDEO STUDY

Two goals of speech writing are to inject a speech with originality and to recognize and convey a focus. If you incorporate originality into your speech, your audience is more likely to listen to and remember your message. You ensure focus by recognizing the purpose and planning the central thesis at the outset of the speech-writing process. Visual aids come into play for both of these goals: they naturally make a speech original, and they can be used to focus attention on particular points.

The accompanying video shows a speech that exemplifies good use of originality and focus. After watching the video, answer the following questions.

1. What is the general purpose of this speech? (Refer to p. 65 for a discussion of how to determine the general purpose.)
2. What is the specific purpose of this speech? (Refer to p. 66 for a discussion of the specific purpose.)
3. How does the speaker intentionally mislead her audience in the introduction?
4. What do you think her goal is in misleading the audience?
5. What is the speaker's central thesis? (Refer to pp. 67–68 for a discussion of central thesis.)
6. What visual aids does the speaker use to illustrate her points?
7. How does she help the audience visualize her statistics?
8. In what ways is this speech original? In what ways is it focused?

6

Discovering Information

After reading this chapter you will be able to:

- complete a personal inventory
- use the library to find books, locate periodicals, peruse government documents, and take advantage of the reference collection and the vertical file
- accurately and completely record information
- do informational interviewing
- compare and contrast the various types of supporting information: facts, examples and illustrations, statistics, opinions, and personal experience
- be ethical in your selection and use of information to support your speeches

David needed a topic for his speech. Three things that caught his attention led him to his final choice, "People should recycle." Sitting in the classroom just before class started, he observed one of his classmates throwing the wrapper of a Snickers bar in the garbage can. In the hallway after class, he watched students walk by a big yellow recycling bin for cans; ignoring it entirely, one student tossed his soda can on the ground outside the building when he finished the contents. Third, David was powerfully affected by an instructional video called "The Choice Is Yours" (distributed by The Ohio Department of Natural Resources [1992]), which was shown in one of his classes. David decided to choose recycling as his speech topic.

David set up his topic, general purpose, specific purpose, and central thesis in the following manner:

Topic:	Recycling (title uncertain at this point)
General purpose:	To persuade
Specific purpose:	To convince my class to recycle (This will be further refined, perhaps, as additional information is collected. The main points have not been determined yet.)
Central thesis:	Awareness and action are necessary if we are to change our society's view of recycling.

These provided David with at least a temporary working plan. Setting up his ideas gave David some focus for the next process: finding information.

Now that he had his focus, David could direct his attention to the questions he needed to answer:

1. What are the main issues or points of interest I need to cover?
2. What do the respected authorities on this topic say?
3. What are the most recent developments on this topic?
4. How can I adapt my topic to the special concerns or special interests of my audience?

David was a freshman at the university, and this was his first semester on campus. So as he looked for information for his speech on recycling, he was introduced to the campus library facilities as he went through the essential steps of finding information. If you are familiar with topic research techniques and with the facilities and the wealth of information available at your library, you may not need to perform all the steps that David did and that we are about to describe. However, the purpose here is to take you on a journey of finding information—even though libraries will be different, available sources may vary, and access to sources will differ. David's progress will be closely followed in this chapter because his search offers an example of how to evaluate pertinence, variety, and recency of sources.

PERSONAL INVENTORY

Before David began his library investigation, he conducted a personal inventory. A *personal inventory* is a review of one's own knowledge, experience, and interests. For example, David noticed the examples of the Snickers wrapper, the soda can, and the video he had seen. Also, David's uncle worked for a landfill, and David not only was able to interview him but also rode in his uncle's truck to visit a landfill—a good experience that he would be able to use in this speech.

A personal inventory should begin as you look for a topic: What am I interested in? Would my interests make a good speech? Once you have selected a topic, a further personal inventory might include some of these questions:

1. What do I know about this topic?
2. What personal experiences do I have that relate to this topic?
3. What experiences could I seek that would give me more information on this topic?
4. Whom do I know who could provide me with information on this topic?

LIBRARY INVESTIGATION

Usually the library is the next step in the process of finding information after the personal inventory. Often the number of available library resources is overwhelming. With books, periodicals, government documents, and a wide variety of reference works available, it is hard to know where to begin. The best starting point may depend on the topic. A new topic, for example, might require a periodical (newspaper and magazine) search. Books might provide a broad overview of a general topic and possible ways to narrow and focus the subject. However, choosing the ideal place to begin is much less important than getting started.

Because the library has so many resources, some of your search will lead you to paths that do not provide useful information. This should not deter you; simply start another search. Library collections differ, and research is an intense process. However, the easiest place to start is often the card catalog or computer, where a list of the library's book holdings can be found.

Finding books

David's first goal was to find out if his library had any books or other material on the topic of recycling. His library's computerized catalog was its guide to the holdings of all the university's libraries. The online catalog listed all the books, pamphlets, periodicals, sound recordings, and manuscript collections in every branch on campus. Other indexes and databases gave David additional information about newspapers and periodicals. The computer was fast and easy to use; all David had to do was follow the instructions on the screens. He found many books listed on his topic. One by Richard A. Denison and John Ruston, *Recycling and Incineration* (Island Press, 1990), first caught his attention. Then, following the alphabetical listing, David noticed a book by Al Gore called *Earth in the Balance* (Plume Printing [The Penguin Group], 1993). Then he saw one by Brenda Platt, Christine Doherty, Anne Claire Broughton, and David Morris titled *Beyond 40 Percent* (Island Press, 1991), and another book looked interesting as well.

Once David had written down the call numbers of the books from the computer screen, he was able to go to the floors and locations where the books could be found. The advantage of going to get the books was that David could look over related books as well. (Most library computer systems provide a way for the user to view all books on a shelf without having to physically go to the shelf itself. However, David preferred to inspect the books themselves.) At the area where the books were located, David also found a book by Talbot Page, *Conservation and Economic Efficiency* (Johns Hopkins University Press, 1992), and one published by Malcolm Pirni entitled *Ohio Department of Natural Resources Study* (Columbus, OH, 1993), which had many statistics he would be able to use. Because David was from Ohio, he recognized that Ohio-related statistics would be of special interest to his listeners. David was pleased because he already had a terrific start—probably more information than he would be able to use. But he did not stop looking.

Locating periodicals

David wanted to find out if there were recent articles or newspapers about recycling. Upon asking the reference librarian, David was told about Proquest. Proquest's *Periodical Abstracts*, *ABI/Inform*, and *Newspaper Abstracts* are computer databases of indexes to magazines, journals, and newspaper articles. *Periodical Abstracts* and *Newspaper Abstracts* provide references to popular (not scholarly or research-oriented) articles on general subjects like recycling. *ABI/Inform* indexes both popular and more scholarly articles on business subjects. David learned that the ProQuest databases are searched by specific time periods. Because he wanted recent information, he searched for January 1992 to the present.

Again, just as it did for access to books, the computer screen guided David through his search. The reference librarian also had a "How to Use" pamphlet for each of the databases he wanted to use. He found these publications helpful, and they streamlined his search. David found several interesting articles in journals he might not have otherwise examined. For example, in the periodical index he found Thomas G. Donlan's editorial, "Take My Garbage Please: We Can Care for Mother Earth with Dollars and Sense," in *Barron's* (April 19, 1993, p. 10). He also found "Creating Incentives: A Survey of Waste and the Environment," written by the editors of *The Economist* (May 29, 1993, p. 13). In addition, he found Geoff Scott's "Turn on to the 3 R's of Today" in *Current Health* (October 1993). In the newspaper index he found Kenneth Chilton and James Lis's "Recycling for Recycling's Sake: A Waste of Time and Money" in *USA Today* (May 1993). His search was worthwhile.

After David had used the periodical index to locate the articles he wanted to read, he checked the magazine titles in the main online computer he had used to look for book holdings. He had to make certain his library owned copies of the magazines he wanted to read. The main online computer catalog told David which years of the periodicals were available in the library, their format (paper or microform), where they were shelved, and additional publication information and subject headings.

To get microform material David had to go to a special desk. There library staff obtained the microfiche and microfilm for him and helped him locate particular periodicals, showed him how to use the microform readers, and assisted him with the printers and photocopy machines.

The Heart of the Matter

Finding information for a speech is rather like doing effective detective work, trying to solve the mystery of the missing information. Your job as a speaker is to discover the whereabouts and nature of your sources. Like a detective, you begin with some direction: a topic, general purpose, specific purpose, and central thesis. And if you think like a detective, you will ask questions, pursue sources, get answers, and, finally, solve the puzzle of the missing information.

Discovering government documents

After finding books and periodicals, David's next stop was the government documents section, which contained U.S. and Ohio government publications on nearly every topic imaginable. U.S. government publications were organized according to the agency that issued them and were given a call number by the Superintendent of Documents (referred to as a SuDoc number). The reference area of the library had special catalogs and indexes to locate documents; many documents were also listed in the online computer catalog. David's library offered easy-to-read pamphlets describing how to find government documents on the shelves. Not only was David able to find the *Ohio Department of Natural Resources Annual Report* (Columbus, OH: 1992–1993), but volumes two and three of *The Clean Ohio Report* from 1990 and 1991 were also available—great sources, he thought, for Ohio laws and a short history of recycling programs in Ohio.

Using the reference collection

David also visited another area of the library to get information on his topic. The reference collection included indexes to periodicals, book reviews, and essays, as well as both general and subject-specific encyclopedias. Although he didn't need them at this time, it also contained bibliographies on particular subjects, telephone directories, and other directories of businesses and organizations. The fact books and statistical sources housed in the reference collection might help him out, too.

Having up-to-date information on recycling was important to David; being unaware of recent events could damage his credibility. For the most recent information, he started with the *New York Times Index*. He thought that *Facts on File*, which reports on current events weekly by topic categories, might also provide useful additional material. And although David knew it might not be quite as current as these two sources, the *Statistical Abstract of the United States*, published annually since 1878, would provide the standard summary of statistics on the social, political, and economic organization of the United States. Numerical data and other miscellaneous facts also were readily available in the *World Almanac* and the *Information Please Almanac*. He would come back to these sources if he needed to later.

Learning about the vertical file

David's final library investigation was the vertical file. Here, under the topic of recycling, he found a number of brochures and other kinds of unpublished material like clippings, pamphlets, and advertisements from local businesses. All of this material was grouped simply by topic area and filed alphabetically, so it was easy to find and to use.

RECORDING INFORMATION

One thing David remembered as he moved through this process of finding information was the need to take careful notes. If he didn't, he would have to return to these sources or databases to recopy the necessary information. Because digging for information is time-consuming, it is important to work efficiently.

David had learned a system for taking notes in his high school English course. Students were to use two different kinds of index cards, one for the bibliographic information (a source card) and one for the information (an information card). When students first encountered a valuable new source, they were to write complete bibliographic information at the top of the source card.

As a guideline for taking notes, David already knew what bibliographic form his instructor preferred. The box shows two different styles; whichever form you choose, follow it consistently. Also, remember that *all* the information is necessary—not just part of it; it should be listed in exactly the order as is shown. The same sources are shown here in both APA (American Psychological Association) style and MLA (Modern Language Association) style so that you can see the differences between the styles. If you take notes using the MLA style, you will have all the information to convert this style to APA style, but the reverse is not true.

In addition to the bibliographic information at the top, the source card includes information on the author, book, or periodical and a summary or evaluation of the book or periodical. Once you do this for a source, you will not have to do it again.

On the information card, on the other hand, David recorded the information from each source, but he put only one item on each card. Each card began with a heading that identified what was on the card. "Background information," "latest statistics," and "local information" were some headings that provided a quick reference. Then David added a brief listing of the source and the page number. Next came the information itself; one source can require a number of cards. As David was doing his research he did not know exactly what material would be useful to his speech, so he wrote down far more information than he would be able to use. This practice actually saves time because you don't have to return to a source. The really frustrating situation is remembering a piece of information that you failed to copy down and not remembering the source at all.

INFORMATIONAL INTERVIEWING

One source of current information for speeches is interviewing. David could interview his uncle who worked at a landfill. In order to use his time with his uncle well, David planned some of his questions in advance. This way he knew he would remember to ask the essential questions:

- "What is the effect of recycling on landfills?"
- "Why is recycling important to our landfills?"
- "How have landfill operations helped to encourage recycling?"
- "How would you evaluate the progress of recycling in our area?"
- "How could public awareness of recycling be increased?"

Planning questions in advance of the interview has several advantages. First, David could make sure most bases would be covered. Sometimes it is hard to think logically when the interview is in progress; thus, whatever planning that speakers can do will make the interview easier and more comfortable. Second, planning the interview will make the interviewer look credible. A credible interviewer is likely to get more information from an interviewee. Third, planning questions in advance allows interviewers to take up less of the interviewee's time; this shows courtesy and respect. Remember, the interviewee has been kind enough to give you some of his or her time.

When you conduct an informational interview, make sure you let the interviewee talk. The whole point is to get information. A tape recorder is helpful, but be sure to get the interviewee's permission first. Also watch your nonverbal communication. How you dress, for example, can make a difference; so can how you sit, how you talk, how alert you appear, and how responsive and responsible you are. Finally, make sure you go over your notes immediately after the interview. The longer you wait, the more information you will forget.

TYPES OF SUPPORTING INFORMATION

What kind of information should you look for as you research your speech topic? This section discusses the most common types of information: facts, examples and illustrations, statistics, opinions, and personal experience. Although a certain kind of speech may appear to need more of one kind of information than another, speeches that hold attention usually depend on a variety of support. Supporting information differs from visual aids (charts, graphs, and so on) in that the supporting information is the sub-

Two Styles for Bibliographic Notes

APA Guidelines

Books:

Strunk, W., Jr., & White, E. B. (1979). *The elements of style* (3rd ed.). New York: Macmillan.

Gonzalez, A., Houston, M., & Chen, V. (Eds.) (1994). *Our voices: Essays in culture, ethnicity, and communication.* Los Angeles: Roxbury.

Periodicals:

Engen, P. (1993, December). The nation and recycling: An examination of alternatives. *U.S. News and World Report,* pp. 56–58.

Although the *Publication Manual of the American Psychological Association* (*APA*) does not give a form for listing interviews within the references section, the following might be used as a general guideline. It is the same form used by the *MLA.*

Interviews:

Roberts, David F. Personal interview. 23 October 1994.

Bailey, JoAnn C. Telephone interview. 10 December 1994.

MLA Guidelines

Books:

Strunk, William, Jr., and E. B. White. *The Elements of Style.* 3rd ed. New York: Macmillan, 1979.

Gonzalez, Alberto, Marsha Houston, and Victoria Chen, eds. *Our Voices: Essays in Culture, Ethnicity, and Communication.* Los Angeles: Roxbury, 1994.

Periodicals:

Engen, Perry. "The Nation and Recycling: An Examination of Alternatives." *U.S. News and World Report,* 5 Dec. 1993: 57.

If you need to cite works other than books, periodicals, and interviews, you should consult the respective style manuals. They give far more information than can be presented in this space. Almost all citation needs are covered in these two style manuals. If you will be writing research papers, you might want to purchase a style manual. They are handy resources to have available. Different disciplines use different manuals, however, so you need to do some investigating before making a purchase.

stance or evidence of the speech. Visual aids are often used to present the supporting information to the audience, but they are supporting devices, not supporting information.

Facts are things that have actual existence; that is, they are pieces of information that can be observed or sensed. They are usually at the core of what we consider to be true. For example, we know that teeth can become decayed. We also know that there are cause–effect relationships between the amount of sugar consumed and tooth decay and between regularity of brushing the teeth and tooth decay. These are bits of truth we know to exist, and they can be checked against reality by consulting a dentist, talking to others, using personal experience, and reading. Anything indisputable is a fact.

A speaker who wanted her audience to believe that grades are bad used these facts: First, grades are given. Second, grades cause undue competition (this was one of the premises on which she wanted to build her case). Finally, she asserted that grades can be used by instructors to manipulate their students; she would need to prove this premise in order for it to be considered a fact. Most speeches depend on facts as part of their foundation for gaining understanding, seeking belief, or obtaining action. Facts are the basis of reasoned discourse.

Examples and illustrations

Examples are instances or cases in point. A brief, specific instance is known as an example. An *illustration* is a longer, more detailed example told in narrative form. Examples and illustrations can clarify a point you have made, make a point more direct or relevant to an audience, show how an idea has been or could be put into practice, add interest, and hold audience attention. David, for example, planned to begin his speech with the examples of eating a Snickers bar and throwing the wrapper in the trash and drinking a soda and throwing the can on the ground.

When you create an example for a specific purpose, it is known as a hypothetical example. For example, David might say in his speech, "Let's see what the profile of a typical recycler might look like," and then talk about all the things this person would do as part of his or her dedication to recycling.

Illustrations are stories of facts and events—little stories within the speech. Illustrations depend on three things for their effectiveness: clear thought, intense emotion, and vivid language. They are powerful because they portray real people in real situations. Sometimes when an illustration is used a hush comes over the audience. A speaker talking to a college audience about hazing achieved this response when he used the illustration of a college student who died after a three-day initiation spree. A grand jury found the organization the student was pledging morally responsible for the death of the initiate. According to the speaker, the initiation spree included this alcoholic hazing:

> The five initiates consumed the following over the three days:
> 16 gallons of wine, six quarts of tequila, four quarts of gin, four
> quarts of bourbon, two quarts of liqueur, and one bottle of 190-proof
> Everclear—a preparation used to treat acne.

It is easy to see why this illustration caught the attention of listeners.

Statistics

Statistics are numeric representations of groups of examples or facts. They are simply numbers that summarize large bodies of information effectively and concisely. They are powerful for these reasons:

1. Numbers carry weight. In general, people respect statistical evidence.
2. Citing statistics adds to a speaker's credibility. People tend to admire speakers with numbers at their fingertips.
3. Statistics condense a lot of information into a concise statement.

However, numbers should be used sparingly. They are often difficult to conceptualize, and they can turn off listeners. Statistics need to be compared with something listeners can visualize. For example, one speaker reported that the United States produces more than 143 million tons of household, commercial, and institutional garbage per year. Most people cannot comprehend 143 million tons. Even if the speaker said the United States produces more garbage per year than steel (about 126 million tons), this still would not be impressive. Instead, this speaker said the United States produces enough garbage in a year to fill the New Orleans Superdome from floor to ceiling twice a day, including weekends and holidays, for a full year. In this way, her listeners had not only a way to picture this immense quantity but a way to remember it as well.

Opinions

Opinions are views, judgments, or appraisals about facts, events, or beliefs. David wanted to use an opinion from his uncle for his speech. His uncle had said, "The main problem with recycling seems to be that we, as a society, don't want to spend the extra time it takes to separate trash." This would be considered an *expert opinion* because his uncle worked at a landfill. If David had sought the opinions of fellow students about recycling, their thoughts would be called *lay opinion*. And the editor of David's local paper would have an *editorial opinion* about recycling. Finally, an opinion given under oath is called *testimony*. For example, if David could find someone who had testified on the need for recycling, then he would have testimony to support his speech as well.

Personal experience

Personal experience is an excellent source of information. Whatever your topic, you should first discover how much you already know about it. But before relying too heavily on this kind of evidence, you should recognize that it is an effective attention-getter, but it has two major weaknesses.

First, if you appear young and inexperienced, people may doubt or question your experience. Often as speakers we need more credibility and thus more substantial information. Personal experience is not weighty, nor does it have what might be labeled substantive content. Second, one or even two examples may be exceptions to the rule. That is one reason statistics are so powerful: One number in statistics can represent so many cases. In contrast, a personal experience carries little logical weight when you are trying to prove something or make a point. Although its emotional weight may be substantial, when you are making an important argument, it would be wise to seek sources other than, or in addition to, yourself.

A NOTE ON ETHICS

While we are discussing cautions about the use of personal experience, a warning is in order regarding the use of any evidence. When data are derived from sources other than yourself, you must cite the sources. This adds to a speaker's credibility; and *not* citing the source of borrowed ideas and information is known as *plagiarism*. Passing off the ideas or words of another person as your own without crediting the source is literary theft. Most plagiarism occurs when a lazy, unimaginative, or desperate speaker takes another person's speech or adapts a magazine article and then delivers it as if it were his or her own. Such dishonest performances cannot be condoned.

SUMMARY

This chapter has discussed how to find information by taking a personal inventory, doing a library investigation and recording information, and conducting informational interviews. Library investigation includes finding books, locating periodicals and government documents, and using the reference collection and the vertical file.

The types of supporting information discussed in this chapter included facts, examples and illustrations, statistics, opinions, and personal experience. To illustrate as many of these as practical, David's speech has been included here.

Sample Speech

General purpose: To persuade
Specific purpose: To convince class members to reeducate themselves, reduce consumption, reuse when possible, and recycle.
Central thesis: Awareness and action are necessary if we are to change our society's view of recycling.

The Four R's of Recycling

Introduction (attention step)

David just finishes eating a Snickers bar as he is called upon to give his speech. He puts the remaining portion in his mouth and tosses the wrapper on the floor as he goes to the front of the room to start his speech.

David used his personal experience here.

How many of you, after eating a Snickers bar or drinking a Coke, think about how you are going to dispose of the wrapper or can? Some of you will throw it in the nearest garbage can, or you will simply throw it on the floor or ground. If you are like most Americans, you don't think about recycling.

Do you recognize this symbol? It is the symbol used to promote recycling. On a product it indicates that recycled materials have been used. If you haven't seen it, pay attention to some of the products you use, like this shampoo or this lotion. The recycling symbol is on a majority of products you use.

Recycling is recovering discarded products and packaging materials for reuse and processing into new products.[1]

Body of the speech (need step)

Statement of the problem. We need to change the way we handle trash. In a recent article in *Current Health*, Geoff Scott said that in the last 35 years alone, Americans have doubled the size of their waste streams.[2] By the year 2000, it is figured that Americans will produce more than 200 million tons of garbage each year. Safely disposing of this waste is a growing problem. Today, almost 67 percent of the waste stream ends up in the ground in landfills and dumps, and 16 percent is burned in incinerators.[3] Fact is, only 17 percent of our waste is recycled.

And if you think this problem does not affect you, listen to this. We are Ohioans, and the Ohio Department of Natural Resources states that in 1993, Ohioans generated almost 14 million tons of solid waste—about one ton for every person in the state.[4] If that is hard for you to imagine, then picture this. Think of the 4,000 miles that separate Northern Maine from Southern California lined bumper-to-bumper with tractor-trailer trucks full of just the garbage created in Ohio in *one* year.

Explanation of the problem. The reason recycling is the most important component of our waste system is that it plays a major role in conserving our landfill space. My uncle, Mr. Harvey S. Gumpert, owner and manager of Gumpert's Landfill, says, "Recycling saves energy, and it conserves our natural resources as well." In the interview I had with him, he said, "The main problem with recycling seems to be that we, as a society, don't want to spend the extra time it takes to separate trash."

In an editorial in *Barron's* magazine, the editor agreed with my uncle. The editor said, "The number of curbside pickups of recyclables has quadrupled since 1988, but many of us are still lazily throwing everything into one sack to set out for the landfill."[5]

A video I saw in another class called "The Choice is Yours" showed that recycling all recyclable materials uses less energy than using raw materials.[6] It saves the time and expense used to discover and break down the raw materials.

Proof that the problem exists. What do we throw away? According to an article in *Omni* magazine, U. S. motorists throw out 1.3 billion gallons of used motor oil a year.[7] But the biggest part of the waste stream is not oil, plastic, glass, or food. It is paper. Forty percent of our trash is newspapers, magazines, old phone books, packaging material, and junk mail.[8] Paper

---

Marginal annotations (left column):

More personal experience here.

Definition.

Clear statement offered. This is a fact.

Here are three impressive statistics.

Application to specific audience.
Statistic.

Great image created here.

Expert opinion here. Note how David works in his interview.

Editorial opinion here.

Personal experience with the video here.

Fact.
Fact.
Facts.

Statistics.

does not decompose quickly. In one landfill scientists found 40- to 50-year-old newspapers in mint condition.[9] Another 25 percent of home waste is from food and yards. Over 80 percent of our waste can be recycled.[10]

Fact stated by expert.

What's the problem with throwing all of this away? Our landfills continue to fill and close. According to Al Gore, in *Earth in the Balance*, "Out of 20,000 landfills in the United States in 1979, more than 15,000 have since reached their permanent capacity and closed."[11]

Historical anecdote.

Relationship of problem to your audience. We didn't ask for this problem; it has been passed on to us by previous generations. As early as 1889 there has been concern shown toward our disposal of waste, and now, in 1993, we have just hit a peak.[12]

Personal opinion.

If we don't do our part today, there will be no succeeding generations tomorrow. It is our duty to recognize and take action against this serious problem that affects each one of us daily.

Satisfaction step

Plan of action. The best way we have to control our solid waste problem is to first reeducate ourselves and then to reduce, reuse, and recycle.

Expert opinion.

Explanation of the plan. Education is a big part of the recycling effort. According to my uncle, schools in this area are taking an active role in the environmental movement. He is often asked to speak to local schools about recycling. According to an editorial in *American City and County*, a magazine, the Environmental Protection Agency and the Alliance for Environmental Education have teamed up to launch an environmental education initiative aimed at third and fourth grade students. Materials have been sent to 70,000 classrooms across the country.[13]

Fact.

Fact.

Expert opinion.

In *Current Health*, writer Geoff Scott says, "Turn on to the three R's today."[14] To help *reduce* the waste stream, we must stop automatically throwing things away so less goes to the dump. To *reuse* means we need to get more than one use out of a product to help reduce the waste stream. For example, plastic cups, knives, forks, and spoons can be washed and reused just like plastic table cloths. Recycling is a form of reuse. To *recycle*, we need to take the time to separate the trash and dispose of it properly.

Examples.

Expert opinion.

Countering arguments against the plan. Platt, Doherty, Broughton, and Morris in their book *Beyond 40 Percent*, state that opponents to recycling argue that recycling programs, first, are too expensive. Second, they argue there are no markets for recycled material. And, third, they argue that recycling can handle only a small portion of the waste stream.[15] It seems that many people are afraid of change. If recycling can do *any* good for our environment at all, if it can contribute to helping future generations, if it can save time, money, and energy, then it is worth it.

Personal opinion.

Visualization step

Personal opinion and great image.

Think of our world as our body and pollution as an infection. Cleaning up our habits, persuading industrial giants to clean up their acts, and convincing business and the government to sponsor education programs will help prevent the infection from taking over and destroying the body. When we restructure our goals like this, we allow Mother Earth to catch her breath before we lose ours.

Expert opinion.

According to the Ohio Department of Natural Resources, recycling would reduce the massive amounts of trash going to landfills and incinerators by as much as 50 percent.[16] This reduction, too, will help reduce the amount of garbage that goes across state lines looking for available landfills. My uncle

Expert opinion.

says, "Any help will be useful."

Conclusion (action step)

I am looking at you as my peers. We have a responsibility to this generation as well as the next—a responsibility to take action. Awareness and action must begin with each and everyone of us. Recycling takes such a little amount of time—less

Expert opinion.

than two minutes a day according to the Ohio Department of Natural Resources. If you are unsure about recycling a particular object, a symbol will be present—a symbol that rewards you

Personal experience.

for your concern. I know that you can change your habits; I have already started changing mine. Just remember, after reeducation: reduce, reuse, and recycle.

Expert opinion.

Let me leave you with a quote from Al Gore, from his book *Earth In the Balance*. Gore says, "Unless we find a way to dramatically change our civilization and our way of thinking about the relationship between humankind and the earth, our children will inherit a wasteland."[17]

Speech Notes

1. Brenda Platt, Christine Doherty, Anne Claire Broughton, and David Morris, *Beyond 40 Percent* (New York: Island Press, 1991).

2. Geoff Scott, "Turn on to the Three R's Today," *Current Health*, October 1993, pp. 24–26.

3. Scott, pp. 24–26.

4. *Ohio Department of Natural Resources Annual Report* (Columbus, OH: Ohio Department of Natural Resources [Public Information Center] 1992–1993); *Ohio Department of Natural Resources Study* (Columbus, OH: Malcolm Pirni, 1993); Talbot Page, *Conservation and Economic Efficiency* (Baltimore, MD: The Johns Hopkins University Press, 1992).

5. Thomas G. Donlan, "Take My Garbage, Please: We Can Care for Mother Earth with Dollars and Sense," *Barron's*, April 19, 1993, p. 10.

6. *The Choice is Yours*. Videotape. Developed by the Ohio

Department of Natural Resources (Columbus, OH, 1992). 30 min.

7. George Hobbe, "Greasing the Wheels of Progress," *Omni*, September 26, 1993, p. 27.

8. Scott, pp. 24–26.

9. Scott, pp. 24–26.

10. Richard A. Denison and John Ruston, *Recycling and Incineration* (New York: Island Press, 1990).

11. Al Gore, *Earth in the Balance* (New York: Plume Printing, The Penguin Group, 1993).

12. "Creating Incentives: A Survey of Waste and the Environment," *The Economist*, May 29, 1993, p. 13.

13. Editorial, *American City and County*, August 26, 1993, p. 16.

14. Scott, pp. 24–26.

15. Platt, p. 41.

16. *Choice Is Yours.*

17. Gore, p. 348.

Chapter Questions

1. Pick a topic that you would like to give a speech on, and perform a complete personal inventory.

2. Select a topic (it could be the one in Question 1), and investigate it in the library, looking for books, periodicals, government documents, reference books, and vertical file material.

3. As you complete your library investigation, use the suggestions offered in this chapter to record your information on index cards.

4. On the topic you have selected for Questions 1 and/or 2, conduct an information interview. Plan some of the interview questions in advance.

5. As you research a speech topic of your own choosing, try to find at least one example of each type of supporting information: facts, examples or illustrations, statistics, opinions, and personal experience.

6. Critique David's speech. Try to emphasize David's use of supporting information as you answer the following questions:

   a. Did David find convincing information? Was it sufficiently varied? Why or why not?

   b. Would you be convinced by David's presentation (from the information offered here)? Why or why not?

   c. Were there points in the speech that were not well supported? If so, what were they? How could he have better supported them?

   d. What do you think of the way David incorporated his sources into his speech?

Further Reading

John C. Reinard, *Introduction to Communication Research* (Dubuque, IA: Brown & Benchmark, 1994).

> This author says that research is not library work, statistics, or field observation. It is an argument—a process by which you answer questions and try to draw conclusions from information gathered about message-related behavior. In this book Reinard trains students to gather research evidence, to develop research arguments, and to think critically about them. Although aimed at scholarship, the insights are valuable.

Mary John Smith, *Contemporary Communication Research Methods* (Belmont, CA: Wadsworth, 1988).

> Although focused on scholarship, the insights Smith offers regarding research in the field of speech communication are valuable. This book offers a rich and varied assortment of research methods.

Don W. Stacks and John E. Hocking, *Essentials of Communication Research* (New York: HarperCollins, 1992).

> These authors include chapters on asking and answering questions, getting started in library research, using computers in research and analysis, and bringing research together in writing. This is a user-friendly, down-to-earth, practical guide for scholarly research.

Words in Action: VIDEO STUDY

Information is the meat of a speech and can come in the form of facts, opinions, or personal experiences. The accompanying video gives two examples of speeches that depend heavily on information—one by President Dwight D. Eisenhower and the other by President George W. Bush. After you watch the video, answer the following questions regarding the speeches.

1. How does Eisenhower's use of statistics help him keep the attention of this audience?
2. Name the types of information Bush uses to support his actions. List examples of each type from the speech.

Organizing Information

After reading this chapter you will be able to:

- understand the need for order

- discern the main points in a body of information

- compare and contrast the four main methods of organization (topic, time, space, and problem–solution)

- outline your ideas appropriately

- use a sample outline as a model and as a base for analysis and evaluation

Listening to and comprehending a disorganized speech are especially difficult.[1] Unfortunately, many speakers devote too little time to organizing their speeches. This chapter and the next discuss the essential ingredients of organization. Listeners find it difficult to concentrate on the spoken word; thus, speakers must give listeners a framework to help them maintain focus.

This chapter discusses the need for order, laying the foundation for your speech, discerning your main points, organizing your speech, and outlining ideas.

THE NEED FOR ORDER

Planning a speech and providing a framework for that speech are similar to planning a trip or a vacation. You need to know when and where you will be going and how long you will be there. This information allows you to predict how much you can plan to see and how fast you will need to move from place to place. Once the framework is provided, then the detailed planning can be done: getting the tickets if you plan to fly, planning the route if you plan to drive, securing accommodations, and arranging what will be seen. As an active traveler, I have discovered that the more I plan a trip, the more successful the results are likely to be. I have found that a trip cannot be overplanned. Just as with speeches, too much planning has never been a problem.

As you plan your speech, think about taking your listeners on a trip. As you read a book, the chapter title, the main headings, the subheadings, the transitions, and the summary are often what guide you through a chapter. But the journey through a chapter is easier than the journey through a speech because with a book you can proceed at your own pace and even go back if you miss something. Listeners do not have those luxuries. As a speaker, you need to make your topic clear, erect appropriate signposts to guide listeners through your ideas, label the main points to which listeners need to pay attention (and even some minor points they may find interesting), and then in the conclusion summarize the main points of interest they have encountered and remind listeners why they made the trip. As you will discover if you ever try to "wing it," listeners have little patience for a random, spontaneous, unorganized presentation that shoots off in all directions with no purpose, no thesis, and no direction. Planning is the key to good organization. For each and every speech, no matter what length or purpose, plan an introduction, a body, and a conclusion.

Organization leads to clarity. But the most essential point of the analogy between providing a framework for a speech and planning a trip or vacation is this: If the speech doesn't move listeners toward some meaningful and recognized goal, they will lose interest in it. Although they do not always have to see their final destination, they need some sense that they are progressing toward something. That final destination provides listeners with closure or gratifies them through accomplishment. And the more effectively they are led, the better the payoff for you and for them.

Your reward for preparing a successful speech is that you will grab listeners' attention, guide them through your presentation while holding their attention, and bring them satisfied to your conclusion.

LAYING THE FOUNDATION

Before organizing information for your speech, you need to accomplish several things. Consider the following checklist for laying the proper foundation:

____ Have you selected and written out a clear, specific purpose and a central thesis for the speech?

____ Have you analyzed your audience so you have a clear idea of how much audience members already know about your topic and how listeners feel about it?

____ Have you gathered enough information to fill the required time limit for the speech? Have you gathered enough information to allow you to choose from many ideas so that you can avoid having to include information only because it is all that you have?

Remember that reading and listening to ideas are not the same. Readers can take their time, can reread passages they do not understand, and can see ideas in the context of other ideas—the relationships between thoughts. Listening, however, is a one-time event. Listeners take in less detail than readers, so help them at all points during the speech. This is important when you select a framework for the speech, and as you'll see in the next chapter, it's crucial when you design transitions to guide listeners from one point to the next. By selecting a clear organization, you will solidify for listeners the relationships among ideas.

DISCERNING YOUR MAIN POINTS

The *main heads* of the speech are like the hinged ribs of an umbrella over which fabric is stretched: They provide the structure of the speech. If an umbrella rib becomes bent or broken, the entire shape of the umbrella is changed. If you think of the central pole of an umbrella, the ribs are second in importance, just as the main points of a speech are second in importance to the central thesis. To make certain that the shape of the speech will serve its purpose—that it will do what you want it to do—you must select and phrase your main points with great care. If the central thesis and specific purpose have been phrased carefully in a dynamic and interesting way, the main points may already be clear.

For example, what would be the main points of a speech developing the specific purpose, "To explain to the class how riding a bicycle can save fuel for society, reduce pollution, and save money for the rider because of fuel and bicycle costs"? They would probably look like this:

I. Riding bicycles could generate an enormous reduction in gasoline consumption.

II. Riding bicycles could significantly reduce air pollution.

The Heart of the Matter

Think of the job of organizing ideas as being like the job of a photographer. You must try to position the camera for a wide-angle picture of the subject. Certain features will be left out, certain features will be prominent and clear, and others will recede into the background and become a blur. But the wide-angle perspective is important as you begin to make some early decisions about organizing what you have found. Later in organizing you will want to zoom in and magnify particular areas or characteristics of the larger picture. Those decisions are just as important as the ones here, but it is essential to start with the big, overall picture.

III. Riding a bicycle could save the rider the cost of fueling and maintaining a car; the rider would also save because bicycle prices are low compared with car prices or the cost of regularly using public transportation.

You may be wondering how to find the main points of your speech. The following checklist may help. The checklist items are independent of each other; they are not arranged in a series. Any one of them may help you determine your main points:

—— As you gather and review information, see if the ideas themselves dictate or suggest some kind of orderly arrangement.

—— Sift all of the ideas you would like to present, and pare them down so that you can identify the most important and the least important ones.

—— Determine which points you have supporting materials for. For a short speech, no more than three or four should be selected.

—— If you still cannot find the main points, write the important or the interesting ideas you have discovered on three-by-five cards. When you have a stack, sort them into piles by seeing which ones are related to each other. Now write a short statement that reflects the main emphasis of the cards in each pile. This will be a main point.

Once you find the main points, use these rules to phrase them:

1. Use complete sentences, not sentence fragments or phrases.
2. Use simple sentences that are specific and to the point.
3. Use vivid language to produce a strong, clear impression.
4. Use parallel structure; the same sentence parts should occur in corresponding positions.

ORGANIZING YOUR SPEECH

The body of your speech is the central or principal part that must carry out your intent. The essential information, or content of the speech, is conveyed in the body. Using a method of organization imposes structure on the content. In addition, listeners will remember your ideas better if the main points are arranged in a logical sequence. Studying the various methods of organization may also help you discover your main points.

Generally, you will follow one of four basic speech patterns when ordering your main points. Any of these patterns can be used to organize the whole speech, any major segment of it, or relatively brief developments of ideas, explanations, amplifications, or arguments. The patterns are topic order, time order, space order, and problem–solution order.

Topic order

This is one of the most common organizational patterns. In topic order each main point develops part of the specific purpose. For example, Mindy developed a specific purpose that read, "To make my audience aware of the personal, social, and spiritual benefits of self-assessment." There will be three main points:

I. What are the personal benefits of self-assessment?
II. What are the social benefits of self-assessment?
III. What are the spiritual benefits of self-assessment?

All of these main points develop part of the specific purpose, so Mindy has used topic order organization.

In following topic order, the main points may also follow some logical order. For example, they may go from what is considered least important to most important, or from specific to general. The speaker decides the order of the points; this is not a function of the topic. Let's say the speaker has selected the specific purpose, "To show concerned citizens how alcoholics can recover." With this purpose the speaker could decide to do any of the following:

- Follow a step-by-step procedure showing how alcoholics are detoxified.
- Take a typical recovered alcoholic back through the process of recovery.
- Describe the various organizations that help and how they can be contacted.
- Detail the physiological and psychological changes in the alcoholic that must be reversed.
- Prove that interpersonal relationships (a possessive mother, domineering father, or spouse who keeps the mate dependent) directly affect the alcoholic.
- Show that the drinker must be motivated to want treatment, and describe the variety of motivators that work.
- Describe how prescription drugs can help alcoholics recover.

As you can see, there are many possible approaches that could satisfy the speaker's specific purpose. The speaker chooses an approach as he considers the audience for which the speech is intended, his own needs or information, and the occasion on which the speech is being given.

Topic order can be used in either informative or persuasive speeches.

A speaker talking to the relatives of an alcoholic, for example, might try to get those relatives to look at their own behavior and to examine their relationships with the alcoholic (a persuasive purpose)—that is, to get them to take action. The speaker could use mother, father, and spouse as main points, further explaining the role of each in the speech.

A topical outline usually phrases the main points as parts of the topic, as definitions, as causes, or as reasons. Because topic order is used so often, here is an example of each style:

Phrasing main points as parts of the topic. When the specific purpose is phrased so that the main points are included within it, the topical outline evolves as parts of the specific purpose. For example, the specific purpose "To introduce my listeners to theater as a career, as an educational tool, and as a way to polish important communication skills" has three clear parts that would make selecting the main points of the speech easy. Mindy's speech on the personal, social, and spiritual benefits of self-assessment used the parts of her topic as main points.

Phrasing main points as definitions. When the specific purpose is phrased with an emphasis on explanation, definitions will often emerge. For example, a music major phrased her specific purpose like this: "To explain to nonmusic majors the musical instruments of an orchestra." Excluding new electronic ones, she grouped the 26 instruments into three major categories and organized her informative speech with an emphasis on definitions:

I. Wind instruments create sound vibrations when air is blown into or across them.
II. Percussion instruments produce sound when struck in some manner.
III. Stringed instruments produce sound when a stretched string is made to vibrate.

Phrasing main points as causes. When the specific purpose is phrased with a focus on effects, causes can make up the main points. For example, when the specific purpose reads, "To help the audience understand how the weather can have a negative effect on one's mood," the topic order would be based on causes:

I. The weather can aggravate a medical condition (heart condition, allergies, and so on).
II. The weather can cause stressful effects.
III. The weather can cause adverse reactions in people taking drugs or medication.

Phrasing main points as reasons. When the specific purpose is phrased with a focus on reasons, the speech is most often persuasive. For example, a speaker might wish to pursue the following specific purpose: "To prove to the class that grades motivate students." The main points would be the reasons why the speaker feels grades are valuable. It is sometimes useful to add a *because* after the purpose statement; this also helps to make certain that all the main points are parallel:

I. (because) Grades are important rewards for work.

II. (because) Grades serve as a measure for students to determine their own success (or lack of it).

III. (because) Grades are an accurate reflection of the competitiveness that exists in our society.

A topic order based on reasons works for persuasive speeches that attempt to prove that an idea, event, or thing is good or bad, right or wrong, important or unimportant, beneficial or detrimental, and so on. The form is as follows, with speakers inserting whatever idea, event, or thing is appropriate:

Specific purpose: "To convince my audience that _____ is justified"

(because)

I. _____ can help society.

II. _____ can help each one of us personally.

III. _____ can contribute to our future.

The topic may be education, sports, self-improvement, physical fitness, or any other that a speaker considers worthwhile. If he or she wants to convince an audience that a movie is worth (the value) seeing, it can be framed in a similar manner with the "because" statements indicating the topics: action, acting, realism, photography.

Time order

This pattern is sometimes referred to as chronological order, and it is especially useful in informative speeches. It should be used when the main points follow a chronological or reverse chronological sequence. Use this organizational pattern when it is important that listeners see a sequence in the ideas or events in your speech. For example, you would use this pattern to show:

• How to do something (play a sport)
• How to make something (build a piece of furniture)
• How something happened (passage of a law; re-creation of an accident; the evolution of an idea)
• How something works (a high-quality CD-ROM word processor or the Boeing 777)

To speak about a specific purpose such as "To explain how to overcome procrastination," you might develop the main points like this:

I. Know the event about which you procrastinate.

II. Identify the emotional consequences you experience while procrastinating.

III. Objectively view your problem and dispute your irrational beliefs to effect changes in your behavior.

Space order

Like time order, space (or spatial) order is used primarily in informative speeches. It should be used when the main points reveal or indicate a spatial relationship. When an instructor explains the various parts of an outline—introduction, body, conclusion—she might use space order to organize the presentation, just as a music instructor might use space order to explain the parts of a musical instrument or a banker to show what the various numbers on a check mean.

When you want to explain an event, place, thing, or person in terms of its parts, space order is usually appropriate. Audiences will remember your descriptions best if you proceed logically. That is, if you are emphasizing the arrangement or function of the parts, you should move from top to bottom, left to right, outside to inside—or in any constant direction that will allow listeners to follow the presentation. For example, if you chose to describe the anatomy of a grain of wheat, you might use space order (outside to inside) in the body of the speech:

   I. The grain or kernel of wheat is covered by a thin shell—the pericarp.
  II. The next several layers—the bran coat—are generally reddish brown in color.
 III. Inside the bran coat is the main food storage organ, called the endosperm, which consists of starch and protein (gluten).

A speaker talking to a group of new freshmen used space order to describe the campus library:

   I. The main use areas of the library are on the first floor: circulation, reference, reserve section, and food.
  II. The secondary use areas, which have the most popular books, are on the next two floors.
 III. The least used areas, those that contain the specialized collections and rare books, are at the top of the library.

Problem–solution order

This organization scheme is most appropriate for persuasive speeches. It is more specific than the other orders because the pattern itself dictates the order of the main points. It is effective because it follows the way people generally think. For example, if listeners were going to accept or act on the solution to a problem, they would first need to know the following:

   I. What is the problem?
     A. Does it require a change in belief?
     B. Does it require a change in behavior?
     C. Does it require both?
  II. What are possible solutions?
     A. What are the strengths of each?
     B. What are the weaknesses of each?
 III. What is the best solution?

A. Is it reasonable?

B. Is it practicable?

C. Will it solve the problem?

IV. Is this solution the best way to solve the problem?

A. Has it worked before?

B. Has it worked in other places?

C. Are there better ways?

Let's examine a speaker's use of this pattern. The speaker's specific purpose was "To convince listeners that individuals should take a hand in decisions about having surgery" (arguing against leaving such decisions to doctors). The following problem–solution format was used for this speech:

I. Nearly 1 out of every 10 Americans will be advised to have surgery this year; a significant number of these surgeries will be unnecessary.

II. Possible solutions include avoiding surgery altogether, getting second opinions, or just taking doctors at their word.

III. Patients should challenge doctors until they are sure that the operation in question is appropriate.

IV. When patients, rather than doctors, make the choices, there will be less deformity, discomfort, disability, and risk of fatal complications because of unnecessary surgery.

Another possible pattern would be a problem–causes–solution order. Using this order, you would describe the problem itself, list the causes for its occurrence, and then give a solution. This order is often appropriate for listeners who are unfamiliar with the problem. For example, a teacher might use this format in the classroom when seeking to change an already established classroom procedure:

I. (Problem) There has been little original material submitted in the papers.

II. (Causes) This lack of originality has occurred because students are too dependent on the readings assigned and are not offering their own insights and suggestions.

III. (Solution) This lack of originality can be solved if you include a section in your papers labeled "Critique," and in that section you place your personal reactions and suggestions to the authors of the readings.

OUTLINING IDEAS

The final stage in organizing information (except for writing out introductions, transitions, and conclusions, which will be discussed in the next chapter) is to put the ideas into outline form. An *outline* indicates the principal features and various parts of the speech and their relation to each other. Here's how you would show the relationships in an outline designed for a speech with three main ideas and two or three subdivisions under each main idea:

I. First main point

   A. A first major subdivision of I

      1. A first minor subdivision of A

      2. A second minor subdivision of A

   B. A second major subdivision of I, parallel with A

   C. A third major subdivision of I, parallel with A and B

      1. A first minor subdivision of C

      2. A second minor subdivision of C

      3. A third minor subdivision of C

II. A second main point, parallel with I

   A. A first major subdivision of II

   B. A second major subdivision of II, parallel with A

      1. A first minor subdivision of B

         a. A first minor subdivision of 1

         b. A second minor subdivision of 1

      2. A second minor subdivision of B

III. A third main point, parallel with I and II

   A. A first major subdivision of III

   B. A second major subdivision of III, parallel with A

This is an outline for three main ideas. Rarely will the breakdown of points go further than small letters (like a and b under II.B.1). If you need a further breakdown, use arabic numerals in brackets: (1), (2), and so on.

Many people believe that if an A is used, a B must also be used, and if a 1 is used, a 2 must be used as well. A C or a 3 need not necessarily be used. The purpose of an outline is to show divisions: how a major division (main idea) is subdivided or how a minor subdivision is further divided. If an idea cannot be divided, then the point should be written as part of the category directly above it in the outline—that is, the category to which it is directly subordinate. This avoids outlines that list only one subdivision or only one minor subdivision. Although this is a formal rule in standard outline procedure, it is not always followed.

Jeremy spoke about "a wellness lifestyle" to his basic speech class. His specific purpose was, "to describe to class members the components of a wellness lifestyle, the change necessary for a wellness lifestyle, and the benefits of a wellness lifestyle." The outline for his talk is included at the end of the chapter. Notice his consistent support of the principles discussed in this chapter. An analysis of his outline, also included, reveals his adherence to proper outlining procedure.

SUMMARY

This chapter discussed the need for order in speeches. Because reading need not be a one-time event whereas listening is, speakers need to give listeners clearer and more deliberately planned signals than writers need to give to readers. A lucid organization scheme is essential.

Laying a strong foundation for a speech means making certain that a topic, a general and specific purpose, and a central thesis have been determined and written out; a sufficient informational base must also be established. Next you need to find your presentation's main points and phrase them accurately and appropriately.

The chapter concluded by giving tips on how to outline your ideas. A sample speech and outline are presented and critiqued at the end of this chapter.

Sample Speech

The following speech was given by Jeremy to his basic speech communication class and is used here with Jeremy's permission. The analysis in the margin is designed to emphasize the outlining techniques.

General purpose: To inform

Specific purpose: To describe to class members the components of a wellness lifestyle, the changes necessary for a wellness lifestyle, and the benefits of a wellness lifestyle.

Central thesis: Specific benefits can be realized from following a wellness lifestyle.

A Wellness Lifestyle

Introduction

This question is designed to get attention.

Notice that Jeremy has not outlined the introduction to the speech.

Notice how Jeremy previews or forecasts his first point of the speech and its subpoints.

Transition.

Here Jeremy presents his central thesis and then provides a smooth transition into his first main head.

How many of you consider yourselves to be healthy? What is *your* definition of health? When health is mentioned, absence of disease is what comes to mind for most people. However, health is much deeper than that. The World Health Organization states, "Health is a state of complete physical, mental, and social well-being and not merely the absence of disease and [sickness]."[1] A more well-rounded version of health today is known as wellness or maximal well-being, which includes physical, emotional, social, intellectual, and spiritual well-being. Also, it refers to functioning well as a total person, or achieving full human potential.[2]

Today, interest in wellness programs is on the rise. People of all ages are taking their health into their own hands and taking responsibility for fulfilling their individual needs. Anyone can benefit, in all aspects of life, from practicing a wellness way of life. The first step toward achieving wellness is to become aware of its components.

Body of the Speech

First main idea.

I. The five components of wellness:

First subpoint.

A. Physical health is the first component and includes the following aspects:
   1. Eating well
   2. Exercising regularly
   3. Avoiding bad habits
   4. Making responsible decisions about sex
   5. Getting regular medical checkups[3]

Listed in nonsentence form. None had additional supporting data.

B. Emotional health is the second component and includes the following aspects:
   1. Optimism
   2. Trust
   3. Self-esteem
   4. Self-acceptance
   5. Self-confidence[4]

Notice how Jeremy has kept subpoints parallel to each other.

C. Intellectual health is the third component and includes the following aspects:
   1. Openness to new ideas
   2. Motivation to master new skills
   3. Sense of humor
   4. Creativity
   5. Curiosity

In the third subpoint, Jeremy uses parallel structure again.

D. Spiritual health is the fourth component and includes the following aspects:
   1. To enjoy
      (a) Capacity for love
      (b) Compassion
      (c) Forgiveness
      (d) Joy
      (e) Peace
   2. To maintain harmony and balance
      (a) Between oneself and others
      (b) Between inner needs and the demands of the world
   3. To recognize a higher power[5]

Parallel structure is continued in the fourth point.

Jeremy had three subsubpoints, which he kept parallel. He also had seven, third-level subpoints designated with small letters in parentheses.

E. Social health is the fifth component and includes the following aspects:
   1. We need to be needed by loving and supportive people
   2. We need to develop good communication skills
   3. We need to have a capacity for intimacy
   4. We need to contribute to our community[6]

Notice how Jeremy briefly tells what he just did before continuing.

Now that I have provided the five components of wellness, I am going to tell you what a strong wellness program looks like. What would you do to pursue a strong wellness program?

Jeremy's main heads are parallel.	II. The five steps of a wellness program:
	A. Determine what you want to change.
Subpoints are parallel as well.	1. Choose only one behavior or habit.
	2. Work on just that task alone.
Even subsubpoints are parallel.	3. Realize success sooner when just one task is approached.
	B. Determine where you are and where you are going.
	1. Take a week to record your regular behavior.
	2. Now determine where you want to be.
	3. Set up some tentative goals based on this analysis.
Each subpoint is parallel.	C. Make your goals specific.
	1. State them in precise terms.
	2. Be realistic.[7]
Jeremy had brief examples for each of his ideas.	D. Make a plan of action.
	1. State your goal in measurable terms.
	2. State your goal in accomplishable terms.[8]
	E. Measure your success and reward yourself.
	1. Keep a journal.
	2. Reward yourself.
Transition.	Now that you know the five components and the five steps of a wellness plan, what are the benefits likely to be?
The main heads are parallel.	III. The benefits of a wellness lifestyle.
	A. Physical fitness is one benefit.
	1. It's easier to get out of bed.
	2. You view life as more positive.
	3. You are more relaxed under pressure.
	4. You can better deal with negative situations.
	5. You have more energy.[9]
Jeremy's subpoint B is parallel to A.	B. Emotional fitness is another benefit.
	1. It is a positive addiction.
	2. It produces a natural high.
	3. It offers a sense of accomplishment.
	4. It gives a balancing cushion to stressors.[10]
Transition.	We've looked at the components; we've looked at a plan; and now we've looked at the benefits.

Conclusion

Wellness is more than just not being sick; it is a positive state of health. It means taking responsibility for our own health. How? By learning how to stay healthy. By practicing good health habits. By giving up harmful habits. And by responding to our body's warning signs before something serious happens.[11] Everyone reaps the benefits of well-planned wellness programs. Looking good means feeling good. Just remember what Ralph Waldo Emerson said, "The first wealth is health."[12]

Speech Notes

1. Dale Hahn and Wayne Payne, *Focus on Health* (St. Louis, MO: Mosby Yearbook, 1991), pp. 1–3.
2. Lori Turner, Frances Siezer, Eleanor Whitney, and Barbra Wilks, *Life Choices* (New York: West, 1992), p. 9.
3. Paul Insel and Walton Roth, *Core Concepts in Health* (Mountain View, CA: Mayfield, 1994), p. 232.
4. Insel and Roth, p. 232.
5. Insel and Roth, p. 232.
6. Insel and Roth, p. 232.
7. Judith Hurley and Richard Schlaadt, *The Wellness Lifestyle* (Guilford, CT: Duskin, 1993), pp. 12, 14–17.
8. Hurley and Schlaadt, pp. 12, 14–17.
9. Dr. John Piper, Health Education Professor, Interview, November 4, 1993.
10. Piper.
11. *What Everyone Should Know about Wellness* (pamphlet) (South Deerfield, MA: Channing Bete, 1993).
12. Hurley and Schlaadt, pp. 12, 14–17.

Chapter Questions

1. What familiar examples clearly show the need for order in our lives?

2. Why is it essential to lay the proper foundation for a speech before organizing ideas?

3. What other methods might work for discovering main points in a speech?

4. For the following specific purposes, which methods of organization presented in this chapter might work best?
   a. To convince an audience that universal health care should be adopted.
   b. To prove to an audience that welfare reform in this country would be beneficial.
   c. To explain to the class the many uses of desktop publishing.
   d. To explain to the class birth order and how it affects each sibling.
   e. To convince the class that language education is important.
   f. To motivate audience members to make changes in their lives now that will add years to their lives later.

5. In this example a speaker used the topic "Society's Insistence That Women Be Thin." For the specific purpose "to show class members why and how women alter their bodies, why society insists that women be thin, and how society conditions women into believing they have

to be thin," the speaker had accumulated the following main and sub-ordinate points. Can you arrange them in outline form? No transitions are included in the list.

_____ Society tries to make women believe they have to be thin to look socially acceptable through certain products, the fashion industry, and magazine advertisements.

_____ As women become powerful and successful in society, primarily in jobs identified as male, men become intimidated.

_____ The first method women use to alter their bodies is cosmetic surgery, such as breast implants or liposuction.

_____ To prevent losing their power, men teach women to concentrate on the mirror and the scale.

_____ The popular Barbie doll gives young girls false perceptions of what the female figure should look like.

_____ The second method women use is unhealthy eating methods, such as starving themselves and becoming anorexic or practicing the binge–purge methods of bulimia.

_____ Magazine advertisements reinforce the belief that women have to be thin.

_____ Most women feel they have to be thin to achieve personal and societal approval.

_____ The fashion industry says women have to be thin.

_____ Some feel that society insists that women be thin as a backlash to control women.

_____ Men are scared that if women become too successful, they will become too powerful.

6. Provide a thorough critique of Jeremy's speech, "A Wellness Lifestyle." Emphasize the elements of outlining and organization.

Further Reading

James C. Humes, *The Sir Winston Method: The Five Secrets of Speaking the Language of Leadership* (New York: William Morrow and Company, 1991).

Humes emphasizes organization. In Chapter 7 Humes discusses the importance of having a single theme. Chapter 11 discusses the E-A-S-E formula: exemplify, amplify, specify, and electrify. This is an easy-to-read book full of useful, practical advice.

Sheldon Metcalfe, *Building A Speech*, 2nd ed. (Fort Worth: Harcourt Brace, 1994).

Unit Three of this book, "Creating the Structure," includes two chapters: "Organizing the Body of the Speech" and "Selecting the Introduction and Conclusion." These chapters are thorough, full of useful examples, and well written.

Endnotes

1. Messages are better comprehended and are more persuasive if they are well organized. The support for this statement comes from research in the speech communication discipline completed many years ago. See, for example, Raymond G. Smith, "Effects of Speech Organization upon Attitudes of College Students," *Speech Monographs* 18 (1951), pp. 292–301; Ernest Thompson, "Some Effects of Message Structure on Listeners' Comprehension," *Speech Monographs* 39 (1967), pp. 51–57; Harry Sharp, Jr., and Thomas McClung, "Effect of Organization on the Speaker's Ethos," *Speech Monographs*, 33 (1966), pp. 182–83; James C. McCroskey and R. Samuel Mehrley, "The Effects of Disorganization and Nonfluency on Attitude Change and Source Credibility," *Speech Monographs* 36 (1969), pp. 13–21; Arlee Johnson, "A Preliminary Investigation of the Relationship Between Message Organization and Listener Comprehension," *Central States Speech Journal* 21 (1970), pp. 194–207; James F. Vickrey, Jr., "An Experimental Investigation of the Effect of 'Previews' and Reviews' on Retention of Orally Presented Information," *Southern Speech Journal* 36 (1971), pp. 209–19; and Christopher Spicer and Ronald E. Bassett, "The Effect of Organization on Learning from an Informative Message," *Southern Speech Journal* 41 (1976), pp. 290–99.

Words in Action: VIDEO STUDY

Once you have the information for a speech, the next step is to decide on the most effective way to organize the information. For example, you may organize it chronologically, by topic or space, or as a problem and a solution. Although Barbara Jordan's speech on the accompanying video does not follow one of these patterns, it does have a clear organizational structure. After watching the video, answer the following questions.

1. Describe the organizational pattern Barbara Jordan's speech follows.
2. What is the specific purpose of Jordan's speech? How is the organizational structure appropriate to this specific purpose?

Introductions, Transitions, and Conclusions

After reading this chapter you will be able to:

- construct gripping introductions
- use transitions to guide your listeners through your speech
- construct memorable conclusions

A l Gore, vice president of the United States, delivered an address before the Television Academy at the University of California Los Angeles. Notice how he began his remarks as he spoke about the national information infrastructure:

It's great to be here at the Television Academy today. I feel I have a lot in common with those of you who are members of the academy. I was on Letterman. I wrote my own lines.

I'm still waiting for residuals.

At first, I thought this could lead to a whole new image. And maybe a new career. No more Leno jokes about being stiffer than the Secret Service. Maybe an opportunity to do other shows. I was elated when "Star Trek: The Next Generation" wanted me to do a guest shot—until I learned they wanted me to replace Lieutenant Commander Data.

The historian Daniel Boorstin once wrote that for Americans "nothing has happened unless it is on television." This of course leaves out a few major events in our history. But this meeting today is on television—so apparently this event is actually occurring.[1]

Gore demonstrated a number of essentials in both public speaking and effective introductions. First he began with a compliment to the inviting agency, the Television Academy. Next he identified with his listeners by saying, "I feel I have a lot in common with those of you who are members of the Academy." Third, he used humor to gain favor with his audience. The comments about Letterman, residuals, a whole new image, Leno jokes, the guest shot, and replacing Lieutenant Commander Data, as well as the "apparently this event is actually occurring" remark, were all designed with humor in mind. In sum, he designed an introduction that would put both him and his listeners at ease. Because of its informal, chatty nature, it made everyone feel comfortable. Also, it directly countered the popular stereotype that he was "stiffer than the Secret Service."

This chapter discusses introductions, transitions, and conclusions—but not in that order. Conclusions are discussed first because this order naturally follows the development of the body, which comes first. With the body and conclusion prepared, you will know what you are going to introduce. After that you can write smooth transitions. At the end of the chapter a speech is provided, along with critical commentary, to illustrate the use of an effective introduction, good transitions, and a strong conclusion.

Because introductions and conclusions are the first and last things listeners hear, they are important. They represent a vital opportunity to grab listener attention and to leave listeners with a clear sense of the main purpose of your effort. Your speech will not be successful unless you make your introduction and conclusion powerful and effective.

CONCLUSIONS

You are unlikely to know precisely how you want to end your speech until you have constructed the body. A strong conclusion follows naturally, logically, and smoothly from the body. The introduction is not prepared first because it should reflect what is in the body and conclusion, and that may not be known until both are finished. Often the introduction and conclusion are directly linked.

The conclusion of your speech is your last opportunity to make an impression on your listeners. Research has shown that audience members remember what they hear last.[2] You can capitalize on this recency effect by making certain that your main points hit home. A well-planned, succinct

---

The Heart of the Matter

A sense of unity must govern the construction of your speech's introduction, transitions, and conclusion. That is, these aspects of the speech should be viewed as serving one purpose: to make the central thesis clear in listeners' minds. Each part is uniquely designed to contribute to the cohesiveness and coherence of the whole speech so that audience attention can remain focused on the essential content. How the parts contribute to achieving this purpose may differ, but the goal is the same for each: to ensure that listeners hear and understand the central thesis of the speech.

---

conclusion can make a lasting impression. Although a good conclusion is unlikely to save a poor or mediocre speech, any speech will be enhanced by a strong, dynamic conclusion. If you have worked hard on the body, you will not want to see this effort wasted with a weak, ineffective conclusion.

Your conclusion should serve three purposes, although the first two may be combined: It should (1) summarize the speech, (2) leave the audience with the overall purpose, and (3) make an impression. A conclusion can also call the audience to action, make a final plea, or inspire.

Summarizing

Perhaps the easiest conclusion to use is the summary. Here a speaker summarizes the main point of his speech about self-discipline:

> That is why self-discipline—the self-discipline we can get from savoring the moment, taking control of our time, capitalizing on our skills, working hard, taking good care of ourselves, making time for relationships, and encouraging our spirituality—can make such a difference in the quality, the productivity, and the happiness we experience. No one, other than a saint, can be 100 percent self-disciplined all the time, but if we take control of our lives self-discipline can become a habit. It's a habit worth having. Take charge of your life.[3]

Because a simple summary is often not enough, you may want to supplement your summary to heighten your conclusion's impact. Some ways to reinforce a summary are discussed in the section called "Being Impressive."

Stating the purpose

If many listeners leave your speech not knowing what you talked about or not knowing the purpose of your speech, it is probably your fault, not theirs. (If just one person out of 30 or 40 missed the point, it was probably not your fault.) You do not always need to state the purpose of your speech in so many words; sometimes it is clear without explicit statement, and sometimes leading listeners to the purpose can create drama. In general, however, especially for beginning speakers, it is better to state the purpose during the speech and remind listeners of the purpose in the conclusion.

Although you may have summarized or stated the purpose before the conclusion, it can be part of the summary as well. Listeners must know why you were speaking. You are better off including the purpose in the conclusion than taking a chance listeners will get it on their own. Too many speakers assume that their point was obvious. Notice here how Bert Roberts reinforces his central thesis in the conclusion of his speech, "Information Highways Delivering and Shaping: The Multimedia World of Tomorrow":

> For you, new capabilities and applications will reveal themselves in the near term. The multimedia world is about to present you with a host of opportunities.
> Bear in mind that opportunity used to knock. In the multimedia future, it will call.
> When it does, be sure to answer your television...or your PC...or your videophone.
> Whatever device you want. The network will be there, delivering —and even shaping—the world of tomorrow. Thank you.[4]

Just one note on Bert Roberts's final two words. Generally it is thought that you should avoid saying "thank you" to conclude your speech. If your speech is good, the audience should thank you, not you them. Also, some people think "thank you" at the end of a speech is a cliche; that is, there are so many inventive, interesting ways to end a speech that using "thank you" may show a lack of creativity.

Being impressive

Just as with the introduction to your speech, you have at hand many tools to help you shape impressive conclusions. Most of these techniques will work whether the speech is informative or persuasive. Your job, of course, is to select the best method of closing to heighten the emotional impact of the talk, arouse listeners to belief, action, or concern, or plant messages in listeners' minds.

Conclusions can accomplish these goals if they are planned carefully. You may say, "Oh, I don't have to worry about the conclusion. I'll just say whatever occurs to me at the moment." More often than not, such conclusions fail because they are long-winded, unplanned, confused, or nonexistent. The best conclusions are carefully planned, and they depend for their effectiveness on one or more specific techniques such as direct appeal to the audience; challenge; the use of a final example, illustration, or personal note; or the use of a quotation.

Notice in this conclusion how David M. Cooney, talking about stress, combines techniques by making a final direct appeal to his audience and challenging them as well:

> All of us in our daily lives face daunting situations simply because of our exposure to the winds and gales of our society. Those situations can either kill us, literally, or they can make us stronger and better. We can be like the man who can sleep when the wind blows because we have gained control of ourselves and we have empowered the people with whom we work to do their jobs properly. We can create a healthy environment so we don't need to worry about being prepared. Or we can run from incident to incident, developing high blood pressure, offending people, lowering our effectiveness, working longer than we should, and achieving marginal results. You can have either a stressful life resulting in burnout or a successful life resulting in satisfaction. It is up to you.[5]

A more obvious and direct challenge was made by Will Kopp in his speech, "Inventing the Future":

> I encourage each of you to keep learning, keep inventing a better tomorrow, and help make my predictions come true.[6]

Other challenges might include phrases like "Do it," "Try it," "See it," "Be concerned about it," "Think about it," or "Believe it."

In her speech, "More Prepared Than 911," Jody Daugherty, a basic course student, began and ended with examples. Here is the one she used in the conclusion:

> Paul Harvey, on WJR radio, reported this story. Last week a man was working late at his computer when he began having a heart attack. He called his doctor and was put on hold. He typed his emergency on his E-mail, and within 10 minutes a total stranger arrived and administered CPR. After a one-night recovery in the hospital, the man returned home.[7]

In the following speech, Fraser P. Seitel uses a quotation in his conclusion:

> And those who will lead our field into this golden age will be the ones who take seriously these 10 commandments to which I've alluded...and also who take to heart the words—fittingly enough— of the Rev. Dr. Billy Graham, who is fond of saying the following:
> "Never give up.
> Never slow down.
> Never."
> Thank you.[8]

A conclusion often combines techniques like a summary, a challenge, and a final quotation. Introductions can also combine techniques.

INTRODUCTIONS

When you know the importance of first impressions, when you realize the value of grabbing listeners' attention quickly, and when you know that audience members are waiting to see what you look like and to hear what you sound like, then you will realize the advantages of an effective introduction. But a dynamic first impression doesn't just happen; it requires careful planning and preparation.

Use your introduction to get the attention of the audience and to lead listeners comfortably into your speech. This is the time when you are likely to be the most uncomfortable before your listeners because they haven't yet interacted with you. Therefore, you should also use your introduction to put both yourself and your listeners at ease. Use the introduction to establish rapport between you and your listeners and to establish your credibility. For example, why are you qualified to speak on this topic? What do listeners need to know about you that will help them better understand your position or approach? Finally, you need to lead listeners into the main content of your speech. A good introduction provides a hook (the central thesis) on which listeners can hang all the other ideas of the speech. So you see the importance of carefully planning your introduction. You can fulfill the goals of an introduction in any of several ways:

1. Tell a story.
2. Use a startling statistic.
3. Open with a question.
4. Cite an example or illustration.
5. Use an anecdote or a personal reference.
6. Create suspense.
7. Be humorous.
8. Compliment the audience.
9. Refer to the situation or occasion.
10. Cite a quotation or an important opinion.
11. Use a combination of approaches.

Because of the role an effective introduction plays in the success of a speech, examples of each of these techniques are provided to explain and illustrate them.

Tell a story

In his speech titled "Finding the Common Ground," James S. Todd, executive vice president of the American Medical Association, told this story:

> Good afternoon. And thank you to my good friend David Holley for that generous introduction. And thank you for the chance to offer this one doctor's assessment—my diagnosis, if you will—of the debate over health system reform as it stands today.
>
> Now I'm not an economist, and I'm not a public policy planner. But I am a physician, a surgeon, and I've spent a long time working in

our health care system.

For 22 years, back home in New Jersey, I was like a primary care doctor—except it was for surgery. Car wrecks, and gunshot wounds, and more cancers than I care to remember.

Once even a young boy, hit by a train. Not many survive this sort of awful accident. I'll never forget the afternoon when they brought him in. And his family was just outside. Terrified beyond words.

But because we had the equipment we needed, we quickly knew the extent of his injuries. And we knew then what we had to do. Everyone did their job. And he survived. Today he's grown, with a family of his own.

That's just one of the miracles I witnessed firsthand.[9]

Use a startling statistic

Government professor James V. Schall, of Georgetown University, used startling statistics to begin his speech, "The Firefighters Legacy: Duty and Sacrifice":

I will begin my remarks as someone from another city by citing the following passage from the *New York Times*, for August 9, 1994: "The number of New York City firefighters killed or seriously injured in the line of duty this year is the highest in at least a decade, fire officials said yesterday. In the latest incident, Captain Wayne Smith suffered burns over 40 percent of his body, as well as to his lungs, in a Queens fire on Sunday." Captain Smith subsequently died 59 days after the fire.[10]

Open with a question

In this speech to the Grand Rapids Area Chamber of Commerce, titled "Good Writing Is Good Business," Melissa Brown, communication consultant, uses a question in her introduction:

Okay, by a show of hands: How many people in this room *enjoy* writing? [NOBODY]: I thought so. [A FEW]: A lucky few. You don't fool me—I know there are people out there who would rather drink Drano than write anything longer than a shopping list.[11]

Cite an example or illustration

Claudette MacKay-Lassonde, then vice president for corporate affairs at Xerox Canada Limited, began her speech "Butterflies, Not Pigeonholes" with an illustration:

Four months ago last Tuesday, a young female butterfly beat her wings quickly as she soared in the calm air over Hong Kong. The tiny air currents the butterfly's wings set in motion grew as they encountered other forces, evolving into the weather system that has plagued the Mississippi Valley this summer.

That is the theory. A single butterfly's flapping wings can set in motion a chain of events that has a significant impact months later and thousands of miles away. The theory is called the Butterfly Effect.[12]

Use an anecdote or a personal reference

In his speech called "Journalism as a Career," Ken Verdoia combined the use of humor with a personal reference:

> First, let me thank the University of Utah for continuing its support of young journalists in this state through these special seminars, and for letting me be part of your time at this institution today.
>
> Second, let me offer an explanation of why I was selected to speak to you. It's simple: I serve as living proof that a career in journalism must be in the reach of practically anyone.[13]

Create suspense

Judith E. N. Albino, president of the University of Colorado, used suspense to open her speech, "In Transition: Higher Education":

> When America slowly opened its eyes and heard the global call for change, it was waking up to an Orwellian nightmare. What we saw, we wanted not to believe. What we heard, we wanted to ignore. Fast asleep, we had been taking our global competitors for granted. Those of us in this room know all too well the position in which this placed America. Our global competitiveness began stuttering…even faltering. We were left with products the world wouldn't buy anymore, products even Americans didn't want anymore. We ended up where we remain today, with an unfavorable balance of trade.[14]

Be humorous

The opening introduction of this chapter is a fine example of humor by Al Gore. However, beginning speakers are wise not to plan a humorous introduction. If it falls flat, as planned humor often does, it starts the speaker off weakly. It's far better to avoid this than to chance a negative reaction from listeners. Using humor effectively takes a great deal of training and practice; even some experienced speakers avoid using planned humor.

Here James R. Houghton, chairman of Corning Inc. and an experienced speaker, uses humor to open his speech titled "Globalization: Unleashing the Power of People":

> Thank you very much, Frank. At a time like this I get a little worried how to respond to an introduction like that. The only one I've heard that really works is the following: "Frank, thank you for that wonderful introduction. Of all the introductions I've ever had, yours is certainly the most recent."
>
> The other thing that I would say to you up front is that Frank is right, my great-grandfather did found the company, but I have to tell you unequivocally standing here that my current position has nothing

at all to do with my name. It's all sheer brilliance! Now if you believe that, you'll believe anything, I guess.[15]

Compliment the audience

Notice in this speech to the Golden Key National Honor Society, "Self-Fulfillment through Imaging," how the audience was complimented:

> Thank you for asking me to speak. This is my third Golden Key keynote address, and I want you to know I relish these opportunities because these audiences are so special. To me you represent everything that higher education should be. I wish all my audiences could have your intelligence, your commitment to education, and your dedication to principles of personal advancement.[16]

Refer to the situation or occasion

When Newt Gingrich, speaker of the House of Representatives and U. S. Congressman from Georgia, presented the Republican agenda before Congress (January 4, 1995), he opened his speech this way:

> We are starting the 104th Congress. I do not know if you have ever thought about this, but for 208 years, we have brought together the most diverse country in the history of the world. We send all sorts of people here. Each of us could find at least one member we thought was weird. I will tell you, if you went around the room the person chosen to be weird would be different for virtually every one of us. Because we do allow and insist upon the right of a free people to send an extraordinary diversity of people here.[17]

Cite a quotation or an important opinion

In this speech called "The Human Rights Agenda: Dilemma and Opportunity," J. Kenneth Blackwell, treasurer of the state of Ohio, used a quotation in the introduction as he spoke before the Columbus Council on World Affairs:

> Thank you, Pat (Fehring). Almost a half-century ago, the American writer, Gertrude Stein, lay dying. Her good friend of many years, Alice Toklas, asked her, "Gertrude, what is the answer?" To which the dying writer replied—her last words—"Alice, what is the question?"[18]

Use a combination of approaches

Yet another method for constructing an introduction is to combine approaches. Sometimes you might tell a story, use a quotation, add some statistics, and then ask a question. Or you could combine any of the different approaches. The point is to make your introduction interesting, attention-holding, creative, and relevant to the central thesis. Time spent in preparing the introduction is well worth the effort; it will often tell your listeners the significance, relevance, and interest of the whole speech.

TRANSITIONS

Transitions are the glue that holds speeches together. They smooth the flow of ideas. They remind listeners what they have just heard and tell listeners that the speaker is moving to the next idea. They not only link main ideas together but also allow the audience to see how the various parts of the speech relate to each other.

Stated in another way, transitions tell audiences where speakers have been, where they are, and where they are going. If the headings of an outline are the bricks in a foundation, the transitions are the mortar. They are more necessary in speaking than in writing because, as we have discussed, speech is a one-time event; listeners cannot go back, as readers can, to review a section that was unclear. Readers, for the most part, can lead themselves. Listeners must be carefully led.

Transitional Phrases

In the first place	Parallel with that
The first step	Comparable with that
The first matter we should discuss	In the same category
	More important
In connection with this	Next in importance
Together with this	Add to this
It follows then	In addition to
With respect to this	Best of all
Concerning this	As a result
Related to this	Because of this
For example	For this reason
An illustration of this	This can be explained by
A case in point would be	The reason is
To summarize	On the other hand
We have traced	At the same time
As we have seen	Not only...but also
Up to this point	

The main problem with transitions is that they are often unplanned. When left to the last minute or to the time of delivery, transitions are often left out. Delivering a speech produces unexpected stresses, nervousness, or events that do not allow total freedom of thought. Under such conditions, it is easy to forget transitions or to grip your notes tightly and follow them rigidly; and yet the need for transitions doesn't change.

A transition that is not part of the actual outline seldom gets used. And when transitions are not used, the speech appears rough or staccato; with many sharp edges on the speech the audience loses the train of thought, the relationship of points, or the unity and coherence of the whole. You cannot depend on listeners to supply the missing transitions that you should have included. How do you know when a transition is needed? If you are not sure whether one should be used, it is better to insert it than leave it out. Transitions can take many forms. The words, phrases, or sentences you select will depend on the subject matter and the audience. The easiest and shortest transitions are single words that indicate you are moving to another idea: *next, now, further, also, similarly, likewise, furthermore, so, therefore, consequently, thus, certainly, yet, still, nevertheless, besides, first, second, third, finally,* and *last* are all useful, especially when combined with transitional phrases. The problem with single word transitions is that they are short and can easily be missed by listeners. If missed, they have not served the intended purpose. Listeners are left on one side of the river while the speaker has crossed to the other side because the listeners have missed the bridge across the river. Now, with the speaker in foreign territory, listeners may be left confused and disoriented.

Transitional phrases do not differ greatly from transitional words; phrases are just longer and more likely to be heard. The list of transitional phrases shown in the box is far from complete and is not in any particular order, but it should serve as a guide. Pick and choose the phrases that serve your purpose best. As your guide, use the phrases that sound or feel the best; you must be comfortable with them.

A lecturer talking about holding audience attention incorporated transitions into her lecture material in this way:

> All right, we have talked about how to make your message compete [with other stimuli that compete for listener attention] using content and evidence. Now let us look at how to make your message compete using organization. Because attention comes in spurts, in organizing your material it is important to refocus attention. You refocus attention by (1) using transitions, (2) using internal summaries, and (3) continually relating your material back to your thesis.

In this brief excerpt the lecturer uses all three of the techniques she is discussing. She begins by relating the material back to her thesis (how to make your message compete). She then uses a transition (Now let us look), repeats her thesis, introduces her new topic (organization), repeats her new topic area (organizing), and forecasts or previews her next three points. The value of including such transitional material in speech is that it keeps listeners focused on where you have been, where you are, and where you are going.

SUMMARY

Organizing a speech includes preparing an outline and planning a conclusion, an introduction, and transitions. Of these elements, you should write your conclusion first—right after you finish preparing the body of your speech. With the body of the speech so fresh in your mind, it will be easy to summarize, relate the speech back to the central thesis, and leave the audience with a quotation, something to think about, a challenge, or a question. After you have written your speech's conclusion, you will know where you are going, so you will be ready to write your introduction. Next you can link the introduction to the body with a transition and prepare transitions between your main ideas.

You should write out the conclusion, the introduction, and the transitions in full because it is easier to judge their effectiveness and work on them when you can see them in their entirety. Writing out these sections of your speech completely helps assure that they will be well planned and not forgotten because of the stress of delivering your speech. However, do not deliver them straight from your manuscript; it would be better to either memorize these parts or know them extremely well.

Introductions, transitions, and conclusions develop important relationships and maintain your connection with your listeners. The success of your speech depends on these crucial elements.

Sample Speech

The following is a graduation speech by Martha Saunders, assistant professor of public relations, at the University of West Florida. The speech was delivered on October 28, 1993 and is used here with her permission.[19]

Learn to Listen with Your Heart: Farewell to Graduates

Martha begins with a personal example and uses her credibility at the outset of the speech.

In the Department of Communication Arts we spend a great deal of time thinking and talking about words—the meaning of words, the persuasive value of words, the ethical implications of words, and, generally, the impact of words as they are delivered in messages among people. Because of this, I was especially captured by a magazine article a few months ago that discussed how words influence people.

Here Martha sets the stage for what she plans to do in the speech. This is still part of her introduction.

The article suggested that the most important messages that humans deliver to one another are usually expressed in very simple terms. I hope that doesn't shock you now that you've spent these past few years having your minds crammed with complicated thoughts. The article went on to suggest that the *most influential messages* in our language most often come in three-word phrases.

This is the end of Martha's introduction. Now she has cited three examples of what she plans to do in the speech.

I had to agree that three-word phrases such as "I love you" or "There's no charge" or "And in conclusion" certainly were capable of prompting a strong reaction in me, and as I had hoped to impress you with profound thought today, I decided to share with you *three* three-word phrases that I have found useful as I have moved along in my life.

Here is where Martha begins the body of her speech. She begins with transitional words: "the first."
Now Martha uses examples to support her first main idea.
Martha chooses examples with which her listeners can identify.
She really engages her audience.

The first three-word phrase I've found useful in life is this: *I'll be there*. Have you ever thought about what a balm those three words can create?

I'll be there. If you've ever had to call for a plumber over a weekend you know how really good these words can feel. Or if you've been stranded on the road with car trouble and used your last quarter to call a friend, you know how good those words can be. Think about them:

"Grandma, I'm graduating in August!" *I'll be there*.

"Roommate, I'm stuck at the office and can't get to the airport to meet my sister!" *I'll be there*.

"Mom, the baby cries all night and if I don't get some sleep I'll perish!" *I'll be there*.

Recently I was talking with a local businessperson who is occasionally in a position to hire UWF graduates, and she told me the single most impressive thing a job candidate can do is to demonstrate a real interest in the well-being of that business. Someone who will help further the objectives of that organization, whether or not he or she is "on the clock," is going to be a valuable person. In other words, *be somebody who will be there.*

One of my favorite stories about someone who knew how to "be there" is told of Elizabeth, the Queen Mother of England, who was asked whether the little princesses (Elizabeth and Margaret Rose) would leave England after the Blitz of 1940. The queen replied:

> "The children will not leave England unless I do. I shall not leave unless their father does, and the king will not leave the country in any circumstances whatever." *I'll be there.*

She moves to the second three-word phrase with a transition: "the second." Again, she supports her point with examples.

The second three-word phrase I want to present to you is perhaps the hardest to learn to say—I know it was for me and sometimes still is. That is, *maybe you're right.* Think about it. If more people were to learn to say *maybe you're right* the marriage counselors would be out of business and, with a little luck, the gun shops. I know from experience it can have a disarming effect on an opponent in an argument. In fact, one of my lawyer friends uses it often in his closing remarks—and he is a *very* successful lawyer. *Maybe you're right.*

Notice here how she uses personal experience as one of her examples.

It has been my experience that when we get so hung up on getting our own way that we will not concede on *any* point, we are doing ourselves a real disservice. Make life a little easier on yourself. Remember the old saying: "There are a hundred ways to skin a cat—and every single one of them is right." *Maybe you're right.*

Notice that she begins each of her three main points in exactly the same way: "the third phrase." Once again, she uses a personal example to begin her support for this point.

The third phrase I want to introduce to you I must have heard a thousand times when I was a little girl. Whenever I was faced with a hard decision I would turn to my caregiver and ask what I should do. Her response was always the same three-word phrase—*"Your heart knows"*—then she would go on about what she was doing.

"My heart knows?" I would think to myself. "What's that supposed to mean? I need advice here. I need for you to tell me what to do."

She would just smile and say, *"Your heart knows, honey, your heart knows."*

But as I was an imperious child, I would throw my hand on my hip and say, "Maybe so, but my heart isn't talking!"

To this she would respond—*"Learn to listen."*

Here Martha makes the point of her speech clear. She doesn't leave it to chance; she doesn't make her listeners guess. She has now completed her three main points, and she is going to draw them to a conclusion as she moves quickly toward the close of her speech.

This brings me to the point of my speech. You know, life doesn't come in the form of a degree plan. There's no Great Advisor out there who will give you a checklist and say, "Do these things and you'll earn your degree in 'life.'"

To some extent, the page is blank now. You may have a rough outline of where you're headed, but I can assure you, you won't get there without having to make some tough decisions—and decision making is never easy.

You may be able to find people to suggest what you should do, but for the most part, no one will be willing to accept the responsibility for your mistakes. You'll have to make your own choices.

Martha concludes her speech with her advice.

My advice to you today is to *learn to listen to your heart*. The psychologists call this "tuning into our subconscious." Spiritual leaders call it "turning to a higher power." Whatever you call it, there is an ability in each of you to find the right answers for your life. It's there and it's a powerful gift that all the education or degrees in the world can't acquire for you. You've had it all along—now, you're going to have to use it.

And to draw all of her ideas together, Martha has found a quotation for her final thought, and then ends her speech appropriately with a challenge: "Choose well."

In "The Bending of the Bough," George Moore wrote, "The difficulty in life is the choice." Choose well, graduates.

Chapter Questions

1. Why are conclusions, introductions, and transitions so important to the success of speeches?

2. List some ways to conclude speeches that are not mentioned here.

3. If you were trying to get your audience to donate blood because a local American Red Cross blood bank was in short supply, how might you conclude the speech to inspire your audience to donate?

4. What are some unique ways to introduce speeches that were not mentioned in this chapter?

5. If you were asked to give a speech to a group of high school students about the value of a college education, how might you introduce this speech? Why? What material might you use for the conclusion? Why?

6. If you were asked to give a speech called "Public Speaking Should Be a Required Course for All College Students" to a skeptical college administration, how might you begin the speech? How would you end it?

7. Link the following three ideas with transitions. The speaker is introducing the audience to the following three-word phrases: I don't know, I don't understand, and I will learn. Be more creative than simply using "first," "second," and "third."

8. Based on this chapter, prepare a brief speech that would convince a novice speaker of the importance of conclusions, introductions, and transitions.

Further Reading

For other excellent examples of introductions, transitions, and conclusions, readers should examine the speeches in *Vital Speeches of the Day*.

Michael S. Hanna and James W. Gibson, *Public Speaking for Personal Success*, 3rd ed. (Dubuque, IA: Wm. C. Brown, 1992).

　　The chapter called "Beginning and Ending a Speech" offers a number of different ideas speakers can use.

Jo Sprague and Douglas Stuart, *The Speaker's Handbook*, 3rd ed. (Fort Worth, TX: Harcourt Brace, 1992).

　　Sprague and Stuart have written excellent separate chapters on introductions, transitions, and conclusions. Their chapters are short, but they are packed full of good information.

Endnotes

1. Al Gore, "The National Information Infrastructure: Information Conduits, Providers, Appliances and Consumers," *Vital Speeches of the Day* LX (February 1, 1994), p. 229.
2. Gary Cronkhite, *Persuasion: Speech and Behavioral Change* (Indianapolis: Bobbs-Merrill, 1969), pp. 195–96. Also see Ralph L. Rosnow, "Whatever Happened to the 'Law of Primacy'?" *Journal of Communication* 16 (March 1966), pp. 10–31. Cronkhite summarizes research indicating that ideas are better recalled by listeners if they are placed at the beginning *or* at the end of a presentation.
3. Richard L. Weaver II, "Developing Self-Esteem: Effective Leadership Starts from Within," *Vital Speeches of the Day* LVIII (October 15, 1991), p. 21.
4. Bert C. Roberts, Jr., "Information Highways Delivering and Shaping: The Multimedia World of Tomorrow," *Vital Speeches of the Day* LX (February 1, 1994), p. 236.
5. David M. Cooney, "Stress: It's All Up to You," *Vital Speeches of the Day* LX (February 1, 1994), p. 244.
6. Will Kopp, "Inventing the Future: Battelle's Vision of Tomorrow's Technology," *Vital Speeches of the Day* LV (February 1, 1994), p. 247.
7. Jody Daugherty, "More Prepared Than 911." Used with permission. Daugherty cites Paul Harvey, WJR Radio, Detroit, Michigan, April 5, 1994.
8. Fraser P. Seitel, "The 10 Commandments of Corporate Communications: Better Management Understanding of the Communications Function," *Vital Speeches of the Day* LX (January 15, 1994), p. 204.
9. James S. Todd, "Finding the Common Ground: The Path to Health System Reform," *Vital Speeches of the Day* LX (January 1, 1994), p. 178.
10. James V. Schall, "The Firefighters Legacy: Duty and Sacrifice," *Vital Speeches of the Day* XX (April 15, 1995), p. 395.
11. Melissa Brown, "Good Writing Is Good Business: Clear Words Lead to Correct Action," *Vital Speeches of the Day* LIX (March 1, 1993), p. 311.
12. Claudette Mackay-Lassonde, "Butterflies, Not Pigeonholes: Educating Our Young People for the New World of Business," *Vital Speeches of the Day* LX (January 1, 1994), p. 182.
13. Ken Verdoia, "Journalism as a Career: Doing the Job Right," *Vital Speeches of the Day* LIV (February 15, 1993), p. 276.
14. Judith E. N. Albino, "In Transition: Higher Education—Evolving to Meet the Needs of a Changing World," *Vital Speeches of the Day* LIX

(April 1, 1993), p. 372.

15. James R. Houghton, "Globalization: Unleashing the Power of People," *Vital Speeches of the Day* LXI (February 15, 1995), p. 268.

16. Richard L. Weaver II, "Self-Fulfillment Through Imaging: The Me We Want to Be," *Vital Speeches of the Day* LVII (January 15, 1991), p. 216.

17. Newt Gingrich, "Plans for the 104th Congress: The Republican Agenda," *Vital Speeches of the Day* LXI (February 15, 1995), p. 226.

18. J. Kenneth Blackwell, "The Human Rights Agenda: Dilemma and Opportunity," *Vital Speeches of the Day* LXI (November 15, 1994), p. 88.

19. Used with the permission of Martha Saunders and *Vital Speeches of the Day*. See *Vital Speeches of the Day*, LX (October 28, 1993), pp. 201–202.

Words in Action: VIDEO STUDY

A good speech includes an introduction to gain the audience's attention, transitions to map the way, and a conclusion to provide closure. Three video samples accompany this chapter. The first is an example of an introduction, the second is a conclusion, and the last is the beginning and ending of a student speech. After viewing these sample speeches, answer the following questions.

1. What technique does Ann Richards use in her introduction to secure audience attention?

2. During the 1988 presidential campaign, George Bush was fighting the perception that he was a "wimp." How does he use the conclusion of his speech to overcome his opponents' claim?

3. What two objectives does the student speaker accomplish with her introduction?

4. Is the speaker's conclusion strong? Why or why not?

PART III

Making the
Presentation

9

Credibility

After reading this chapter you will be able to:

- understand the importance of credibility to listeners, to speakers, and to a speech's content

- build your credibility by developing a positive speaker–audience relationship

- build your credibility through quality communication

- use specific methods to develop your credibility before a speech

- develop your credibility with regard to your competence

- develop your credibility with regard to your trustworthiness

- develop your credibility with regard to your dynamism

When Ella was asked to speak to her alma mater's undergraduate Future Business Executives club, she worried that the members might not be aware of all that she had done since graduation and that she might not have the credibility she needed to provide them the insights she wanted to. It was as if she had three strikes against her before she even opened her mouth: (1) she was a woman, (2) she was short, and (3) she was African-American. But she had made it! She was told she would have an introducer, so she spent time carefully preparing an introduction for herself that would include all the information she thought it was important for listeners to know: her college preparation, her M.B.A., her work as a junior executive, her work as part of a public relations team, and, finally, her promotion to vice president of public relations. All of these were important to her credibility for giving this speech.

When Scott decided to speak about the salaries of professional athletes, he wanted his audience to know why he was concerned about this topic. Since most listeners had no information about him, he decided to incorporate personal information as examples within his speech. It was clear from his examples that he had been an athlete throughout his educational career, that he intended to go into professional sports after college, and that both his father and his grandfather had been involved in professional athletics. Scott wasn't bragging; but his position regarding the salaries of professional athletes—being in favor of making what one was worth—required listeners to know why his commitment was so deep.

This chapter discusses the importance of credibility and how to build credibility through a positive speaker–audience relationship. Next the qualities of good communication are described, followed by sections on credibility before and during the speech. Finally, competence, trustworthiness, and dynamism are discussed as components of a speaker's credibility.

THE IMPORTANCE OF CREDIBILITY

Credibility is made up of many personal qualities: intelligence, trustworthiness, reliability, competence, and more. When you assess a person's credibility, you are responding to all of these characteristics. Credible people are sometimes referred to as people of good will. We turn to such people for guidance, information, and leadership. Your credibility—the sum of these personal characteristics—is a powerful communication factor, one we react to in ways that may supersede logic, emotion, or other considerations.

This chapter explores how we perceive a speaker's character—how speakers are viewed by audience members. *Ethos* can be defined as the character of the speaker in the eyes of the audience; image, personality, charisma, and ethos all refer to the same thing.[1] No two audience members are likely to view you in exactly the same way, and how you are viewed may bear little resemblance to how you really are. Often there is a discrepancy between your personal self—the way you are in private—and your public self—the way you project yourself to others. Thus, we are dealing here with an image—your image or character in listeners' minds.

When you come before an audience, some listeners may have already formed an impression of you; that is, they may have some prior knowledge of you. This is often true of keynote, graduation, or special occasion speakers who have been asked to speak because of their reputation. This prior impression is sometimes referred to as *extrinsic ethos* because it is credibility established externally (actually prior) to this speech occasion. Sometimes as a listener you are not aware of the extrinsic ethos, but you are informed of it in the program notes or by the introducer, as in Ella's situation. It is still extrinsic to the speech occasion because speakers bring it with them.

The Heart of the Matter

Your credibility depends on the perception of your character in the eyes of every individual audience member. However, every listener is likely to have a different perception or impression. The best way you have to control these perceptions is to do nothing that would in any way detract from a strong and positive impression. This is easier said than done. Does this, for example, mean you have to be perfect? No. What it means, however, is concern and control. You need to dress appropriately, prepare appropriately, act appropriately, and present your ideas appropriately. You must make certain that anything over which you have control makes a positive contribution to your credibility. Awareness and sensitivity to the problem may be sufficient to create the necessary control. You must give this area your attention if you want to be effective; it is one of the essentials of public speaking.

If you are a beginning speaker you are likely to have little extrinsic ethos. Thus, you must earn ethos within the speech occasion. When you create your impression (or character) during a speech, this is called *intrinsic ethos*, earned credibility, or credibility developed within the speech. A good example of this is what Scott did with the examples in his speech about professional athletes' salaries. When you meet people for the first time, they must earn your respect and confidence. The same is true for speakers you hear and see for the first time. Respect and confidence are built through competent handling of both the situation and the material of the speech.

Why is credibility important? First, it determines whether your listeners will believe what you say. It also determines your chances of meeting your speech objective. Often you are able to sell your ideas only to the extent that you are able to build your credibility with your audience. Ideas do not stand alone.

BUILDING CREDIBILITY: THE SPEAKER–AUDIENCE RELATIONSHIP

Much of a speaker's credibility arises from the relationship between the speaker and the audience. That is, you have opportunities to improve your ethos as a result of how you interact with your audience.

Billy and Trevor had been friends since high school. Together they decided to sign up for a public speaking course in college. Neither took the commitment seriously; they considered the content lightweight, the approach silly, and the assignments beneath them. They joked, made fun, and had a good time in class. After each had an early assignment evaluated very low by their classmates, Billy and Trevor talked to the instructor. She informed them that their credibility had been damaged by their immature actions in the classroom, and that very likely classmates were getting back at them for their behavior. They asked what they could do about it, and their instructor suggested they change their behavior.

But the instructor also warned them that their credibility would probably continue to suffer. Credibility is a little like trust in a relationship—it takes a long time to establish it, and when it is broken, it takes an even longer time to rebuild it. In this case Billy and Trevor's classmates did not trust them, and rebuilding that trust might take some time.

There are many techniques for building your credibility. These techniques vary, and so will your ability to use them in different situations. But all must be used in an honest, forthright, and sincere manner; otherwise your attempts at building credibility will be transparently phony.

The first way to build credibility as a speaker is to help listeners feel important. Make them feel they are an important part of your message or of the potential results of your message. Include them in your presentation by using pronouns such as *we*, *us*, and *our*. In her speech titled "Passive Smoke" Alisha ended by saying, "This is our problem and with determination we can solve it together."

Treating your audience courteously is another way to build credibility. It helps them know you think highly of them. For example, be on time; keep your speech within the appropriate time limits; be as brief and to the point as possible so you don't waste valuable listener time; dress appropriately; and express gratitude for any courtesies that have been extended to you.

Remind yourself that your listeners are important. If you truly believe this, your attitude will show. Treat them as special; display acceptance, approval, and appreciation. Try not to dominate them nor to jam your ideas down their throats. Consider them as equals—people who will rationally weigh your ideas and make decisions about them. Treat them better than you would like to be treated if you were in their place.

Notice audience members individually. Pay attention to them. Put them in the spotlight by looking at each of them eye-to-eye when you speak. This makes each listener feel special.

Talk *with* your listeners, not *at* them. Share your ideas with them. Listeners must feel they are a part of your presentation. Extended conversation makes them feel included; formal delivery styles often alienate them.

Be enthusiastic. Enthusiasm is catching, just as its opposite—indifference—is. Sell yourself on your ideas and your message. Allow your leftover energy to be used in movement, gestures, and other constructive, positive activity. Activity indicates enthusiasm as long as it does not distract. Audiences like enthusiasm, and they are more likely to view you as credible if you are enthusiastic about your topic.

Act confidently. If you show confidence, even if you do not feel it, your listeners will respond to you as if you possess confidence. Their response to you, in turn, will help you believe that you have confidence. Make your movements strong and decisive. Command the situation by acting as if you know what you are doing, know what you want, and know how you are going to get what you want. Well-defined, controlled movement works as a self-fulfilling prophecy: Confidence breeds confidence.

- We like people who know what they want and act as if they expect to get it.
- We like people who hold up their heads, look others in the eye, and move as if they have somewhere to go and mean to get there.
- We like people who act as if they have something to say and mean to say it.
- We like people who believe in themselves and act that way.[2]

Let your voice reveal strength. Do not allow your tone of voice to indicate hopelessness or lack of courage. It should reflect boldness, self-assurance, and expressive control. Do not mutter or babble. Also, eliminate such mannerisms as "uh," "you know," and other vocalized pauses.

BUILDING CREDIBILITY THROUGH QUALITY COMMUNICATION

Effective communication is a crucial building block of credibility. As you begin speaking in public, concentrate on the following five qualities of communication. This will keep your mind on your message and not allow you to become sidetracked by aspects of delivery:

1. *Effectiveness*—work at achieving your intended purpose.
2. *Efficiency*—strive to achieve your greatest effectiveness at the least cost. Some speech situations require a high investment in energy; others do not.
3. *Comprehensibility*—communicate clear information as well as clear feelings, meanings, intentions, and consequences.
4. *Validity*—strive for believability in your message:
   a. Create a message that conforms to what receivers know and believe.
   b. Create a message congruent with how your listeners evaluate ideas.
   c. Be a speaker your receivers can support or believe in.
5. *Utility*—make your message useful for both you and your audience.[3]

DEVELOPING CREDIBILITY BEFORE A SPEECH

If you can analyze your audience before you give a speech, you may be able to find out what the audience knows about you and what kinds of things would appeal to them. For example, one speaker knew that he was being asked to speak before an organization because he had given a previous speech before another organization in town. Thus, he was able to use that experience as part of his own introduction. Another speaker discovered most members of her audience had been sorority members when they were in college, so she incorporated her own sorority affiliation into her introduction.

There are at least three things you can do to help develop your credibility prior to a speech. First, you need to be aware of your image in all contacts with audience members before the speech. This is where Billy and Trevor ran into difficulty. It is easy to determine in a speech class whether classmates consider you informed, intelligent, humorous, insightful, argumentative, prompt, lazy, cheerful, or whatever. These perceptions will affect the way your speeches are perceived. The same is likely to be true if you are asked to speak to a group of which you are a member, such as a service organization, club, fraternity or sorority, or professional association.

Even though listeners know little about you, they will make judgments and guesses based on the few cues they have. For example, Lee was asked to speak about his experiences in China before coming to the United States. The executive committee of the chamber of commerce knew little about Lee before they asked him to speak, but his friendliness, professionalism, and confidence in negotiating the arrangements told the chamber of commerce they had chosen a good speaker. When he arrived and was warmly received, his social ease and comfort provided a final positive impression before the speech itself.

A second thing you can do to develop your credibility prior to a speech is to provide your contact person with adequate information about your qualifications. Most people are overly modest when asked for advance publicity information. Those who have to prepare the introduction need a resume that lists background and achievements as well as clippings, testimonials, books, articles, and even a photograph if appropriate. Some speakers write out the entire introduction themselves and tell introducers to feel free to change it or condense it in any way they want. Considering the amount of time it takes to prepare introductions, you would be well advised to both provide all the information *and* write out a complete introduction. It is better to be safe than to try to follow a disastrous introduction.

Finally, a third thing you can do to develop credibility before a speech is to help introducers set a favorable tone. Providing the appropriate information is important, but indicating what information should be stressed may be helpful. Give a phone number where you can be reached by the person who will introduce you so you can answer questions. (Your introducer may also be able to give you information about your audience.)

DEVELOPING CREDIBILITY DURING THE SPEECH

As you gather materials for your speech, begin thinking about how to develop your credibility during your speech. Most beginning speakers do not have extrinsic credibility on a particular topic. The only extrinsic credibility they have, if they are in a public speaking class, is what their listeners know about them from class. Because they have little extrinsic credibility, beginning speakers must earn their ethos within the speech occasion. Speakers we hear for the first time must earn our respect and confidence through competent handling of both the situation and the material of the speech. How can you create a positive impression in the minds of your listeners?

1. *Listeners respond positively if you reveal a solid knowledge base.* This means you must appear qualified, informative, and authoritative. You should have fresh, clear, relevant, and specific supporting material.

2. *Listeners respond positively if you appear trustworthy.* Nobody likes to be treated in a hostile or unpleasant manner or feel that they are being lied to or manipulated. We trust honest, kind, friendly, pleasant people. If you appear earnest and sincere, others are more likely to believe you or act on what you say.

3. *Listeners also respond positively if you appear bold and forceful.* If you are poised, dynamic, and assertive you are more likely to be an effective persuader. If you can exhibit a sense of humor as well, you are even more likely to succeed.

This section elaborates on each of these three characteristics: competence, trustworthiness, and dynamism. We will explore specific ways for speakers to reveal each of these during a speech.[4] For speakers who are relatively unknown, these suggestions should prove helpful. Remember, however, that your goal is to exhibit *genuine* competence, trustworthiness, and dynamism. Attempting to create a false appearance of these qualities is unethical and is likely to fail.

Competence

You exhibit *competence* as a speaker when you come across as well informed and well prepared; when you are able to quote experts effectively and use the appropriate expert vocabulary without showing off; and when you include relevant facts during your speech. Also, if you are well organized and use transitions to help listeners move through the speech easily, you will be perceived as competent.

If you have done extensive research, refer to that effort during your speech. Citing the sources you have consulted for your evidence will demonstrate your competence by showing that you have done your homework. And finally, mention any personal involvement that you have with the topic; that is, describe anything you have done or will do that relates to the topic. For example, Nikki, who talked about personal appearance, indicated in her speech that she was a fashion merchandising major, which added to her competence on this topic. Terry talked about virtual reality and education, and mentioned his experiences in an education class he was taking. Brian noted during his speech about preparing for job interviews that he had eight interviews before he was finally hired.

Trustworthiness

Your listeners will consider you *trustworthy* when they feel they are being treated fairly. For example, are you open with your audience, letting them know some relevant personal details of your life? When Pat talked about child abuse, for instance, she noted that she herself had been an abused child. When Keil talked about alcoholism, he mentioned that his father was an alcoholic. When Missy discussed shyness, she said that she had always been a shy person. (There is no need, however, to reveal intimate details.)

Ask yourself these questions when you want your listeners to trust you: Do you show respect for your listeners? Do you show appreciation for the listeners' current beliefs and values? Do you present your ideas objectively? Because listeners, in general, trust themselves, can you show that your orientation is consistent with that of your audience? Does your nonverbal communication appear positive and consistent with your message? Are you calm, firm, purposeful, and honest? Do you appear to be of good character?

To add to your trustworthiness, if you have taken any personal actions in the past that support your current beliefs and orientation, make certain that information gets into your speech. For example, when Andre talked about cardiopulmonary resuscitation, he mentioned a CPR class he was required to take in preparation for being a summer lifeguard at a local pool. When Erica spoke about skills that coaches must master, she talked about her own background as a basketball coach throughout junior and senior high school. In his speech about rock and roll, Joe mentioned his work as a drummer for a rock band.

Dynamism

Listeners will consider you *dynamic* when they feel you are enthusiastic and energetic. How do you reveal dynamism in your speeches? Here are 10 specific suggestions:

1. *Reveal complete ego involvement with your topic.* For example, when Tony talked about racial prejudice, it was obvious that he truly despised prejudice. Kate, who had been a victim of a serious crime, showed her anger at criminals. Both Tony and Kate were clearly involved with their topics. They were enthusiastic and energetic and took serious positions regarding their speech topics.

2. *Be fluent.* Speech hesitancies such as "uh" or "er" or "you know" weaken dynamism. You do not need to be as polished as a professional speaker, however, you need to try not to distract your listeners with unnecessary mannerisms.

3. *Avoid leaning or slouching on a lectern.* No matter what your attitude, slumping implies laziness or lack of concern and thus weakens your presentation.

4. *Project your voice to the back of the room.* Dynamic speakers are both intellectually and physically powerful.

5. *Project composure and calmness.* Power is not just force. Although in

general extroversion is preferred over introversion, what is most appreciated is behavior that is relevant to the ideas being communicated. Sometimes this is force; sometimes it is calmness.

6. *Deliver your ideas sociably.* That is, you should display your dynamism within the context of good fellowship, friendliness, and camaraderie.[5]

7. *Relate everything you do to one clear, powerful central thesis.* This is much more dynamic than is approaching a topic from several different perspectives at the same time. It would be easy, for example, to select a topic like crime and then try to speak about guns, rape, and theft. A stronger speech, however, would likely take just one of the three issues and perhaps focus on only one aspect of the issue. For example, gun control alone involves different kinds of guns, federal versus state or local controls, the illegal possession of handguns, and many more issues. This strength of focus is similar to the power that speakers derive from taking clear, unambiguous stands on issues.

8. *Use strong evidence.* Choose facts, quotations, and examples that are reliable, honest, and typical. Does your evidence help listeners understand or make a decision? If not, don't use it. Evidence needs to be justified to listeners; that is, they need to know who the authority is, why this authority should be respected, and what position this authority takes on your ideas. Sources of facts and statistics should be identified and their objective worth demonstrated. Evidence that listeners accept will be a dynamic part of your presentation.

9. *Tell listeners what you will do, are doing, or plan to do as a consequence of your involvement with the topic.* This area is one where speakers can easily gain strength, yet it is often overlooked. One of the most dynamic instances of using this suggestion occurred when Malcolm, in a speech about seatbelt usage, described in minute detail the recent accident his parents had been in and how the entire car was totaled around them, yet they survived because both had their seatbelts on.

10. *Speak as though you are vividly realizing your ideas at that moment.* You will appear dynamic if your ideas seem fresh and your words seem to develop spontaneously during your speech. Avoid looking too polished, rehearsed, or memorized.

SUMMARY

Listeners are influenced by your credibility. Thus, you must continually think about the kind of image you have before the speech (extrinsic ethos) and the one you want to project during the speech (intrinsic ethos). Credibility determines whether listeners will believe what you say; it also determines your chances of meeting your speech objective.

To build credibility in speaker–audience relationships, help listeners feel important, treat them courteously, notice them individually, talk with them instead of at them, be enthusiastic, act confidently, and show strength in your voice.

Five qualities of communication that can aid you in establishing credibility are effectiveness, efficiency, comprehensibility, validity, and utility.

To develop credibility before a speech, provide your contact person with adequate information and help introducers set a favorable tone. During the speech you can develop credibility by building competence, trustworthiness, and dynamism.

The effect of any speech is its total impression—a fusion of all the speech's elements. That is why the five critical characteristics of communication are presented in this chapter. Efforts to improve credibility are a critical part of speech preparation and presentation.

Confidence is one of the most difficult elements of credibility for a beginning speaker to achieve. However, the momentum that resulted from any prior success you have had is likely to propel you toward further success. Everyone has had some success in life. Remembering your previous successful experiences will help to counteract worry or fear. Operate from one success to another. Capture the excitement you get from success. Let yourself get excited. In this way you will breed confidence, and confidence in front of listeners translates into credibility.

Chapter Questions

1. Why is credibility an important element for speakers?

2. Why does credibility involve speaker–audience relationships as well as speakers' personal characteristics?

3. What additional elements of the speaker–audience relationship might affect the speaker's credibility?

4. What would a speech that lacks any of the five qualities of communication look like or sound like?

5. Write an introduction to be read before a speech you plan to give.

6. For a speech you are planning, incorporate elements that will promote your competence, trustworthiness, and dynamism.

7. Do you think credibility is more or less important than evidence? More or less important than organization? What about delivery? Emotion?

Further Reading

Sheila Murray Bethel, *Making a Difference: Twelve Qualities That Make You a Leader* (New York: G. P. Putnam's Sons, 1990; paperback edition, New York: Berkley Books, 1990).

> This book's first three chapters have the subtitles "The Secret of Building Charisma," "The Magnet That Attracts Others," and "Building Trust with Your Followers." This well-written book is full of captivating examples and practical suggestions and advice.

James M. Kouzes and Barry Z. Posner, *Credibility: How Leaders Gain and Lose It, Why People Demand It.* (San Francisco: Jossey-Bass Publishers, 1993).

> This well-written and well-documented book is about what it takes to earn the trust and confidence of others.

Endnotes

1. See Kenneth E. Andersen and Theodore Clevenger, Jr., "A Summary of Experimental Research in Ethos," *Speech Monographs* 30 (1963), pp. 59–78. Aspects of credibility are summarized in Michael Burgoon's *Approach Speech/Communication* (New York: Holt, Rinehart & Winston, 1974). See also James C. McCroskey and Thomas J. Young, "Ethos and Credibility: The Construct and Its Measurement after Three Decades," *Central States Speech Journal* 32 (Spring 1981), pp. 24–34.

2. Although good delivery alone may not enhance a speaker's effectiveness, poor delivery can impair audience comprehension, source credibility, or the persuasive impact of a message. See Kenneth C. Beighley, "An Experimental Study of the Effect of Four Speech Variables on Listener Comprehension," *Speech Monographs* 19 (November 1952), pp. 249–58; Gerald R. Miller and Murray A. Hewgill, "The Effect of Variations in Nonfluency on Audience Ratings of Source Credibility," *Quarterly Journal of Speech* 50 (February 1964), pp. 36–44; Kenneth K. Sereno and Gary J. Hawkins, "The Effects of Variations in Speakers' Nonfluency upon Audience Ratings of Attitude toward the Speech Topic and Speakers' Credibility," *Speech Monographs* 34 (March 1967), pp. 58–64; and James C. McCroskey and R. Samuel Mehrley, "The Effects of Disorganization and Nonfluency on Attitude Change and Source Credibility," *Speech Monographs* 36 (March 1969), pp. 13–21.

3. Stephen W. Littlejohn, *Theories of Human Communication* (Columbus, OH: C. E. Merrill, 1978), pp. 51–52.

4. It is clear from one study that this can be accomplished early in the speech. See Robert D. Brooks and Thomas M. Scheidel, "Speech as Process: A Case Study," *Speech Monographs* 35 (1968), pp. 1–7.

5. The conclusion from most of the studies of McCroskey and Young was that there were five dimensions of credibility: competence, character, sociability, extroversion, and composure. See, for example, James C. McCroskey and Thomas J. Young, "Ethos and Credibility: The Construct and Its Measurement after Three Decades," *Central States Speech Journal* 32 (Spring 1981), p. 27.

Words in Action: VIDEO STUDY

Speakers who build credibility with their audience are able to meet their primary objective: to communicate a message. Ways to build credibility include making audience members feel important, being courteous toward them, looking them in the eye, and conveying enthusiasm and confidence in both self and message.

The accompanying video allows you to compare two speakers' abilities to establish credibility with their audience, in this case *you*, the viewer. After watching the video, answer the following assessment questions. You may wish to briefly review Chapter 9 before answering the questions.

1. In his introduction to his speech on gangs, does the speaker establish credibility on the topic? Why or why not?
2. In her introduction to the speech on Venice, does the speaker establish credibility on the topic? Why or why not?

Language

After reading this chapter you will be able to:

- explain why language is so important in speeches
- show why the principle "meaning lies in people" is the foundation for understanding how language works
- use clear and simple language
- accurately select words for your speech
- make appropriate word choices
- use dynamic language
- use five specific guidelines for improving your language

B ob Gower, president and chief executive officer of Lyondell Petrochemical Company, was asked to be the keynote speaker at the scholarship dinner for the College of Business Administration at the University of Houston. Because Bob wanted to appeal directly to his listeners and represent his company in the best light, and because Bob cared deeply about his topic, he chose his language carefully. He wanted to focus on success, on the students' future, and on leadership. But that wasn't all. Bob also wanted to motivate his listeners. He wanted to emphasize positive traits such as good will, high performance, and desire. The following is the introduction he presented. As you read it, notice Bob's language—his choices were not accidental.

> Success in the future will depend, more than anything else, on capable leadership—leadership that not only understands technology and global influences but that also understands the way people think, understands what motivates them, and understands how to get people to perform at their highest level.
>
> The differentiating factors that could be relied upon in the past— factors such as technology, location, and capital—will continue to be important. There is no question about that. But it is doubtful that they will be sufficient by themselves in the future to create success.
>
> Businesses, all organizations, will have to rely more on the good will and high performance of their people, on the desire of people for their organization to succeed.[1]

A concern for language can have three results. First, it can set you apart from others who may not pay special attention to their effective use of language. Second, your speech is likely to make an impression when other speeches do not. And third, your speech is likely to achieve results when other speeches fail. Time spent selecting language is like time spent buying a new car. Not just any car will do: A car must achieve your purpose; a car represents who you are; and the right car will get you where you want to go with color and style.

This chapter is about language and how you should select words for your ideas. First the chapter discusses where meaning lies. The concepts of clarity, simplicity, appropriateness, and dynamism are also explored. The chapter closes with a section on improving language use, with five specific suggestions for improvement. Because language plays such an important role in conveying ideas to listeners, speakers who do not spend time thinking about their language or who do not plan at least some of their language specifically may miss an opportunity to influence their audience.

MEANING LIES IN PEOPLE

One instructor, commenting on the impact he hoped to have on his students, said, "You know, if I can only get my students to understand the concept that 'meaning lies in people,' I will consider my job successful."

Some people think meaning lies in words themselves. However, words are simply triggers. They are stimuli for ideas, nothing more. If you choose the right word, you can trigger an idea similar to but never exactly the same as the idea you had in your own mind when you selected that word.

The beauty of this concept is its focus on the audience. This book has emphasized repeatedly how important it is that speakers concentrate on their audience. You need to select your topic, your facts and examples, your organization pattern, and your language with your audience clearly in mind. Remembering the principle "meaning lies in people" will help you as you labor to find the right words to trigger just the right ideas or images in your listeners' minds.

When you speak, you are not conveying meaning. You are simply using words, or symbols, to stimulate meanings in the minds of your listeners. A word is a symbol because it stands for something else. The words you choose bring forth the many associations each of your listeners has with these words. The meaning of your speech consists of those associations. Think about how many different associations each listener can come up with for the words that you use. As you can see, your choice of words is important if you want some control over the associations listeners draw from your speech.

The best way to understand this concept is through a picture, the "triangle of meaning" developed by communication theorists C. K. Ogden and I. A. Richards.[2] (See Figure 10.1.)

In Ogden and Richards's triangle of meaning, the three points are labeled *thought*, *word*, and *thing*. The broken line connecting *word* (a sym-

Figure 10.1.
An example of Ogden and Richard's triangle of meaning.

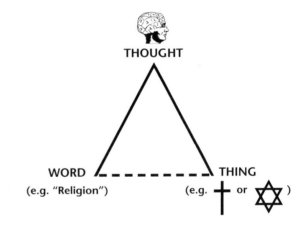

bol) and *thing* (the referent or stimulus) shows that the word is not the thing. There is no direct relationship between a word and the thing it refers to. So when you use words, the only connections between the words you use and the things they represent are in your mind (your thoughts) and in the minds of your listeners (their thoughts). For example, a few years ago a televised public service announcement that supported the anti-smoking campaign showed a person drawing deeply on a cigarette while an announcer talked about the harmful effects of the smoke. The irony, however, was lost on our young son, who went around the house drawing deeply on the end of a pencil, depicting the apparent pleasure displayed by the actor. Our son thought that the announcer's words (spoken in a deep male voice) conveyed pleasure not disdain. The connection for our son between the words in the announcement (symbols) and the thing (smoking) was (his thoughts) the deep pleasure gained from smoking—not the intended warning about smoking's harmful effects. (A call to the television station from us stopped this advertisement from being shown during the early evening hours when many children watched television.)

Because no two people have exactly the same experiences and background, no word (or set of symbols) can evoke exactly the same associations in different people. This is clearly the case with such emotion-laden words as "America," "masturbation," "communism," "homosexuality," and so on. But it is also the case with less controversial words—"vacation," "study," "rights," and many others. In your speech you must try to select words that are likely to have fairly similar associations so that listeners come up with meanings similar to those you intend. To forge communication, a common set of words must be used; and to create understanding, a common set of associations must be attached to those words by both you and your listeners.

ATTRIBUTES OF EFFECTIVE LANGUAGE

Because common associations need to be attached to the words you use so that your listeners will understand what you say, you must select words with clarity, simplicity, accuracy, appropriateness, and dynamism in mind. When your language is characterized by these attributes, you stand a better chance of controlling the associations between the words and the things they represent.

Clarity

Clarity is achieved when you use words that are immediately meaningful to listeners—that is, when there is a close correspondence between your meaning and the meaning evoked in the minds of your listeners. If your speech can arouse specific and definite meanings, you have a good chance of being understood. You must strive to use words that are free from ambiguity and confusion. In the speech at the end of the chapter, notice how Amy selected language with an eye on clarity.

It is difficult to attain clarity in spontaneous speech. Without adequate planning, many speakers tend to ramble, take shortcuts, and make incorrect assumptions about audience knowledge and understanding. In contrast, giving some thought to the language you will use in your speech allows you to be more specific. Try to remember these three suggestions:

1. Have a clear picture in your mind of precisely what you want to say. In many cases this includes the choice of appropriate language.
2. Be able to clarify and elaborate on your ideas through examples, explanation, and perhaps redundancy; be able to say the same thing again using different words.
3. Be receptive to the feedback you get from listeners. Confused looks are easy to detect. Be prepared to use feedback to guide your communication.

Simplicity

Some people think that public speaking is a formal process that requires formal language. This is not true. In fact, simple, understandable words are almost always more effective and ensure greater understanding. In informal conversation we tend to use short, simple words. Public speaking is extended conversation.

Look at Bob Gower's language in this chapter's opening example. The biggest word he used was "differentiating," and that word was unnecessary; he could have simplified his sentence by leaving the word out. A large, stilted, formal vocabulary is likely to cause confusion, create distance between you and your listeners, and distract from your message.

William Strunk and E. B. White, in their popular, short, and effective guide to writing, *The Elements of Style*, say it best: "Do not be tempted by a 20-dollar word when there is a 10-center handy, ready, and able."[3] This does not mean speakers must be trite or childish or talk down to their listeners. Avoiding vague and confusing words can avoid unnecessary communication breakdowns.

How do you attain simplicity? Here are three suggestions:

1. Use your ear as a guide. Be sensitive to the words you use. If a word seems complicated, it probably is.
2. Consider your own vocabulary and background. Do the words of your speech feel comfortable and natural? Do they reflect how you normally talk?
3. Respond to the knowledge and background of your listeners. Strive to approach them at their level of sophistication.

Accuracy

Try to select words that convey what you mean. You will want to fill as many gaps as you can, so the meanings produced in listeners' minds come close to those in your own. Many times you may not say what you mean because you do not give your listeners enough information. When you already know the subject, it is easy to visualize what you are talking about. You may sometimes forget—and don't we all?—that listeners lack your experience. When you refer to an object or event, let your listeners know exactly which object or event is being discussed and provide enough details so that they can understand it. For example, in speaking about increasing campus safety, Lance said the following:

> I have talked to campus administrators who said that campus safety is a major issue and that they are investigating ways to increase student safety while on campus.

But during the question-and-answer period following the speech, it became clear that Lance was not being accurate. First, he could not recall the names of the people he interviewed. Second, he attributed statements to "campus administrators," suggesting that he talked with more than one. When he answered questions, he revealed that he had spoken to only one. Third, Lance admitted that he was unsure whether the administrator actually said that campus safety was a "major issue," or if the person described the issue as "a concern," or as "important." These other words would convey different meanings than "major issue." Finally, when asked about the administrator's statement about "investigating ways to increase student safety," Lance could not remember a single idea. Were any specific ideas presented? Did Lance listen carefully to the person with whom he talked?

Notice how Lance's credibility came into question because of his lack of accuracy. Lance needed to get his facts straight before presenting them to his listeners. Besides omitting details, you can sometimes be inaccurate because you use words unfamiliar to your listeners. When you become immersed in a subject, you begin to pick up the accompanying vocabulary. You know the words and you become so comfortable using them that you may forget your audience may not share your knowledge. Thus, your symbols may have no meaning for them. When two lawyers talk about one of their cases, for example, their language will likely be so technical that outsiders cannot understand what is being said. A legal brief, written in legal language (sometimes referred to as "legalese"), is nearly incomprehensible to those unfamiliar with that vocabulary.

As a speaker, you can attain accuracy if you remember these rules:

1. Limit the number of examples used so that you can give fairly complete details such as names, places, dates, and other facts.
2. Select specific and concrete words that by their nature are accurate and clear. Using the wrong word will confuse your listeners.
3. If you use uncommon or technical words that may be unfamiliar to your audience, define them accurately.
4. Check your statistics for accuracy. Make certain they are correct and that they convey the information you want them to convey.

Appropriateness

Words should be designed for a specific audience, not for just any audience. At the end of this chapter, notice how carefully Amy, in her speech about economics, selected words that she knew her audience would understand and appreciate.

To see how much language can change from audience to audience, think about the words the following speakers used. A speaker talking to a group of actors used the words "blocking," "characterization," "heightening," "improvisation," and "stage business." A speaker talking to media experts used "access channels," "electronic news gathering," "fiber optics," "saturation campaign," and "tiered services." In talking to a group of mental health workers, a speaker used "multiaxial system," "psychosocial stressors scale," "global assessment," and "identifiable exogenous and endogenous factors." The point is not to use sophisticated, technical jargon to impress listeners; just use language appropriate for your audience.

You can follow these five suggestions to help make certain your language is appropriate:

1. Base your choice of words on your audience analysis. Always choose words that have a direct relationship with your listeners.
2. Select material that has audience appeal. Selecting your language is likely to be easier if you speak about facts, examples, illustrations, opinions, statistics, and personal experiences that relate to listeners.
3. Avoid questionable words that you are not sure audience members

will understand. Rather than take a chance on an unknown or confusing word, make another choice.

4. Use personal pronouns such as you, us, we, and our. These give listeners a verbal clue to your interest in them and are likely to make them more receptive.

5. Ask your audience questions. These, too, create the impression of direct audience contact and involvement. When listeners feel involved, they are likely to view whatever else takes place as appropriate.

Dynamism

Dynamic language is vivid and impressive and is often simple. Select language that enhances your content through emphasis and imagery. Words are the attire in which your thoughts are clothed. However, they should not be so fancy that they cause listeners to miss the message. The goal is strength without distraction. Dynamic language can make a message magical.

However, the magic of words comes not from supernatural powers but rather from careful, thoughtful planning and preparation. Some ideas need to be written out carefully. A number of techniques may help make your speeches dynamic.

1. *Antithesis sets one clause or other part of a sentence against another to which it is opposed.* John F. Kennedy said, "Ask not what your country can do for you; ask what you can do for your country." Another example is "It's nice to be important; it's more important to be nice." One student talking about studying used this antithesis: "What counts is not the number of hours you put in, but how much you put in the hours."

2. *Parallel structure occurs when ideas of equal weight are given the same grammatical form.* This technique is also referred to as using continuums, serializing, or stacking. For example, a nontraditional student spoke about raising her children while she was going to school. At the end of the speech she cited part of the famous series of phrases called "Children Learn What They Live," written anonymously:

If children live with tolerance, they learn to be patient.
If children live with encouragement, they learn confidence.
If children live with praise, they learn to appreciate.
If children live with fairness, they learn justice.
If children live with security, they learn to have faith.
If children live with approval, they learn to like themselves.
If children live with acceptance and friendship, they learn to find love
    in the world.

Martin Luther King, Jr., used parallelism toward the end of his "I Have a Dream" speech:

So let freedom ring from the prodigious hilltops of New Hampshire.
Let freedom ring from the mighty mountains of New York.
Let freedom ring from the heightening Alleghenies of Pennsylvania.

3. *Triplets* are lists of three things. They offer a third way to construct dynamic language. For some reason a list of three is always stronger than

either two or four. Here is an example of a triplet: "People are born. People live. People die." If you were to put the advantages of using triplets into triplet form they might read like this:

They aid memory.
They have impact.
They sound right.

One of the most beautiful triplets I know was used by a student to end a motivational speech. She said the author of this triplet is unknown:

If you want to enrich today, plant flowers.
If you want to enrich years, plant trees.
If you want to enrich eternity, plant ideas.

4. *Vivid language* is another way to create a dynamic speech. One component of vivid language is the *active voice*, in which the subject of the sentence performs the action represented by the verb. A sentence that depicts someone doing something is stronger than one that describes something being done. In this latter case, the *passive voice* relies on a form of the weak verb *to be* plus a past participle of a stronger and usually more interesting verb. For example, "Many fragrant gardens were visited by us" is not as strong or direct as "We visited many fragrant gardens." Using the active voice generally results in shorter, more powerful sentences.

5. *Refined language* incorporates subtle distinctions in meaning to create vivid imagery. Specific words are stronger than common, general terms, which are weakened by their frequent repetition and lack of precision. Consider the following examples:

Weak	Strong
walk	stagger, stumble, limp, stroll, stomp, march
sit	plop, perch, straddle, slouch
beautiful	radiant, striking, graceful, stunning
say	shout, exclaim, whisper, stammer, whine

Colorful language will give your speech both potency and flair.

6. *Careful language selections* will include in your speech striking facts, relevant quotations, precise descriptions, graphic illustrations, and thoughts that add surprise, create suspense, or build to a climax. Your choices of supporting material affect the language you will be able to use during your speech, so as you consider including examples, facts, and so on, think about the words you will use to present them.

7. Your *personal imprint* will help make your speech dynamic. As you talk about your views in your own language, your personal style will show. Your unique personality will contribute to the power of your presentation.

In sum, dynamism is more likely to occur if these suggestions are followed:

- Use antithesis, parallelism, and triplets.
- Use the active voice.
- Refine your language.
- Make careful language selections, and select outstanding supporting material.
- Let your unique personality shine through.

> # The Heart of the Matter
>
> It would be great if your vocabulary were sufficient to express any idea or thought that occurred to you. Unfortunately this isn't the case for most people. But the wider your vocabulary, the easier it is to capture and express your ideas. You can expand your vocabulary by reading, observing, and listening, and also through experience. Buy a book, read it, and look up every word you don't understand. Then use those words in conversations. Take the *Reader's Digest* "It Pays to Enrich Your Word Power" tests, and when you learn new words, use them in conversations. Practice. When you catch yourself describing something as "nice" or "good," rephrase the description. Expanding your vocabulary is a matter of wanting to do so. The more vocabulary you have, the easier it will be to both write and speak. And the writers or speakers who can articulate their ideas clearly will be looked to for leadership and will find leadership positions comfortable. The real power of language will be yours if you work to expand your vocabulary.

IMPROVING YOUR LANGUAGE USE

Language habits are hard to change. But the rapidity with which you pick up a common phrase, an advertising slogan, or a movie star's latest verbal mannerism proves that change can and does occur. Just try to control the change so that it operates in the direction of improvement. Rules and formulas offer no solution; however, the following five suggestions may be helpful:

1. Be aware of how others use language. Listen closely to detect the clarity, simplicity, precision, and dynamism in others' words. The better the critic, the better the learning.
2. Monitor your own use of language. Because you use language all the time, you can make constant improvements.
3. Use a dictionary. The healthy habit of using a dictionary will soon be as comfortable as calling on an old friend.
4. Use new words in conversation. Once you have used a new word or phrase, it becomes more natural and is available for further use.
5. Increase your speaking and writing opportunities. For example, start a diary or a journal. Practice allows experimentation and goes a long way toward increasing effectiveness.

SUMMARY

Choosing words carefully is an intricate part of the speech effort. It is linked to audience analysis, originality, strong supporting material, tight organization, and getting audience members to listen to you. Choosing language should not be viewed as separate from the other processes.

This chapter explained how meaning is created in people. Knowing this, you can select words that are appropriate for your listeners. Language is responsible, in part, for your impact on listeners.

This chapter also discussed the concepts of clarity, simplicity, accuracy, appropriateness, and dynamism of language. For each of these concepts, specific suggestions for improvement were offered. Finally, five general suggestions for improving language use were offered: (1) be aware of how others use language; (2) monitor your language use; (3) use a dictionary; (4) use new words in conversations; and (5) seek out new speaking and writing opportunities. Language habits do not change easily.

It is useful to think of public speaking as extended conversation rather than a highly formal and distinct enterprise. Thus, we can capitalize on the positive aspects of conversation such as ease of language use, a natural, comfortable vocabulary, and the normal flow of conversation.

This chapter has emphasized that language makes a difference. Clear, simple, accurate, appropriate, and dynamic language will reinforce and support your presentation and the meanings you intend to evoke in listeners. With effort and planning, your language will work effectively.

Sample Speech

Amy delivered this speech in her basic speech communication class. It is used here with her permission. In this case, there is no critique of the speech. However, notice her use of language. Ask yourself whether she has selected clear, simple, accurate, appropriate, and dynamic language.

General purpose: To persuade
Specific purpose: To persuade my listeners to do something about underpaid teachers
Central thesis: Teachers around the world are being underpaid, and something needs to be done for these men and women who are responsible for our next generation's education.

A Lesson in Economics

Introduction (attention step)

Christine's interview with Mr. Hale was going great. She had impressed him right away with her easy-going personality and, most importantly, with her strong college background. In addition, Christine was giving all the right answers to all of Mr. Hale's questions.

Finally, the conversation turned to what Christine thought was one of the most important issues of this job—her starting salary. Mr. Hale slid a copy of the school system's contract across his desk into Christine's hands. Carefully, she took the contract and began to scan down the page, only to let her eyes stop when she came across a dollar figure. When she did focus on the amount, she almost dropped her jaw.

Christine couldn't believe it! She understood that she wasn't in the highest-paying profession, but she thought she was worth more than the starting figure the school board gave.

The feeling that the fictional character named Christine got sitting in Mr. Hale's office is the feeling all nonfictional educators have about their salaries. To quote Jennifer Stara, a high school teacher in Los Angeles, "My real hardship as a teacher is not breaking up gang fights, but it is the battle for a decent salary."[1] Teachers all around the world are being underpaid, and something needs to be done for these men and women who are responsible for our next generation's education.

Body of the speech (need step)

Statement of the problem. Teaching is the occupation in which one educates the future. That sounds like a pretty important job, if you ask me. Unfortunately though, a pretty important salary does not go along with it. How unimportant are we talking here, might you be asking? Well, let's just say that a desk assistant at a health club, with no college experience or training, can make equivalent to that of a starting teacher who has four-plus years of a college background.[2] The January 1993 issue of *Working Woman* gave a report of some beginning salaries with a librarian starting at $25,900, an architect at $23,400, and a teacher at just $18,200.[3] Furthermore, the *Chronicle of Higher Education* cited that the average teacher salaries went up just 2.5 percent in 1992–1993, which failed to keep pace with inflation, which was 2.9 percent.[4] I should note that throughout my speech when I refer to teachers, I am discussing public school educators. Catholic, or other private school, teachers make substantially less than those in public schools, with differences reported to an average of almost $10,000 lower.[5]

Explanation of the problem. With the statistics I just gave, it's no wonder that the number of students graduating annually from teacher preparation institutions has been drastically reduced.[6] In fact, the National Commission on Excellence in Education cited low teachers' salaries as a major reason why talented college graduates are not attracted to the field.[7] Even though some of us hate to admit it, we live in a materialistic world, and the only way to obtain the material things we want is through a well-paying job. Of course college students will not be interested in teaching, where material possessions won't come as easily as in other professions.

College students who consider a career in education are not the only ones fed up with the low salaries offered. It is also the teachers who have many years of experience under their belts. In 1986 the *Journal of Teacher Education* found that 38 percent of experienced Alabama teachers were seriously considering leaving the profession and that 58 percent of them cited low salary as an important reason.[8] What society as a whole doesn't understand is that teachers put a considerable amount of their paychecks back into their classrooms. In recent years, educators have calculated the amount of money they have donated to their schools only to come to the conclusion that they have been used.[9]

Proof that the problem exists. To bring this problem even closer to home, teachers in Napoleon, Ohio, are also sick and tired of being underpaid. Napoleon educators, according to an article in the *Toledo Blade*, are demanding a 24 percent raise over three years in an attempt to bring their salaries in line with those of their peers in neighboring school districts. The school board's final offer provided only an 8 percent increase over three years.[10] Because no agreement between the two could be reached, the educators protested their low wages by setting up a strike that began on October 13, 1993, and continued for eight weeks, just ending this last Tuesday. However, an end to the strike does not mean an agreement has been reached. It is stated in Ohio that teachers can strike only for a period of eight weeks, and then the issue must go before the State Board of Education for them to vote on. As of today, Napoleon teachers are still awaiting news from Columbus.

Relationship of the problem to your audience. But I'm not in education, nor do I live in or anywhere near Napoleon, you might be saying to yourselves. Okay, I understand that. But take some time and think about your future. Some of you might want children, and all this controversy between school administration and the teachers could influence their education. Keep in mind that teachers are not paid by the hour like doctors and lawyers.[11] All the extra time an instructor puts in after school is strictly on his or her "free time." Teachers are becoming more receptive to this idea, and with it they have become more and more frustrated. Many teachers have stopped caring, and in turn they have stopped spending extra time after school to give extra help to those who need it.[12] In addition, some have altered their lesson plans so they can make time to grade those extra papers in class instead of dragging them home each night.[13] No longer, too, are they willing to volunteer to attend outside of school events. These actions by your child's teacher will take away from your child's education. Does it concern you? It certainly should.

Satisfaction step

If any of us were to sit in a room where there were a few educators and a few school board members present, we could easily come to some conclusions. The first would be that the teachers are sick and tired of being promised that if they take a small raise now, it will be made up for later.[14] It is because the "later" never seems to come, and they know that. The school board members, on the other hand, believe the money in the school systems should be spent on other programs and not on the teachers.

Plan of action. We all wish money grew on trees. If it did, it would keep both of these two groups happy. The school board and administrators could fund all the programs that their little hearts desired and, at the same time, pay the teachers what they are worth. The educators could go to work each morning knowing that they have finally been given a fair deal. They could give just time to their lessons and know that the extra work and time they were putting in were not only beneficial to students, but, too, part of their job rather than an invasion of their free time. But since money trees are only in our dreams, a solution must be reached.

Explanation of the plan. How about having professional sports programs sponsor some of the school organizations and activities that the school districts traditionally spend all their monies on?[15] Both in San

Francisco and Chicago the school districts have caught onto this idea, and they no longer totally support all their programs. People today are always saying that sports figures are our children's heroes, so this is a great way for the children to feel even closer to those whom they look up to. At the same time, the schools will be saving money, and this extra cash can then be put where it belongs—into the educators' paychecks.

Countering arguments against the plan. Many people feel that teachers should just accept their pay because, in reality, they have the advantage of the school calendar—days off over the holidays and three months off during the summer.[16] However, many school districts have lengthened the school year so teachers are now working the days just like any other nine-to-five job.[17] Others argue that teachers have favorable daily working hours.[18] But what they fail to keep in mind is that every night teachers have to bring home papers to grade and lesson plans to make up for the next day.

Visualization step

As I mentioned earlier, teachers have already taken action against their poor salaries by altering their lesson plans to squeeze in time for paper grading. This is just a small step in educators' rebellion. If nothing is done for these men and women, an even bigger step might be taken. Who's to say they won't just stop teaching altogether and start providing handouts for their students to fill out, so they can grade them right there in the classroom? This will end all forms of creative teaching and learning. Many people believe our educational system is bad now, but just wait until these students come up our nation's educational ladder.

On the other hand, if teachers were just to get the decent salary they deserve, all frustrations on their part would disappear, and the educational system could return to where the child's imagination was properly nourished. Even educational leaders readily admit that salaries must be improved if schools are to attract and hold superb teachers who inspire the future generations.[19]

Over 20 years ago former President Jimmy Carter said, "No poor, rural, weak, or black person should ever again have to bear the additional burden of being deprived of the opportunity for an education, a job, or simple justice."[20] We don't want to deprive anyone of an opportunity for an education, but simple justice works both ways. Simple justice means paying teachers what they deserve.

Action step

The best thing you, as a citizen of your city and an alumni of your school district, can do is to take action by attending open school board meetings and voicing your concern there. I understand many of you reside here in Bowling Green for most of the academic year, and you are not willing to go home for your school district's monthly meetings; however, B.G.S.U. does get out a month earlier than everyone else, so how about attending that last meeting in May?

In the future, your child might be unfortunate enough to have a teacher who has been burned by his or her school system one too many times, and this will in turn affect your child's full learning process. However, with your help, teachers can fight for the decent salary they deserve so that your child does not have to be the loser in this situation. Simple justice means paying our teachers what they rightfully deserve. I hope this lesson in economics has made this clear for you.

Speech Notes

1. Jennifer Stara, "I'm Not Working for Free Anymore," *Glamour* 91 (February 1993), p. 114.
2. Ruth Mayer, "You Have to Start Somewhere," *Mademoiselle* 99 (October 1993), p. 158.
3. Alyssa A. Lappen, "1993 Salary Survey," *Working Woman* 18 (January 1993), pp. 41–43.
4. Denise K. Magner, "American Association of University Professors Survey Finds Salaries Rose 2.5% in 1992–1993," *Chronicle of Higher Education* 39 (April 14, 1993), p. 19.
5. Valerie E. Lee and Julia B. Smith, "Gender Equity in Teachers' Salaries: A Multilevel Approval," *Educational Evaluation and Policy Analysis* 12 (Spring 1990), p. 58.
6. Allan C. Ornstein, "Teacher Salaries Look Good for the 1990's," *Education Digest* 56 (December 1990), p. 23.
7. Lee and Smith, p. 58.
8. Robert E. Rowsey, "Perception of Teachers' Salaries and Nonsalary Benefits," *Journal of Teacher Education* 37 (March 1986), p. 42.
9. Stara, p. 114.
10. John Lis, "Napoleon Teachers Leave Desks, Pupils, Strike for More Pay," *The Toledo Blade* (October 14, 1993), p. 1.
11. Stara, p. 114.
12. Stara, p. 114.
13. Stara, p. 114.
14. Lis, p. 1.
15. Stara, p. 114.
16. Rowsey, p. 44.
17. Rowsey, p. 44.
18. Rowsey, p. 44.
19. Rowsey, p. 44.
20. John Bartlett, *Familiar Quotations*, 16th ed. (Boston: Little Brown, 1992), p. 753.17.

Chapter Questions

1. What did you think of the language used by Bob Gower in the introduction of his speech? Did this language make you want to hear more from him? Why or why not?

2. If you were to make a suggestion to Bob on how he could improve or add to the language he chose, what suggestions might you make?

3. Was the principle "meaning lies in people" new to you? Why is it a useful way of looking at meaning? How would it help speakers?

4. How do the concepts of clarity, simplicity, accuracy, appropriateness, and dynamism provide guidance for the proper choice of words? Can you think of another criterion that could be added to this list?

5. If you were to improve your language, how would you go about it?

6. Using language as your focus and the concepts discussed in this chapter as your guide, evaluate Amy's speech. What were her strengths? What were her weaknesses? How could Amy have improved her speech?

Further Reading

Jane E. Aaron, *The Essential Handbook for Writers* (New York: Harper-Perennial, a Division of HarperCollins, 1994).

> Aaron has written a portable and indispensable guide to writing. Her guide covers matters of style, grammar, usage, punctuation, mechanics, and research. This is a short, easy-to-use guide full of valuable examples.

Ray Bradbury, *Zen in the Art of Writing* (Santa Barbara: Joshua Odell, (1994).

> Here is a book to spark your creativity. In 11 stimulating essays, Bradbury, the well-known author of novels, stories, plays, television programs, musicals, essays, and poems, discusses the pleasures of writing. Bradbury presents writing as a celebration, not a chore. This is neither a technical nor a how-to book; rather, Bradbury shares the delights of discovery. Fascinating material that all readers will find interesting.

Bonnie Friedman, *Writing Past Dark: Envy, Fear, Distraction, and Other Dilemmas in the Writer's Life.* (New York: HarperPerennial, a Division of HarperCollins, 1993).

> This book offers readers an opportunity to experience the emotional side of the writer's life. When you need to access the memories, images, and ideas inside you that will make your messages personal, powerful, and persuasive, this is the book that will free your spirit. This supportive, intimate, reflective book offers comfort and understanding and is both interesting and wise.

Endnotes

1. Bob G. Gower, "Leadership: March Off the Map," *Vital Speeches of the Day* LXI, no. 3 (November 15, 1994), pp. 79–81. His introduction appears on page 79.
2. C. K. Ogden and I. A. Richards, *The Meaning of Meaning* (New York: Harcourt Brace Jovanovich, 1930).
3. William Strunk, Jr., and E. B. White, *The Elements of Style*, 3rd. ed. (New York: Macmillan, 1979), p. 76.

Words in Action: VIDEO STUDY

A good speaker chooses words carefully, keeping in mind that in some cases, the same word conveys different meanings to different people and that simplicity is often the best technique for attaining an audience's understanding. As you will see in the video selections for this chapter, dynamic language can make a speech special and memorable. Methods for making a speech dynamic are on pp. 143–144. After watching the video, answer the following questions.

1. Give some examples of John F. Kennedy's use of antithesis.
2. Can you find an example of parallel structure in Kennedy's speech?
3. Can you find an example of triplets in Kennedy's speech?
4. What metaphor does Mario Cuomo employ to criticize his political opponent?
5. Where did Cuomo discover this metaphor? What does he accomplish using this metaphor?
6. How does Cuomo create antithesis in his speech?
7. What analogy does Sarah Weddington use to emphasize her point? What makes this analogy effective?

11

Delivery

After reading this chapter you will be able to:

- know what qualities result in an effective presentation

- understand the characteristics of effective delivery

- assess your articulation and pronunciation, rate and pause, pitch and inflection, loudness or volume, and quality

- recognize the importance of general attractiveness and dress to effective delivery

- assess your facial expression, eye contact, bodily movement, posture, and gesture

- compare and contrast the memorized, manuscript, impromptu, and extemporaneous styles of presentation

- rehearse for effective extemporaneous delivery

- use repetition, organization, regrouping, and note taking to remember your speeches

When Maria stood to give her first sales report, she began to appreciate the value of the public speaking class she had taken in college. In that class she had learned how to collect evidence, organize data, and present her ideas clearly and enthusiastically. Now all the time she spent preparing and giving speeches for her public speaking class was finally paying off. She knew her material well and was poised, comfortable, and effective. She had the attention of her peers as well as that of her supervisor. The positive comments she received on her presentation made her feel like a permanent member of the sales team—even though she had been with this company for just six months.

Bill and his wife, both just out of college, had purchased their first home in a suburb outside a large industrial town. Soon they discovered that a large discount department store was planning to move in directly across the street from the entrance to their housing development. They thought the store would depreciate the value of their new home, bring strangers into their neighborhood, and increase traffic problems.

They called the township and found out that a public hearing on the store's move was to be held in two weeks. Bill circulated a petition and began preparing an opposition speech. During the first week, he prepared the outline and adjusted the wording. During the second, he delivered his speech to his wife, friends, and neighbors, continually improving his delivery until the night of the hearing.

No other speaker was as convincing as Bill. As his conclusion he showed the petition signed by 90 percent of his neighbors. The audience of 100 citizens applauded loudly and long. Later Bill was told that his speech, the petition, and the response he received had convinced the owners of the discount store to look for another location. They did not want to move where they were not wanted.

Both Maria and Bill knew the importance of delivery to a public presentation. You can gather the best material and put ideas together in the most effective manner; but if you do not deliver the ideas effectively, no material or organization can carry the weight of a presentation. Delivery is like a catalyst in a chemical reaction: It initiates the chemical reaction and enables it to proceed.

How can a speaker ensure an effective presentation? This chapter explores this question, discussing both vocal and physical characteristics of effective delivery. The differences between manuscript, memorized, impromptu, and extemporaneous speeches are clarified, and four techniques that should help you improve your memory are presented.

HOW TO MAKE AN EFFECTIVE PRESENTATION

Although delivery creates more anxiety than any other aspect of public speaking, most people put off practicing their delivery until the last minute, or they fail to practice it at all. Many students say, "I don't mind doing all the preparation. It is getting up before the audience that scares me!" This is a common concern.

Thorough preparation and practice for the speech are the most effective methods for reducing nervousness. Speakers who procrastinate, who do not take the processes of preparation and practice seriously, and who do not anticipate the effects that standing in front of a live audience can create are often the ones who suffer the most nervousness. Anxiety cannot be eliminated, but it can be controlled and constructively channeled.

The best way to ensure an effective presentation is to prepare and practice. A speaker cannot be too prepared. The more time and energy you can put into your speech, the more confident you will be. Specific methods for rehearsing the delivery of your speech are presented later in this chapter. Making an effective presentation is within the grasp of anyone who wants to make the effort. There is nothing magical, mystical, or mysterious about it. With methodical preparation, anyone can deliver an effective speech.

The Heart of the Matter

Delivery is composed of voice, appearance, and movement, but it can be greater than the sum of its parts. Delivery is best when it is *not* the focus of your or your audience's attention. The best delivery is a natural, comfortable extension of your personality, manner, and unique abilities. When you focus on delivery, on the other hand, it becomes awkward and contrived. If you have a good topic, sufficient planning and preparation, and a desire to convey an important message to listeners, your delivery will naturally be appropriate to the message, context, listeners, and your intentions. Delivery is best when it brings your ideas to life and makes the whole presentation more than the sum of its individual parts.

CHARACTERISTICS OF EFFECTIVE DELIVERY

Delivery can be broken down into its three major components: voice, appearance, and movement (including movement of face, eyes, and body). As a speaker, you are on display. Every twitch of the eyebrow or wrinkle of the nose can be perceived and will probably be interpreted. To avoid sending inadvertent cues, you must exercise control. Of course, you cannot control every cue, but with experience and the knowledge that even minor cues elicit distinct meanings, you can become aware of your behavior and how it affects the impression you want to convey.

Become aware of your voice

Voice here refers not to your words but to how you say those words. Variations in the physical characteristics of your voice (such as articulation, rate, pitch, loudness, and quality) greatly influence how listeners perceive your emotional states, attitudes, emphasis, and transitions. Even though these perceptions are subjective and may not be accurate, they nevertheless affect listener understanding of messages. Thus, changes in your vocal characteristics can aid you in conveying moods or feelings, drawing your audience in (or tuning them out), revealing your attitudes, providing emphasis, or indicating transitions.

Your voice punctuates your speech. Notice, for example, how you raise your voice slightly at the end of a question and pause briefly at the end of a sentence or idea. You may even hurry your pace or raise your voice slightly for a sentence that would be written with an exclamation point.

Variety in your voice is a key to holding attention. Just as physical movement catches people's attention, so do changes in the voice. But, although you want to avoid monotony, you must be careful not to vary your voice just for the sake of holding attention. Changes should be clearly tied to the message you want to get across. Otherwise changes may distract by calling attention to themselves. The vocal characteristics over which you can exert control include articulation and pronunciation, rate and pause, pitch and inflection, volume, and quality.

Articulation and pronunciation. These can affect the clarity of the sounds you produce as you speak. Both can result in either clarity or confusion, and both depend, in part, on how you use your organs of speech. *Articulation* creates distinct sounds in speech; *pronunciation* is how correctly you create the sounds of words. You can articulate a word distinctly and still pronounce it incorrectly. The phrase "et cetera," for example, is sometimes said as "ec-cetera." The articulation is clear but wrong because the correct pronunciation is "et'-set-a-ra."

Most articulation problems result from either laziness or rushing to get words out. Enunciation becomes blurred if you do not establish the correct placement of your lips, tongue, and jaw—your articulators. Instead of *going to*, you may say *gunna*; or perhaps you say *wanna* instead of *want to* or *I dunno* instead of *I don't know*. These are common shortcuts. American pronunciation also includes frequent substitutions, such as a *d* for a *t* in *water*, which is generally said as *wader*. In some regions of the United States people tend to substitute *d* for *th* in such words as *these* and *those* (*dese guys* and *dose ladies*). Another common error is dropping the *g* from *ing* endings: *winnin* for *winning* or *goin* for *going*. Many of these errors can be corrected if you simply monitor your use of language.

In addition to articulating carefully, you must pronounce words correctly. Your best guide here is to listen to educated speakers in your region; pronunciation varies from one geographical region to another. Another valuable tool is a dictionary. Correct pronunciation is important because a mispronounced word calls attention to itself and quickly distracts listeners from your message. The mispronounced word becomes a message by itself. If you are not sure how a word is pronounced, ask someone else to say the word or look it up. If you still feel uncertain, perhaps you can substitute another word.

Rate and pause. These aspects of speech serve different purposes and have different effects. They are linked because you can vary rate by interjecting more pauses or by decreasing the number or length of pauses. A *pause* is a temporary stop, break, or rest. Pauses affect rate as does the duration of the sounds of your speech. *Rate* is simply how quickly you speak.

The rate of your speech affects how well your listeners are able to comprehend your messages. If you speak too quickly you may not be understood; if you speak too slowly you may create boredom, put your listeners to sleep, or lose their attention as their thoughts drift. Variation in rate is the key to holding attention. Although 125 to 150 words per minute is usually considered a satisfactory rate of speaking, you must plan to adjust your speaking rate to the size of the room, the possible use of a microphone, audience reactions, the speech occasion, and the material you are presenting.

A change of rate can affect the feeling or tone you are conveying. When Lee wanted to emphasize an important concept in his speech on the need for nuclear energy, he slowed down, changing the rate at which he spoke each word and emphasizing each word separately. When Lisa wanted to build excitement or surprise in her speech about the need for women to learn methods of self-protection, she sped up her rate. In Monty's speech about the high cost of dying, he conveyed a somber, gloomy mood at a slower rate.

As you set the rate of your speech, you also need to remember to pause. Pauses provide emphasis and indicate transitions between ideas. In addition, if you ask listeners to think about the answer to a question you have posed, pause to allow time for a mental response. If you use parenthetical expressions or other asides, you can set them off by pauses, too. If you tell a story, pause to add emphasis just before you deliver the punch line or moral to the story.

But as useful as they are, pauses can also cause problems. For example, they can distract if they are misplaced. If they signal a mental blank such as losing your place, they can disrupt your flow of ideas. Pauses can also cause distraction if they are filled with unnecessary verbalizations such as *uh, er, like, you know, okay,* and *right*. Eliminate unnecessary vocalized pauses. Instead of using an unnecessary word in place of a pause, you should simply be silent—no noise, just a break or hesitation.

Pitch and inflection. *Pitch* is the highness or the lowness of your vocal tone. Your pitch is determined by the vibration of your vocal folds. Slow vibrations (like the vibration of the strings of a bass violin) produce a low pitch, whereas faster vibrations create a higher pitch. These differences contribute to the meaning of speech and help to create our unique voices.

As you vary your pitch, you make use of inflection. *Inflection* involves changes or variances in pitch. Thus, as you raise or lower your voice to add emphasis, to ask a question, to make a point, or to gain attention, you are using inflection. If your speech makes no use of inflection, listeners are likely to call your voice monotonous.

Monotony is sameness in tone or sound. Not only is monotony a powerful sedative for listeners, it also robs words and phrases of their meaning. A monotonous voice that is a result of many years of conditioning is not easily changed. If you have a monotonous voice, you can add expression by working with a tape recorder; observing and imitating others who are expressive; and, in general, practicing at varying your inflection.

Volume. *Volume*, an obvious vocal characteristic, is the relative loudness of a voice. When your volume is insufficient, no one can hear you. But if you speak too loudly, you can cause physical discomfort.

You must find a comfortable volume that satisfies listeners and suits the situation and topic. However, it is change in volume, not the volume itself, that holds attention. Listen to a piece of music played by an orchestra, and notice the many changes in volume (crescendos and diminuendos) that occur throughout the piece. Imagine how the piece would sound without these changes. A speech needs the same variety to keep from becoming dull and tedious.

Quality. The *quality* of a voice includes those characteristics that belong to the voice and make it distinctive or unique. Obviously your voice can affect the meaning of a message. For example, how you say "I love you" can change how it is received and the meaning it conveys. Vocal quality also affects your impression of speakers. Unfortunately, people are stereotyped by their voice type. For example, you probably do not attribute as much authority to a high, nasal, whiny, or weak voice as you do to a low, clear, strong one. Often people have little control over their voice quality; yet your impressions of voices are still related to these features. The problem, of course, is that superficial judgments of people by the quality of their voices can be highly inaccurate. A person of courage and enthusiasm may have a thin, weak voice, just as a deeply committed, passionate person may have a monotonous voice. And a voice that shows genuine sincerity and enthusiasm may hide a person who is unprincipled, deceitful, and dishonest. The voice can serve as both a map and a mask.

Voice quality is not easily changed because it is created partly by physical characteristics such as the shape of your larynx and the size and shape of your mouth, nose, sinus cavities, and so on. But although vocal quality is largely inborn, it can change throughout your life. Tension or nervousness can also cause subtle changes, as when your voice becomes thin or strident because of taut throat muscles. Anger can produce a harsh or breathy quality. As you become involved in your message, your voice reflects your emotions and the sentiments you are feeling.

Become aware of your appearance

Your *appearance* is how you look—your general appearance—as well as how you dress. Attractive people generally make better persuaders; that is, people like to listen to an attractive person more than an unattractive one.[1] However, if you judge speakers' credibility by their general appearance— matters (except for dress) that may not be within the total control of speakers—you are basing decisions on irrational and irrelevant factors. Attractive people are not necessarily honest, well-informed, or intelligent.

Concern for your dress and grooming is different from general appearance because you have control over these features; thus, they communicate something. As a speaker, you must try to dress appropriately so that your attire does not distract from your message.

Become aware of your movement

Movement includes both facial and bodily motion. Controlling your movements is crucial because your listeners will be sensitive to them.[2] Often you will be unaware of the messages that your motions convey. But, listeners who hear your verbal message look to your face and body for nonverbal reinforcement or lack of reinforcement. If your message is disturbing, for example, listeners will look at your face and body to see how disturbed *you* are. If verbally you indicate wild enthusiasm but fail to reinforce that message with your face and body, listeners must decide which message to believe. Often they will believe the nonverbal component of your speech more readily than they do your words.

Facial expression includes all the nonverbal facial cues to which listeners attach meaning. The face is one of the most revealing nonverbal sources for cues; it shows speakers' attitudes toward listeners, toward the topic, and toward themselves.[3] The face is one of the most important sources for revealing your sincerity; from it listeners often can tell whether you like them. A warm, pleasant attitude is easily conveyed—and easily faked. Listeners can tell whether you are enthusiastic or deeply concerned about your topic from facial cues. In addition, your face can convey a wide range of emotions: confidence or doubt, courage or fear, happiness or sadness, surprise or expectation, love or hate. Facial expressions are sometimes referred to as affect (feeling) displays, which is why it is important for you to be concerned about conveying the proper feelings that will appropriately reinforce your message.

Facial expressions are important in revealing your emotion. Without them, you lose a significant part of the strength of a communicative effort; the animation will be missing. People who show little or no facial expression often lack other aspects of nonverbal behavior such as bodily movement and vocal variety. Such a lack of animation may be read by listeners as apathy or boredom.

If you really are bored with your topic, you should change it rather than try to fake interest or animation. Listeners who suspect or detect a false display of emotion will be distracted by it and will likely pay little attention to the ideas of the speech. If your lack of animation results from inhibitions (shyness, for example), you can gain some energy by "psyching yourself up." Techniques for generating energy include the following:

1. Make sure you have had enough sleep.
2. Practice thoroughly so you feel confident.
3. Use positive self-talk.
4. Concentrate on the ideas you want to share.
5. Realize that your listeners have never heard these ideas expressed in just this way before.
6. Strive to make your delivery fresh and new as you speak.
7. Act alert, confident, and as if you are in charge.

Eye contact is the amount of time you actually look your listeners in the eyes. If you refrain from looking at your listeners eye-to-eye you can elicit a variety of negative reactions: "You don't care about us," "You are lying," "You are unsure of your ideas," "You lack confidence," "You are scared," "You have no experience in public speaking." You may think these reactions do not matter; however, if your goal is to have some effect on listeners, these reactions distract listeners from your intent and make reaching your goal more difficult, if not impossible.

Weak eye contact makes you look insincere, uncomfortable, and insecure. The eye contact you use must say to listeners, "I believe in my subject, and I want you to believe in it too." Good eye contact means looking at listeners 85 percent of the time, even if you are reading a speech from a manuscript.

The key to effective eye contact is to deliver your ideas not to an audience but rather to individuals in that audience. That is, you must connect with one individual at a time by looking them in the eye. You must establish a communicative bond with them. The highest compliment listeners can pay to you, no matter the size of the audience, is remarking that they felt you were talking directly to them.

Bodily movements include all body motion to which listeners attach meaning. They can be divided into three categories: general movement, posture, and gestures. All are important because your body is likely to be the first nonverbal channel noticed by listeners—before you even open your mouth.

General movement is used here to refer to body movement that is not related to posture or gesture. Movement stimulates attention. People are attracted to motion. As you are sitting in a lecture hall, notice how many heads look up when a person comes in late. Thumb through a magazine and look at the advertisements. Often those depicting action grab the most attention.

Because movement attracts attention, you must take care that your movement reinforces and enhances your message and does not distract from it. Awkward, inappropriate, and distracting movements can and do occur, and audience attention is just as easily drawn to these as it is to movements that are graceful, appropriate, and reinforcing.

General movement should be comfortable and natural. Its effect on listeners should be subliminal, not overt or obvious. When listeners notice your movements, they are distracted from the verbal message, and your message, purpose, or central idea suffers. Thus, movements should not call attention to themselves.

Meaningful movement of the body usually occurs when speakers move from one idea to another. Often it accompanies a transition. This can be as obvious as moving while saying, "Moving to the next idea, then…" or as subtle and quick as a one-word transition such as "Next" or "So" or "Thus." Movement to either side of the lectern (or to the center) usually signals a change from one point to another in the message.

You also can use movement to emphasize an idea. For example, Claudio moved closer to his audience when he said, "I'll bet you're wondering what all this has to do with you." Sara, talking about the need for her generation to make a commitment to change, said, "But *we* cannot afford to make such mistakes, can we?" as she leaned closer to her listeners to make her point.

It is up to you when to move. All of your movement should be appropriate, natural, and comfortable. But to summarize the suggestions, you should move

- to reinforce and enhance your message
- when you move from one idea to another
- when you use a transition
- to make an idea more emphatic
- to make a point sharp and definite

Posture is the position or bearing of the body as a whole. While you wait for a bus or train sometime, watch the way people carry themselves as they walk. Often you can tell the importance of people's mission by their posture. Those who feel their mission is important will stand erect; their posture could be characterized as bold, aggressive, and alert. They look important by the way they hold themselves. Similarly, to show your audience that your message is important, you must hold yourself erect and alert. Allowing your shoulders or back to slump will be a nonverbal cue suggesting lack of concern, lack of caring, or lack of importance.[4]

Posture is important not only during your actual presentation but also as you move to and from the lectern. Remember to use what feels comfortable for you. The drill sergeant stance can be as distracting as the slouch. Both can be inhibiting because it is difficult to move other parts of the body when you are postured at either of these extremes. Be comfortable, which means being alert and ready to respond.

Gestures are the use of the arms and hands as the means of expression. Gestures are probably the part of bodily movement that is most inhibited by fear of public speaking. A person who uses gestures lavishly in normal one-to-one conversations sometimes freezes or becomes inhibited in front of listeners. Knowing this, you should plan considerable practice and rehearsal. The best way to practice is by using videotape so that you can view and evaluate your gestures. A second method is to rehearse in front of a mirror. A third is to ask others to criticize and evaluate your gestures.

Here is a rule of thumb regarding your gestures: Don't plan your gestures, but plan to gesture. As with all bodily movement, planned nonverbal behaviors may appear counterfeit. Unless yours are natural, they may look artificial and awkward. To increase your comfort, practice gestures in informal conversations. Most people do not gesture enough in public speaking.

STYLES OF PRESENTATION

A *style of presentation* is simply the way you plan to deliver your speech to your audience. The style of presentation may be part of a class assignment; it may be dictated by the speech occasion; or it could depend on your comfort or personal preference. For example, when Jennifer was asked to eulogize her best friend, who had been killed in a car accident, she spoke from a manuscript not only so the words would be carefully planned but also so she could better control her emotions. Whenever Rob was asked to speak, on the other hand, he felt most comfortable memorizing the speech. His background in theater made this approach natural, easy, and effective for him.

The most common delivery styles are memorized, manuscript, impromptu, and extemporaneous delivery. Each is discussed in this section, with some specific requirements mentioned. Each style has its strengths and weaknesses; these are described so that if you are given a choice of style you will be able to select the most appropriate one. And because the extemporaneous style tends to be the most common, a specific approach to practicing it is offered.

Memorized delivery

In *memorized delivery* the speaker learns the entire speech word for word. When you commit a manuscript to memory, you can polish the wording of ideas and look at listeners while you deliver the speech. To memorize a speech you must go over it many times, much as actors do to learn their lines for a theater production.

Memorized delivery has other benefits as well. It gives you freedom to move in front of listeners because you are not tied to a manuscript or lectern. It allows you to concentrate on your delivery of ideas. Since the words and ideas have already been selected, your primary job becomes bringing those ideas to life. Thus listeners hear a fluent set of ideas that appears natural and spontaneous.

However, one problem with memorized delivery is that the speech often sounds memorized. Few people can successfully master the technique. A speech that sounds memorized has a negative effect on listeners. Often it sounds boring, dull, and monotonous—as if the speaker doesn't care. Natural spontaneity is the final goal of memorization, and memorizing a speech so well that it sounds natural and spontaneous requires much time and energy. It is best for beginning speakers to avoid this style.

The other major problem with memorizing is that in mastering the wording you learn a specific word order. Any mistake then requires that you backtrack or skip ahead to recall that specific word order. The focus is on the words—not *any* words, *the* words—and thus three facts may become apparent to listeners: (1) You have not mastered the content, (2) you can provide no additional insight into the topic, and (3) you have allowed for no on-the-spot adaptation to the audience or the occasion.

If you must give a memorized speech, here are 10 suggestions:

1. Rehearse orally, learning the sequence of ideas and practicing expressions until they become fluent.
2. Record the speech on tape (audio or video) and listen to playbacks.
3. Strive to grasp the material as a whole rather than working on individual sections or points. Learning speeches as a whole takes advantage of the internal logical and sequential properties of the lines and minimizes omissions in performance.

4. Give the material your complete attention. Isolate yourself from distractions in early rehearsals. After giving it full concentration, try to add distractions that approximate the actual speaking situation.

5. Use many short practice sessions rather than a few long ones.

6. Make certain you know the subject thoroughly. This base of information assures numerous associations between words and ideas.

7. Concentrate on the ideas so that you do not sound like you are just repeating words.

8. Maintain the appearance of spontaneity and flexibility. Avoid appearing stilted, formal, rigid, and inflexible.

9. Maintain a conversational pace. Many speakers who memorize hurry their words and thus lose naturalness.

10. Keep a vision of your listeners in mind as you rehearse. The purpose of the speech is to help them see more clearly, have more information, or respond in some way.

If you memorize you must develop confidence so you don't lose your place in your speech. Thus, you must feel comfortable and in control of the situation. You must plan to spend great amounts of time with the manuscript because only in this way can full memorization occur. All of these suggestions will help your memorized speech to not sound memorized.

Manuscript delivery

In *manuscript delivery* the speech is written out in full and then read aloud. Just as with the memorized style, the wording can be carefully planned. To prepare for using this style, you should proceed in much the same way as you would to memorize your speech. The speech must be well rehearsed so that delivery can sound spontaneous and natural and so that you are not tied to the manuscript.

Presidents, heads of state, and other dignitaries give speeches from manuscripts to avoid mistakes that might result from the wrong choice of words or improper sentence construction. This form of delivery is also used by network newscasters, who read the manuscript from the TelePrompTer™. The better the newscaster is at reading, the better he or she is received by viewers. Other benefits of the manuscript style include

- availability of the words. If you forget material, the words are readily accessible.
- complete prior preparation. You can carefully and completely prepare the exact wording of ideas.
- possible last-minute preparation. You can couch your ideas in clear, appropriate language, even just before a performance.

The problem with this style of delivery is that the written words become a crutch. You begin to like having the whole speech written out in front of you. Even when you know the material well, you often become dependent on the manuscript. Listeners, on the other hand, do not like listening to someone read; speakers who read are often boring and uninteresting. A speech that is read often lacks energy, stimulation, and the natural spontaneity needed to hold attention. When a speech is written out, it lacks on-the-spot audience adaptation and the flexibility that usually accompanies a free and natural delivery.

If you must prepare a manuscript speech, prepare it as if you were going to give an extemporaneous speech from notes. This can be accomplished in two different ways. First, write the speech as if you were speaking. Second, prepare an outline or notes and practice with them. As you give the final speech in practice, record the effort and type the manuscript from the tape. You can polish the wording from the tape as necessary. Using both methods of preparation ensures an oral style of delivery rather than a written style.

Once you have prepared a manuscript, practice with it. The goal of this practice is to become so familiar with the material that you do not have to give the manuscript your full attention as you present the speech; rather, you will be able to maintain eye contact with the audience. This may require three or more run-throughs at this stage.

As you present your information, your eye contact with the audience will tell you when and if you need to change the speech from what is written. Unless there are restrictions on how far you can deviate from the written manuscript, feel free to adapt to changing circumstances. Remember that listeners do not like to be read to; thus, the more you can make the manuscript speech appear to be delivered from notes, the easier it will be to maintain audience attention and interest—which is your goal.

When you are putting words on paper to use before the audience, remember the goal is to have a clear, readable product. Type the manuscript in double or triple spacing. It will be easier to read, too, if you can use a typewriter or a computer and printer that will adjust the font size. Since 12 point is standard, a font size of 14, 15, or 16 points should be sufficient. If it is larger than 16, you will have difficulty getting enough information on a page. Some people find capitalizing all words to be useful. If some words are difficult to pronounce, spell them in a way that will help you know them when you come to them; hyphenate and accent them as necessary. Sometimes it is useful to underline them in red in the manuscript. Then, when you see them coming, you can mentally prepare for them.

You should also highlight or underline places in the manuscript that need emphasis. Use special marks to indicate pauses (//) or places where you need to speed up (-----) or slow down (//////). Do not allow a sentence to be carried over between two manuscript pages; as you read such a sentence unintended pauses can occur.

Number your pages clearly; if you drop the manuscript, it can then easily be put back into order. Also, numbers help you double-check to see that all pages are in order before you begin. When you finish pages as you read, pull them to one side rather than lifting them up from the lectern or turning them over, which can cause unnecessary distraction. Never place material on the back of a manuscript page. Finally, it is wise to make a last-minute check to be sure you will have a lectern on which to place your manuscript.

Impromptu delivery

Impromptu delivery is done on the spur of the moment. No specific preparation is involved. An instructor, for example, might give students several ideas to choose from, allow a few moments for them to collect their thoughts, and then have each of them speak about one of the topics.

The reason for the generally poor quality of impromptu speaking is simply the surprise factor. Good impromptu speaking is rare because speaking without preparation, in general, is weak. While anyone can get up and speak on just about anything, the results usually reflect the lack of planning. But impromptu speaking can be very good. It can, for example, capture your emotions and passion at the moment. It can reflect your years of experience and background information. It can unveil all that is personal and vivid for you. Even further, it can provide an immediate, real, direct, and spontaneous experience that builds on present feelings and thoughts.

Impromptu speaking is not recommended for formal speech assignments. Few people, especially inexperienced speakers, handle this style well. It is foolhardy to leave preparation to chance—this is like throwing out all the information in this book and depending on glibness and personality to pull you through. Most listeners expect speeches to reveal the depth and substance that comes from prior thinking. Most speakers need planning to offer listeners material worth listening to and to establish their own delivery.

However, on some occasions impromptu speaking is expected. This could occur in a business meeting or in a club or association, for example, when someone is asked to make a report on the spur of the moment. Impromptu speech could also occur in a church, synagogue, or temple when a member wishes to express a prayer, share an insight, or propose some action; or in the classroom when a student wants to express an opinion, ask a question, or share some information. The chances are that you will face an impromptu speech situation. How can you plan ahead to make it successful? Here are five suggestions:

1. *Anticipate the situation.* What are the chances you might be called on to speak? Might you be given an award or recognition? Have you been away? Taken a trip? Received an award or special recognition elsewhere? Have you recently acquired new information or a new perspective? A new job or promotion? Do you have a special skill, talent, or ability? If you know you *may* be called on, plan a few remarks. Organize some ideas and some relevant observations. Know whom to recognize or thank.

2. *Listen carefully.* Follow what is being discussed or what is being said by others. If you are asked to speak, what others before you have said may either provide you with material or suggest some relevant information or experience. If you think you may be called on for a reaction, brief notes may help you respond effectively. Stating any of the following with clarity and directness will indicate strength and may be an effective approach:

"I think the previous speaker has overlooked an important point."
"I feel that this argument tends to be a weak one."

"I believe the speaker is correct as far as he (or she) went. What he (or she) failed to say was..."

"There seems to be some inconsistency here."

"Let me just add a couple of additional examples that may help clarify the situation."

3. *Control yourself.* Relax. Breathe regularly. Remember that fear builds on itself. If you can squarely face the situation at hand, appropriate material is more likely to occur to you. Is more information needed? Is there an issue that needs resolving? Is there a question to answer? If you can have the question restated, you will gain a couple of moments to collect your thoughts.

If you lead off with a strong central idea and then support it with some specific examples, you can conclude by restating the opening idea and briefly summarizing your major points. In essence, this is the quick and easy organizational scheme of (1) telling them what you are going to tell them, (2) telling them, and then (3) telling them what you told them.

If you have nothing to say, everyone will appreciate your contribution most if you simply and graciously admit it and add nothing. Too many speakers with nothing to say use up a great deal of human time and energy in saying that they have nothing to say. Sometimes you even have to listen a long time to find this out. The best approach is to say, "I'm sorry, but I don't have anything to add to what has already been said."

4. *Organize your thoughts.* As has already been suggested, your ability to quickly and efficiently gather your thoughts will help you control your emotions. The least that can be expected of impromptu speakers is that they frame a simple, sensible sentence and support it with an example or two. Consider using a ready-made outlining principle such as past, present, and future; who, what, when, where; principle and demonstration; or cause and effect.

Most material for impromptu speaking comes from personal experience. Bring your full background to bear on the situation—your education, reading, conversing, observing, experiencing, thinking, traveling, and questioning. The greater your experience, the more likely you will have grist for the impromptu mill. Develop a knack for swiftly arranging your remarks, and remember to keep the conclusion short and to the point. Summarize, restate your thesis, and sit down. The three B's are pertinent here: Be brief, be to the point, and be seated. Then you won't be the fourth B: boring.

5. *Be positive.* Much of your success in public speaking depends on your having the proper mental framework. A negative attitude drains off energy, whereas a positive one channels it in the right direction. This is not to suggest that a positive attitude guarantees positive results; nothing can do that. But it does provide a sense of mission and responsibility and energizes the spirit.

Try to put everything into the proper perspective. Listeners recognize that this is an impromptu situation. Nobody expects a polished production. If you are asked to improvise, remember that others *want* your firsthand observations or reactions; this is a compliment to your ability. Display of speaking skill is not as important here as an honest, immediate observation.

Extemporaneous delivery

Extemporaneous delivery, the ideal style of delivery, allows you to prepare and practice thoroughly but also allows the exact wording of the speech to be determined at the moment of utterance. However, speakers who give an extemporaneous speech once and then keep repeating the speech the same way fall into the same traps as if they had memorized it. The advantages of extemporaneous speaking are strong:

- You can prepare thoroughly and then look free and natural in performance.
- You can readily and spontaneously adapt to the situation and to the audience.[5]
- You are free to move in front of listeners as long as you can see your note cards.

How can you rehearse or practice your speech using the extemporaneous style of delivery? First, prepare an outline at least a day in advance of a short speech (up to five minutes in length) or two to three days in advance of a longer speech. Then convert the key parts of the outline to note cards or to a *key-word outline* that reflects the full outline but uses key words only. Read through your outline several times to become familiar with the structure and flow of ideas.

Now you can begin actual practice. Check the time you begin to speak. Using your notes as necessary so you do not miss key ideas, begin speaking. Do not stop until you complete the speech. Then check the time again to see how long the speech took. Now look at your outline and analyze your effort. Were key ideas omitted? Were some ideas discussed for too long or too short a time? Did all ideas receive proper clarification and support? And did you imagine the presence of your future listeners to help you aim your efforts?

Although you seldom will need to give a speech using no notes or outline, it is wise to begin working toward a goal of not using them. Beginning speakers tend to use their notes as they would a manuscript—as a crutch. Sometimes too many ideas are put onto a note card and then the note card is used too much. Notes should contain only key ideas or key words and phrases designed to trigger your memory—the fewer and briefer, the better. Short speeches should require only a single 3-by-5 note card; a 10-minute speech might require two or three such cards. In addition to key words or phrases, you might want to write out a brief quotation or an important statistic. Write on only one side of your note cards; you should never have to turn cards over for more information because this distracts listeners. Also, notes should be written large enough to be seen from a distance.

As you continue practicing, use your notes just as you will in your final speech. Refer to them only when necessary. Try to say the speech differently each time you rehearse, using the ideas on the cards to trigger your words. That way, when you actually deliver your ideas before listeners, you will have many different options for phrasing your ideas; you will not be frozen into a single word order or word choice as often occurs when speeches are memorized. The purpose of saying ideas differently in each rehearsal is to give you a variety of options when you stand before your listeners.

Here is a note about using lecterns: Lecterns are designed to hold your notes—nothing more. They are best limited to this purpose. The more familiar you are with your notes, the less confined to the lectern you will be, and the less you will have to look down at the lectern and break eye contact with your listeners. A lectern should be just as subtle and unrecognized as notes or other delivery cues. It is only a prop, but it can easily become a distraction or a barrier between speakers and listeners. Like all other nonverbal elements, lecterns need to be used with efficiency and ease; this can be accomplished with practice.

REMEMBERING YOUR SPEECH

Isn't it too bad that human beings are not born with photographic memories? All you would have to do would be to flip a mental switch and whatever you entered into your memory bank would be remembered precisely as entered (and this section would be unnecessary). Unfortunately, most humans do not have photographic memories, and trying to remember ideas in front of audiences presents difficulties.

An example of how memory can fail when least expected occurred at a Boy Scout meeting. The scoutmaster was ready to introduce the guest speaker—a man almost everyone in the audience already knew because he was the town's fire chief. And yet, after announcing the topic of the speech and some of the speaker's background as the fire chief was coming to the front of the room to speak, the scoutmaster forgot the man's name.

Fortunately, although embarrassed, the scoutmaster did not panic. He simply said, "I'm sorry, I have drawn a complete blank on your name," and the fire chief, still walking toward the front, quickly helped him out. The audience smiled, the fire chief smiled, but there was no laughter or need for serious embarrassment. The incident merely proved that people are fallible. However, the scoutmaster learned an important lesson. From then on (and there were many opportunities to put the lesson into practice), he kept the name of the guest speaker (familiar or not) on a piece of paper in front of him. Interestingly, he never had to use the piece of paper; its presence gave him the confidence he needed to remember the names.

When asked what they fear most about standing before an audience, most students will respond, "Forgetting what I have to say" or "Drawing a blank." How many times have you forgotten someone's name just minutes after you heard it? Public speaking requires remembering many ideas for 5 or 10 minutes in front of an audience. The fear is common and real.

How do you remember ideas? There are a number of techniques:[6]

1. The first is *repetition*. When you want to remember the name of a person to whom you are introduced, repeating the name over and over will help you remember it. When you receive directions from a gas station attendant ("go two more blocks on Warner, turn right on Main, go to the third traffic light, turn left, and it will be the fourth house on the right"), repeating them several times will help. And when you have ideas to remember, the same advice will help you remember them.

2. The second technique is *organization*. Organized ideas are easier to

remember than unorganized ideas; in other words, organization helps both speakers and listeners. One way to remember ideas is to use alliteration, which is simply repetition of the initial consonant sound in two or more neighboring words. For instance, in a speech about conservation the speaker used four R's: Reduce, reuse, repair, and recycle. When teaching students to fly, instructors often preach the four C's: climb (keep the nose of the airplane up), communicate (keep the channels open), confess (tell all you know), and comply (follow directions).

There are other effective organization devices besides alliteration, such as mnemonic devices. For example, Barry wanted to remember the five stages of the grieving process, so he formed a sentence with the main ideas he had to remember: Deny anger by bargaining depressed acceptance. It didn't make much sense but it helped him remember the stages: denial, anger, bargaining, depression, and acceptance.

If you find some kind of order among or between ideas you will more easily remember them. One simple order is personal, social, and cultural. Sometimes order can be discovered where it wasn't directly intended. For example, in the directions just given by the gas station attendant, notice the order: two on Warner then right, three on Main then left, and then fourth on the right—two, three, four; right, left, right. Admittedly, it isn't always this easy, and directions often are given poorly; but finding order can help.

3. The third technique is *regrouping*. When I began to work with ideas for handling anxiety, I had 18 separate, seemingly unrelated ideas. I wasn't certain how many categories they would fall under, but I decided to try three—attitude, preparation, and presentation—that seemed to work. Eighteen was too many to remember and too many to list, but three is easier. I had regrouped the ideas.

Regrouping is an effective technique for remembering ideas because it relates to how many ideas listeners are able to handle. First, it is easier to remember an odd number than an even number. Three, five, or seven items are easier to remember than four, six, or eight. Also, odd numbers tend to be more aesthically pleasing. Second, psychologists have found that seven bits of information is near the limit of what most people can consciously retain at one time.[7] These guidelines should help you group or regroup your ideas to remember them better.

4. The fourth technique is *note taking*. The scoutmaster learned that having a note to help him remember a speaker's name worked well for him. No matter what the event, situation, or type of speech, having notes will help you recall information. If you want to remember it, write it down. This applies to classroom assignments, lectures, interviews, business meetings, briefing sessions, and deadlines. Sometimes the act of note taking is more important than the notes themselves because taking notes is an active process that engages you in listening.[8]

One way to begin the process of taking notes in your everyday life is to make "to-do" lists. This will help you become better organized, plan your activities, and divide your time better between your projects; and it will quickly demonstrate the value of taking notes as a method for remembering ideas.

SUMMARY

Effective delivery plays an important role in public speaking. This chapter addressed the components of effective delivery, including voice, appearance, movement, styles of presentation, and techniques for remembering your speech.

Although delivery is essential in public speaking, it is not the most important element; your message is. Delivery is just a tool to evoke meaning in listeners. If your message does not deserve communication, then effective delivery will be wasted. You are the judge whether your message is worth delivering.

Chapter Questions

1. What additional suggestions do you have for making an effective presentation?

2. Prepare a speech and deliver it before a videocamera. After viewing your presentation, write a thorough critique of the vocal characteristics you employed. How effective was your vocal variety? Articulation and pronunciation? Rate of delivery? Use of pauses? Inflection? Volume? Quality?

3. Write a critique of the physical characteristics you displayed in the speech you taped for Question 2. How effective was your appearance? Your movement? Facial expressions? Eye contact? Posture? Gestures?

4. Compare and contrast the four styles of delivery discussed in this chapter: memorized, manuscript, impromptu, and extemporaneous. Which do you think would be most comfortable for you? Why?

5. What role does delivery play in public speaking? How does it compare in importance with a speaker's credibility, evidence, and central idea?

6. If you had a choice between listening to a speaker who had excellent delivery but weak content or one who had excellent content but weak delivery, which would you choose? Why?

7. What memory techniques have you developed that are not mentioned here?

8. Which of the four ways mentioned for remembering ideas is likely to work best for you? Which is likely to work poorly? Why?

Further Reading

Roger E. Axtell, *Do's and Taboos of Public Speaking: How to Get Those Butterflies Flying in Formation* (New York: John Wiley & Sons, 1992).

Axtell includes chapters on "To Read, or Not to Read?" "Getting Physical," and "Appearing on Television." These chapters deal specifically with elements discussed in this chapter. Although intended for the businessperson, his suggestions will help any speaker come across as intelligent, articulate, confident, and likable. Axtell's examples are contemporary and useful.

Joe Ayres and Tim Hopf, *Coping With Speech Anxiety* (Norwood, NJ: Ablex Publishing Corporation, 1993).

After an overview and a discussion of why anxiety occurs, the authors include three major sections: cognition, affect (emotion), and behavioral factors. The techniques listed for coping include rational-emotive therapy, cognitive restructuring, visualization, systematic desensitization, flooding, rhetoritherapy, and skills training. A well-written, practical book supported with numerous references.

Virginia P. Richmond and James C. McCroskey, *Communication: Apprehension, Avoidance, and Effectiveness*, 3rd ed. (Scottsdale, AZ: Gorsuch Scarisbrick, 1992).

After their overview and a chapter on misconceptions, these authors discuss shyness; communication apprehension; the impact of apprehension, shyness, and low willingness to communicate; and communication avoidance. Their final chapter on reducing apprehension and anxiety discusses specific treatment approaches.

Endnotes

1. See Judson Mills and Elliot Aronson, "Opinion Change as a Function of the Communicator's Attractiveness and Desire to Influence," *Journal of Personality and Social Psychology* 1 (1965), pp. 73–77; R. N. Widgery and B. Webster, "The Effects of Physical Attractiveness upon Perceived Initial Credibility," *Michigan Speech Journal* 4 (1969), pp. 9–15.
2. See Paul Ekman and Wallace Friesen, "Head and Body Cues in the Judgment of Emotion: A Reformulation," *Perceptual and Motor Skills* 24 (1967), pp. 711–24.
3. See Paul Ekman and Wallace Friesen, "Nonverbal Leakage and Clues to Deception," *Psychiatry* 32 (1969), pp. 88–106.
4. See Albert Mehrabian, "Orientation Behavior and Nonverbal Attitude in Communication," *Journal of Communication* 17 (1967), pp. 324–32; and Albert Mehrabian, "Relationship of Attitude to Seated Posture, Orientation, and Distance," *Journal of Personality and Social Psychology* 10 (1968), pp. 26–30.
5. Both audience comprehension and satisfaction are enhanced when speakers attend to audience feedback. See H. J. Leavitt and R. A. H. Mueller, "Some Effects of Feedback on Communication," *Human Relations* 4 (1951), pp. 401–10.
6. I am indebted to Rudolph Verderber for the four main ideas of this section. See Rudolph F. Verderber, *Communicate!*, 7th ed. (Belmont, CA: Wadsworth, 1993), pp. 172–75.
7. George A. Miller, "The Magical Number Seven, Plus or Minus Two: Some Limits on Our Capacity for Processing Information," *Psychological Review* 63 (1956), pp. 91–97.
8. Andrew Wolvin and Carolyn Gwynn Coakley, *Listening*, 3rd ed. (Dubuque, IA: William C. Brown, 1988), p. 215.

Words in Action: VIDEO STUDY

When you have gathered your information, organized it into a speech, and carefully chosen the language you will use, it is time to consider the delivery of your speech. The presentation style is often determined by the occasion of the speech. For example, a formal introduction generally is not delivered extemporaneously.

After watching the accompanying video, answer the following questions. These questions give you an opportunity to examine how occasion influences the type of style employed and to assess the effectiveness of the speaker's delivery based on the discussion in this chapter.

1. Analyze Bill Clinton's delivery. Which presentation style does Bill Clinton use in this instance? How is it appropriate for the situation? What makes his delivery effective or ineffective?

2. Analyze Geraldine Ferraro's delivery. Which presentation style does Geraldine Ferraro employ? How is it appropriate for the occasion? What makes her delivery effective or ineffective?

3. Which presentation style does the student use for her speech? In your opinion, is it effective?

12

Visual Support

After reading this chapter you will be able to:

- explain the purposes of visual support from a listener's perspective, from a speaker's perspective, and from a content perspective

- offer six suggestions for using visual support

- compare and contrast 10 different types of visual support

- select appropriate visual support, know its purposes, and understand exactly how to use it

Sergio, a 30-year-old returning student, sells knives to pay his way through school. As part of his sales presentation his company provides him elaborate visual support that he uses as he talks with his customers. These visual aids demonstrate the various qualities of the knives (sharpness, durability, and looks), highlight special knife sets and combinations, and, near the end of the presentation, show a variety of payment plans. His talk is carefully scripted, but he has learned to be flexible and respond to customer questions and concerns as he proceeds through his visually supported presentation.

Louisa is president of her student body. As one of her campaign promises, she said she would urge administrators to install emergency help lines (telephones that can be used in emergencies) around campus. Because of the importance of this issue to her and to the student body, she has had the aerial view of campus buildings in the college catalog enlarged to the size of a poster and she has marked in red the places on campus where the help lines need to be installed. She will use the poster to accompany her speech to administrators.

Ming is giving an informative speech to her public speaking class about Chinese characters. Her purpose is to give her American audience some knowledge about how Chinese characters differ from English. Ming has drawn the Chinese characters for her first name, the sun, the moon, a tree, a forest, and a table on poster board. She has divided her talk into three sections: the history of Chinese characters, the nature of Chinese characters, and the elements of Chinese characters.

Sergio, Louisa, and Ming are putting to work an important educational principle: People learn better as the number of senses through which they receive data is increased.[1] Using visual support is one of the most effective techniques for adding clarity to speeches. This chapter discusses the purposes of visual support, offers suggestions for using it, and compares types of visual support.

THE PURPOSES OF VISUAL SUPPORT

Visual support is not an extra element that is added on to speeches as epilogues are to books. Throughout human history people have communicated through visual images. Think, for example, about the paintings on the walls of prehistoric caves, the inscriptions left on tombs since the beginning of time, and even the billboards along highways. As a result of movies, television, computer screens, and videogames, people have not only become accustomed to receiving visual images but also expect them. Not making visual aids an integral part of your speech may be a missed opportunity for enhancing understanding.

A *visual aid* is an instructional device (such as a chart, map, or model) that appeals chiefly to vision. When the prefix *audio* is added to the phrase, it includes sounds used as instructional material appealing to our ears. Audiovisual aids amplify speeches by clarifying, explaining, and adding information. This chapter discusses visual support first from a listener's perspective, then from a speaker's perspective, and finally from a content perspective.

A listener's perspective

Besides increasing the number of channels through which people receive information and satisfying listener expectations, visual support serves several other purposes. Listeners are more likely to pay attention to you and remember your information. A study by the Wharton School of Business found that "on average, people retain about 10 percent of a presentation communicated through words alone, whereas the effective use of visual aids increases retention up to 50 percent"[2] (see Figure 12.1). You are also more likely to persuade your listeners if you use visual support.[3]

In addition, visual aids cause movement and change during a speech; that is, when you use them, you must do something besides talk. Visual support holds audience attention because it adds variety. Thus visual support increases listener interest, stimulates listener thought, and involves listeners.

A speaker's perspective

Still another purpose is served when you use visual material: It increases your credibility. Well-prepared visual aids show that you know what you are talking about and have put time and effort into your presentation. When your credibility is enhanced like this you have a greater chance of success.

Effective use of visual support offers you other advantages as well. Because large quantities of information can be condensed in graphs and charts, you are able to cover more information. Using visual support also gives you something else to do during your speech; it can help you vary the pace of your presentation, create listener interest, stimulate thought, and maybe even inject some humor into your presentations.

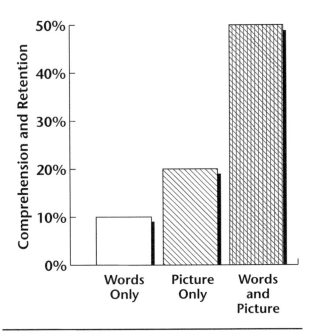

Figure 12.1.
Comprehension and retention of presentation with and without visual support.

A content perspective

Visual aids also increase the effectiveness of the information you are presenting by clarifying or illustrating something the audience may find difficult to understand. For example, Candace wanted to explain how researchers are able to use DNA as a "genetic fingerprint." Without the enlarged pictures of DNA, her explanation would never have been understood. Jeffrey showed pictures and diagrams of the internal features of a

Figure 12.2.
A line graph can be used to show monthly fluctuations in the GNP, sales of an industry, or a region's employment.

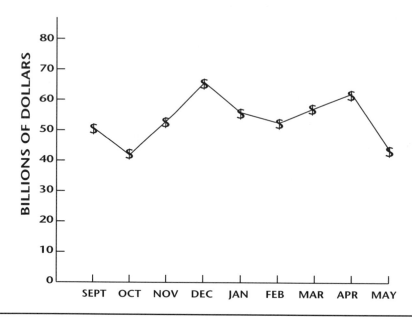

nuclear reactor. And Manuella showed her audience pictures sent back from the Hubble Telescope.

Visual support can help you compare facts and statistics. You can see this in the business section of a newspaper as analysts discuss the economy (see Figure 12.2). As another example, Steve, in a speech about caffeine, showed how human alertness or attention progresses during a normal day. Then, with a second line in red on the same chart, he plotted what happens under the influence of caffeine.

Finally, you can use visual support to show trends over time. For example, Alvaro used a chart to show his university's expenditures on minority recruitment over the past 20 years. He was able to show how the school's concern for minorities was increasing. Tammy used a chart to show the rise in salmonellosis cases over the past 10 years as she spoke in reference to a local outbreak of salmonella poisoning.

Whether visual support assists listeners, speakers, or the content being presented, it clearly supplies benefits to your presentation. However, you should follow some guidelines if you plan to use visual aids during your speech.

SUGGESTIONS FOR USING VISUAL SUPPORT

Several basic principles govern the use of visual support. Regardless of the type of aid you plan to use, your presentation will benefit from these suggestions.

1. *Rehearse with your visuals.* They should never be used for the first time in the actual presentation. For example, Angelena had videotaped different vacation spots. When she tried to play the videotape before the class, she could not make the playback work, and her verbal explanations of the vacation locations could not compare with actually seeing them. Practice using the equipment in conditions similar to those in which you will actually use the visual support. What if there was no handy electrical outlet for the videotape machine, and what if Angelena had no extension cord?

If you are using charts or graphs, set them in front of the room and make sure they can be seen from all angles and from the back. Remember to plan how you will support or attach the chart or graph. When Phil brought his chart to class for his speech about the effects of pollution on people, he brought no tape to attach the chart to the wall or chalkboard. He put it in the chalk trough of the chalkboard, but with no tape to attach the top, the chart kept bending and falling. After Phil tried three times to make the chart stand by itself, the situation became comical—until someone offered some chewing gum. Think ahead: Are chalk and erasers available for the chalkboard? Are there tacks for the bulletin board? Speakers need to carefully plan their use of visual material.

2. *Let listeners see your visual aid only when you are talking about it.* If the audience can see your visual aid before you present it, they will be distracted. For instance, Joelle brought a cage of gerbils for her speech about household pets, but she brought nothing to cover the cage. As it sat on the table in front of the audience, listeners were mesmerized by the gerbils turning and bumping one another off the wheel. If Joelle had put the cage under the table or had been able to cover it, her speech would have been more effective because she could have showed the cage when she talked about it and put the gerbils out of sight when she was finished talking about them.

3. *Make certain your visual aids are large enough for all audience members to see.* Jason's speech on automobile safety (see Figure 12.3) was quite strong until he came to his second visual aid, which consisted of several snapshots of an accident he had been involved in. Unfortunately, the snapshots were so small most audience members could not see them.

Figure 12.3.
A strong and simple visual aid.

Auto Safety

1. Use seatbelts.

2. Avoid alcohol.

3. Check equipment.

A related problem is using chart or graph colors that do not show up well. Rebecca was showing the class the increased cost of prosthetics (artificial replacements for missing body parts), but on her chart she had written figures in yellow, which could not be seen even in the front of the room. (She explained that all she had when preparing the chart the night before class was a highlighter.) Even though the colors may not be as pretty, it is better to select black or dark blue for charts and graphs because they are easy to see. In addition, lines need to be bold or broad rather than thin and narrow.

4. *Keep visual support simple.* A complex visual aid can cause confusion. Wendy's speech about horoscopes provided an example. To illustrate the concept of the rising sign, she showed the class an enlarged rising sign chart so that she could explain ascendants. The twelve sun signs were listed down the left column, and the twelve rising signs were listed across the top of her chart. If you read across to locate the birth time range, there were two numbers in every box. Then you had to follow the column up to the rising sign listed at the top of that column. Although Wendy explained how to use the chart, it had so much information on it that many listeners became confused and distracted.

Some guidelines for keeping visual support simple may help here.

- *Do not put too many details on the visual aid.* Perhaps Wendy could have simplified her chart or, if not, chosen different visual support.
- *Color-code the different parts for easy identification.* For example, when Todd spoke about NBA rookie salaries, he selected a different color for each year from 1990 to 1995.
- *Include only the basic, necessary elements.* When Christine talked about the depletion of the ozone layer, she did not show a diagram of our solar system or even of our entire planet. She showed only part of the earth and its relationship to the stratospheric ozone layer that protects it. This was simple and to the point.

5. *Talk to listeners, not to the visual aid.* Remember that visual support, no matter how effective, does not explain itself. Listeners need you to interpret it. Tell listeners what to look for, how to interpret the lines, what the figures, symbols, and percentages mean, how to understand the complete picture, and how parts relate to each other. As you do this, look at the listeners, not at the visual aid.

6. *Use visual support with discretion.* Too much of a good thing can have detrimental effects. If your speech could use numerous visual aids, you must decide which are the most important points that need emphasis or explanation. Most visual support is another form of emphasis; and if you emphasize everything, nothing stands out. Visual support cannot substitute for effective speaking.

Finally, here are a few words of advice about passing visual aids around. There are three problems with passing things around during a speech. First, the mechanics of distribution often distract listeners from the speech. Second, listeners often are prompted to think about, react to, or even talk about the material they hold in their hands. And this creates the third problem: Speakers often lose control of some of their listeners, who stop listening or talk among themselves. The best suggestion, of course, is to pass around handouts only *after* your speech.

But if you do plan to pass something around, make sure all members of the audience have the same thing. For example, you could photocopy a complex chart or graph, as well as making one large one, so that all audience members have a copy. An added advantage here is that listeners will have something to take away with them. One speaker talking about how to get the most out of college put the suggestions together in a formal contract so listeners could both follow the speech and have a copy of the contract when the speech was over.

If your speech is complicated with many details to communicate, you might use a handout. This could be a copy of your outline or just a summary of the important material; either will help listeners follow along. Pamphlets and brochures are also valuable because they reinforce your message later.

The visual support that will work best for *any* speech is one that is colorful and creative. Think about what you would like to see if you were listening to your own speech. Try to create something that would satisfy your own high standards.

The Heart of the Matter

When looking for visual aids to use in a speech, many people tend to ask, "What visual aids can I find?" or "What visual aids are available?" This is a little like giving a perfunctory speech just to fill an assignment. To find the best visual aids, ask one central question: "What visual aids will best support, enhance, or reinforce the central thesis of my speech?" Then find or construct that ideal support. Visual aids should help listeners see more clearly or understand with greater accuracy: "Aha, *now* I see what you mean!" They should not be used if they do not serve that specific and well-defined purpose. Otherwise, they will distract or confuse and should be eliminated.

TYPES OF VISUAL SUPPORT

Visual support helps amplify or expand your speech because it offers a new dimension. Here are some ideas for possible visual aids:

The object. Showing an actual object itself has a strong visual impact. When Greg gave a speech about the anatomy of the human brain he brought a brain in a jar to class. In addition, he used a plaster replica to point out parts that could not be seen on the brain in the jar. Seeing an actual brain noticeably affected Greg's listeners.

A model. Modeling how a device or apparatus operates, or its basic design, is an effective technique. Greg used a model of the human brain to point out its parts. Alphonso had male and female plaster models for his speech encouraging people to protect themselves from the virus that causes AIDS.

The chalkboard. Most drawings should be completed before listeners arrive, then covered and revealed only when appropriate. If you use the chalkboard, chalk lines must be sufficiently distinct to be seen by all audience members. Carla used the chalkboard for her speech on diet because she had so many facts and figures to convey. She talked about different body frames, basal calories, calorie intake, necessary servings, and serving sizes. The chalkboard helped her display facts and figures clearly to her listeners.

Graphs. Graphs are handy to show relative sizes or amounts. *Line graphs* show two or more variable facts. *Bar graphs* show the relationship of two sets of figures. *Pie graphs* show percentages. *Pictorial graphs* (or *pictographs*) represent statistical data in pictorial form by the size or number of symbols. Almost any issue of *USA Today* will provide a number of examples of pictographs.

Diagrams. If you want to show inner workings of objects or external aspects, diagrams are effective. For example, for his speech about computers, Paul used a diagram of the inner workings of a computer. Diagrams, of course, vary in complexity. Three-dimensional views often provide a great deal of information. Computer-generated diagrams are now within the reach of anyone with access to a computer and printer.

Charts. A chart is ideal to show the parts of an organization or the structure of a business. For her speech called "Understanding the University," Michelle used an organizational chart that began at the top with the president, then moved down to the academic vice presidents, and then showed the deans, the department chairpersons, and the faculty (see Figure 12.4).

Transparencies. *Transparencies* are displayed from an overhead projector. You can produce them beforehand or draw them as they are projected in front of the audience. Transparencies are inexpensive and easy to prepare, use, and transport (see Figure 12.5). Most photocopiers can produce transparencies from an original print; they can then be customized and colored for effective presentation.

Transparencies are often the most effective visual aid as well as the cheapest and easiest to produce. They can be as complex as multicolor, multifoil overlays graphically created by computers with an online plotter; or they can be as simple as colorful displays made in three seconds on a copier.

Slides. Slides offer variety and, like transparencies, can be used repeatedly. Because they are generally more expensive to produce than transparencies, they are often perceived to be a more professional medium. When Juan used slides to enhance his presentation, he used a simple process to build

Figure 12.4.
Organization chart of a university.

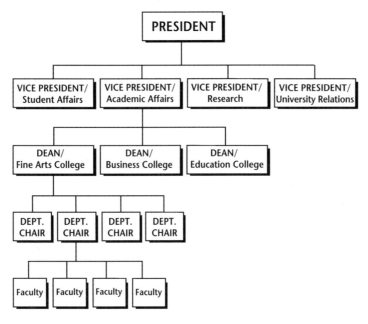

up his main ideas. His first slide presented his first idea in yellow on a dark blue background. The second slide retained the first idea in white, with the second idea now in yellow. The third showed the first two ideas in white and the third new idea in yellow. This technique is especially useful when listeners must take notes on a presentation; it allows them to catch up easily if they fall behind the speaker.

Films and videos. The advantage of films and videos is that they add sound to moving images. Although professionally produced films may be expensive, videorecorders make this medium far more available. For example, for her speech about space and distance Melissa videotaped people on campus standing, sitting, and sharing space with others. She used the videos to help describe the "bubble" of space that people usually keep around themselves as they talk with others. (She burst the bubble when she showed several couples kissing at the end of her video.)

The computer. Although you can use a computer before your speech to produce charts, graphs, slides, and transparencies, a computer can also be used for live presentations. Several software packages now enable speakers to project shows onto large screens. Multimedia software combines sound, animation, and images with text and graphics in an interactive package that is both exciting and visually stimulating.

Figure 12.5.
An example of a transparency.

THE FLASHING RED LIGHT EXAM

- Do you spend more than 20% of your take-home pay on monthly installment bills, not including mortgage payments?

- Do you regularly receive second notices?

- Have you recently borrowed cash with your credit card to meet household expenses?

- Do you find it impossible to put money into a savings account?

- Are you currently being telephoned by a bill collector?

- Do you secretly suspect that your credit card spending has gotten out of control?

- Are you worried about your debts?

- Is there frequent stress at home because of overdue bills?

If you answered "YES" more than once, then the red light is flashing for you.

From David A. Peoples, Presentations Plus, 2nd ed. (New York: Wiley, 1992), p. 103.

SUMMARY

Visual support plays a strong role in enhancing the quality of presentations. This chapter discussed the purposes of visual support from a listener's perspective, from a speaker's perspective, and from a content perspective.

Suggestions were provided for using visual support, including the need for rehearsal, letting listeners see visual aids only when they are being talked about, making visual support large enough and simple, talking to listeners and not to the visual support, and using visual support with discretion. Some pointers were also provided for passing material around the audience during a speech. The basic overall guideline for the use of visual support is to make it colorful and creative.

Finally various types of visual support were discussed. Speakers have numerous types of visual aids to choose from. Transparencies are often the easiest, most efficient, and inexpensive.

Your selection of visual support should be based on the central idea of your speech and how the visual will enhance that central idea. It should also be chosen based on your comfort and confidence. Remember to rehearse with it. And finally, remember that the greatest visual support of all is you as the speaker.

Chapter Questions

1. What are the purposes of visual aids?

2. Can you think of any suggestions for using audiovisual aids that are not mentioned here?

3. Prepare a speech for which you will use a visual aid. How can you ensure that your use of the visual support will be successful?

4. Compare and contrast the different types of visual aids. Which do you think would be easiest to use? Most difficult?

Further Reading

Robert R. H. Anholt, *Dazzle 'em with Style: The Art of Oral Scientific Presentation* (New York: W. H. Freeman and Company, 1994).

There are only four chapters in this 200-page paperback, Chapter 3 is called "Visual Displays: How to (and not to) Use Them." Anholt's suggestions are practical and useful.

Lani Arredondo, *The McGraw-Hill 36-Hour Course: Business Presentations* (New York: McGraw-Hill, 1994).

Arredondo devotes nearly 25 pages to the use of audiovisual materials. She orients her material around seven key concepts, and she provides straight how-to descriptions. Her examples include case studies.

David A. Peoples, *Presentations Plus*, 2nd ed. (New York: John Wiley & Sons, 1992).

Almost 70 pages of this 288-page paperback are devoted to audiovisual aids. Peoples uses many illustrations to demonstrate his explanations in a "do as I do" approach. Great examples and a high-energy writing style make this a valuable book.

Endnotes

1. Research shows that people taught by methods using both visual and oral channels have better recall immediately after the presentation and also after time has elapsed. People who only heard the message had an immediate recall of 70 percent and recalled only 10 percent after three days. Those taught both visually and orally had an 85 percent immediate recall and 65 percent after three days. See Robert Craig's article in the *Kansas City Times*, April 19, 1967. Craig is chief of the United States Public Health Service Audio-Visual Facility. This research is reviewed in Wil Linkugel and David Berg's *A Time to Speak* (Belmont, CA: Wadsworth, 1970).
2. This study was cited in Lani Arredondo, *The McGraw-Hill 36-Hour Course: Business Presentations* (New York: McGraw-Hill, 1994), p. 177.
3. "A study by the University of Minnesota concluded that presentations using visual aids were 43 percent more persuasive than those without visual support." As cited in Lani Arredondo, *The McGraw-Hill 36-Hour Course: Business Presentations* (New York: McGraw-Hill, 1994), p. 177.

Words in Action: VIDEO STUDY

Used effectively, visual aids involve listeners, enable a speaker to simplify and condense large amounts of information, and help vary the pace of a speech. In addition, they help an audience remember your message.

The accompanying video demonstrates how visual supports can enhance or detract from a speaker's presentation. Before answering the questions below, you may wish to review pp. 176–179, "Suggestions for Using Visual Support."

1. In what ways do the visual aids used by the MRI speaker contribute to her presentation?
2. Analyze the type and use of support employed by the speaker who talks about New Jersey.

PART IV

Types of Presentations

Informative Speaking

After reading this chapter you will be able to:

- compare and contrast the three types of informative speeches

- know how to make an effective informative speech

- understand how to emphasize the important points in your speech

- use five guidelines for answering questions from listeners

When Andrew took his part-time job at the gas station across town from a famous fort, he had no idea that he would be giving the same public speech several times a day. "How do you get to Fort Meigs from here?" was the question, and Andrew soon developed a clear explanation.

Conchita's first job was managing a fast food restaurant. Because the turnover of part-time help was so great, Conchita found that explaining how to do the various jobs to new employees was one of her most important tasks. She liked seeing the immediate results of her explanations; either new employees were able to do the jobs well because of her explanations, or they needed additional help.

Min Min's first teaching job was as a graduate teaching assistant while she earned an advanced college degree. Because she worked in a large course under the direction of a professor, her primary job was explaining course assignments to freshmen and sophomores. She discovered that presenting the significant details of the assignments in the clearest order was most effective.

Andrew, Conchita, and Min Min learned how to explain ideas to others. In all three cases, the primary goal was to explain a concept or process clearly. Because they were in knowledgeable positions, they were called upon to convey information they had acquired. And because you are going to college and will soon have a college degree, you will be considered more informed than others with no college background; thus, you will be looked to for advice, comment, and information.

As a student, you will be giving reports, discussing course topics, and explaining complex ideas. In business you may be asked to provide facts and figures relating to a company's performance. At a general sales meeting you may need to tell people about new products, services, pricing schedules, and sales and advertising plans. Artists and musicians may have to explain innovative patterns, trends, and methodologies. In other words, there isn't a nook or cranny in our society where people can hide from information.

This chapter offers insight into the purposes and processes of informative speaking. First we discuss types of informative speaking, second, we review methods of organizing informative speeches, third, we offer advice for making an effective, informative speech, and finally, we look at the process of answering questions.

TYPES OF INFORMATIVE SPEAKING

Your primary purpose in an informative speech is to share knowledge and create understanding. Your talk is likely to take one of three forms: description, demonstration, or explanation.

When your goal is to describe

If your goal is to paint a clear picture of a specific activity, object, person, place, or concept, you will use a *descriptive speech*. Your speech, then, will be designed to provide a clear and vivid impression through accurate and informative material. Description makes an impression that will be remembered by your listeners because of the images created. And the point of your descriptive speech is to provide listeners with new information. For example, Dustin described the experiences he had in job interviews. Jody described her work as a cosmetics specialist in a major department store. Although it was difficult for her, Nichole spoke about how she mourned when her grandmother died. She talked about the six R's of healthy mourning: recognize, react, recollect, relinquish, readjust, and reinvert. Nichole described her experiences so vividly that her listeners could feel her emotion.

To provide an accurate picture of what you are describing, you must make listeners mentally see the size, shape, weight, color, composition, age, condition, and location of your subject. The more specific your information, the more likely it is to leave a lasting impression. Descriptive information should enable listeners to visualize whatever is being described. As a speaker, you should err on the side of too much information rather than not enough.

When you develop a descriptive speech, remember that although effective language is essential, your language must not be so picturesque or florid that it becomes distracting. Your emphasis should be not on the beauty of the language but on the informative intent of the message. Language, like delivery, must serve as a vehicle, not as an object to be viewed or admired for its own sake. Strive for clarity without sacrificing sincerity.

When your goal is to demonstrate

If you want to show your listeners how to do something or how something works, you give a *demonstration speech*. You hear demonstrations often. For example, advertisers on television show you how products work, salespeople show you how to put products together, and instructors tell you how to do assignments. A trip to a bookstore will reveal hundreds of self-help books that tell you how to do everything from growing spices indoors to studying for the Graduate Record Exam (GRE). Anita, a member of the college golf team, showed class members how to properly swing a golf club. David used his background in interior decoration to show class members how to arrange and decorate their dormitory rooms. In one class different students talked on how to take notes, how to read, and how to study for examinations.

Most demonstration speeches follow a time order (discussed in Chapter 7), which illustrates a sequence of ideas or events. Some examples of this order would be directions for how to play a game, how to prepare a recipe, or how to put together a toy, bookshelf, or deck chair.

When your goal is to explain

When you want to inform listeners of ideas or policies, you use a speech of *explanation*. Ideas and policies are more abstract than the topics appropriate for speeches to describe and demonstrate. Much of our communication includes explanations, such as those given by teachers, preachers, doctors, lawyers, and businesspeople. All professions and vocations depend on this form of communication because it is so often necessary to explain ideas and policies to others.

Explaining means giving understanding. That is, if you want to explain a concept, idea, or process, your goal is to get listeners to understand that concept, idea, or process. If listeners can remember it and apply it on their own, you have succeeded. The more complicated your subject, the more care you must give to the explanation.

In her speech, "2001, A Retailing Odyssey: Confronting the Consumer of the 21st Century," Wendy Liebmann, president of WSL Marketing, Inc., first provided an explanation of retailing in the '90s:

> The rebirth began in the '90s. Remember the Mall of America with its Knottsberry Farm, gigantic Snoopy, and roller coaster rides? Remember the Disney and Warner Brothers stores with multimedia, larger-than-life Daffy Duck running amok, and Superman flying from the ceiling? With Bugs Bunny videos, dolls, jackets, mugs, and ties? And there's no forgetting the Nike store with a half court all ready for that quick game of one-on-one before you bought your latest sneakers.
>
> Remember Barnes & Noble bookstores where the experience and pure joy of reading enveloped you? With comfortable armchairs to plonk down in and read undisturbed, and an in-store coffee bar to re-fortify you? Or Williams-Sonoma with cooking demonstrations and free, fresh-baked cookies? Ah, the smell of it. That was just the beginning.
>
> Those retailers who are succeeding in the 21st century understand that retailing is no longer just a function of real estate or inventory management or planogramming. They remember the days of being merchants. They remember the excitement of satisfying their customers.
>
> Yes, they have learned from and embraced new technology, using it to better manage their business. But most importantly they have used it to communicate with and better service their customers and they have never forgotten what it is to be a customer themselves.

What makes this effective as explanation is the detail Liebmann provides. She is appealing to her audience of retail executives with specific information they can identify with and understand.

ORGANIZING INFORMATIVE SPEECHES

As we discussed in Chapter 7, listeners will remember your ideas better and your speech will be more effective if your main points are arranged in a logical sequence. For an informative speech you will generally follow one of three basic speech patterns: topic order, time order, or space order. To review, *topic order* requires that each main idea develop part of the specific purpose. The main ideas are typically phrased as definitions, causes, or parts of the topic. For example, if your specific purpose were to tell your audience about the nutritional components of a peanut butter and jelly sandwich, your three main points might be the amounts of protein, fat, and carbohydrates in this type of sandwich.

Time order, sometimes called chronological order, should be used when the main ideas can be arranged in a time sequence or a reverse time sequence and when you want listeners to see this sequence of ideas or events. For example, you would use time order to explain the process of making a peanut butter and jelly sandwich. *Space order* should be used when you want to explain an event, place, thing, or person in terms of its parts, and those parts hold some definable space. If your speech were about the components of a banana split, you could discuss the banana, the ice cream scoops, and the toppings as three space holders.

The Heart of the Matter

The essence of informative speaking is keeping the goal of imparting information in mind as you figure out how to achieve that end. You must increase understanding beyond what your listeners already know. As an informative speaker you must not only be well informed on your topic, you must also have some knowledge, or some combination of ideas, that your listeners do not presently have. And your speech must give your listeners that information.

MAKING AN EFFECTIVE INFORMATIVE SPEECH

The best advice for making a strong informative speech is to use the principles and guidelines offered throughout this textbook thus far. Beyond that, however, a number of ideas specific to informative speeches may provide additional assistance. Most are not new; they are offered here in the context of informative speaking.

Recognize and adapt to audience knowledge

Although you don't always know how much your listeners know about a subject, your goal should be to recognize and adapt to their level of prior information and knowledge. Find out as much as you can: The more you know about the knowledge base of your listeners, the easier it will be to link your ideas to their interests, needs, or goals and the less likely you will tell listeners what they already know. Construct your speech with their level of knowledge in mind. Select your main ideas, choose your supporting material, and define important terms with specific reference to your listeners. Here are three important guidelines.

First, follow the code of news reporters: "Never overestimate the information of your audience, never underestimate the intelligence of your audience." Second, don't assume your audience will understand your meaning; explain things clearly and thoroughly. Third, as you construct your speech, ask yourself, "Will my topic be clear to listeners who are hearing it for the first time?"

Give listeners the right amount of information

Sometimes we select topics that are too broad or topics that involve too much information. For example, Chi Su chose to tell her classmates about Chinese culture—a topic far too broad for the time limit. Even when Chi Su focused the speech on differences between Chinese and U.S. education, it still included too much information for the time limit. Only when she narrowed it to perceptions of education in China and the United States was she able to provide the right level of information for listeners within her time limit.

Think about how much information *you* can handle during a speech and make your choices based on this insight. Next, look for a variety of information, not just facts and statistics. Third, make your information interesting by relating the numbers and statistics you do use to things audience members will understand.

Try not to be too technical

How technical you can be depends on your audience analysis: How much do your listeners know? As you select your topic, think about what you can explain to your audience in the time you have and think about the language you will need to use to develop your explanations. For example, Regina was a chemistry major, and in a classroom speech she wanted to explain the history of chemistry and the contributions it has made to her listeners' lives. She titled her speech "Chemistry's Contributions: From Soap to Satellites" and talked about chemotherapy, fibers, plastics, resins, dyes, insecticides, anesthetics, and hormones using language within most listeners' knowledge and understanding.

Involve your listeners in your speech

If you can involve your audience in your informative speech, you will increase both their interest and their ability to recall your points. There are a number of specific methods you can use to encourage listener involvement:

- *Encourage informality.* Walking among listeners, establishing eye contact with them, and becoming sensitive to their feedback can give you valuable information.

- *Incorporate questions and probes into the material.* These tie listeners to the material directly and these require some specific response. Questions you might ask include: Can you cite examples from your own life for what I'm talking about? How would you explain this concept in your own words? Can you cite an example of how you might apply this idea?

- *Use rhetorical questions, which require no overt response.* For example, How many times have you..., Do you ever remember seeing..., When was the last time you...? Giving listeners a chance to verbalize, even if only to themselves, enhances their attentiveness and involvement.

- *Provide additional support and reinforcement listeners can hold or see.* For example, you can hand out outlines, fill-in-the-blank or short-answer questions, or other material related to your speech.

- *Use visual aids to support the presentation.* Slides and transparencies can help speakers organize their presentation and make it more appealing. Allot about two minutes of presentation time per slide. A single sheet of paper with key words on it that identify each slide may be helpful to you as a speaker.

- *Motivate your listeners.* Once you know your listeners' wants and needs, you can motivate them to respond.[2] The same principle applies to learning: People learn best when they are motivated to do so. Thus, the most effective informative speech is one that motivates listeners and makes them *want* to learn.

- *Encourage listeners to learn.* Give listeners a reason for learning the ideas, skills, or information you present. Be specific by telling them *how* it will affect their lives and *what* they can do with the material. Give them definite and practical suggestions that they can consider and apply.

- *Emphasize the important points.* In every speech, some points are more important than others and thus should be emphasized or stressed. Emphasis can be planned (see the box on page 194). The points needing emphasis can be carefully selected, and the type of emphasis also can be determined before the presentation.

More on Language

Remember, your word choices and the level of your talk will be adjusted according to who your audience is. For example, here are two descriptions of the symptoms of a major depressive episode. The first is rather technical and is likely to bore the average listener. The second is likely to have some impact on listeners; it relates the material to the audience more specifically.

1. A major depressive episode is characterized by irritability or loss of interest or pleasure in all, or almost all, activities for at least two weeks. Associated symptoms include appetite disturbance, change in weight, sleep disturbance, psychomotor agitation, decreased energy, feelings of worthlessness, difficulty in thinking, and recurrent thoughts of death or suicidal attempts.

2. A major depressive episode can affect any of you. But there are a number of ways you have to detect it. And with detection, of course, you can get quick treatment. One of the early signs is feeling down in the dumps. This often results in looking sad much of the time. When you just don't care anymore, this is another possible sign. Nothing interests you, and you do not seek out things that bring you pleasure. Others might accuse you of withdrawing. Other signs include not being interested in eating, having difficulty falling or staying asleep, not being able to sit still, and feeling negative about yourself.

Bringing the Point Home

As the speaker, you must be the judge of how important it is for listeners to get a particular point. Then you must determine the best way to put the point across to listeners. Your choice will depend both on how attentive audience members are and on the complexity of the point being made. The following methods of emphasis are arranged hierarchically, with the most important method (most effective) listed first.

1. *Use an indicator before starting the point.* "This is the *most important* point I want to share with you..." "The following idea stands out above all the rest..."

2. *Use an indicator after starting the point.* "Now, let me explain what that point means..." "This may sound confusing or complex, so let me explain it to you..."

3. *Repeat a point once.* This is not a paraphrase. Say the point in exactly the same way twice. Saying it more than twice may have a negative effect.

4. *When appropriate, speak slowly.* A change in speed of delivery or in the speaker's tone grabs the attention of listeners and makes the point.

5. *Use a pause and/or a gesture.* The timing of the pause and gesture must be accurate. If you are emphasizing a single word, the pause should occur just before you state the word, and the gesture should occur with the word: "I want you to notice the [pause] *power* of a strong gesture."[3]

As with all things, emphasis can be overused. When speakers overemphasize, overuse such phrases as "this is important," or depend too heavily on repetition, they are likely to achieve an effect opposite to the one they seek; listeners will doubt or reject the speaker's clues as to what is important.

ANSWERING QUESTIONS

Because you are informing listeners about a topic, they may have questions to ask you during or after your presentation. If your audience is small, you might encourage questions during the talk to promote an informal atmosphere and build rapport with the audience.[4] On the other hand, a larger audience generally requires a more formal presentation, and you would then reserve time at the end for questions.

If you have thoroughly researched your topic, you should feel confident that you are the expert and that you know more about it than listeners do. However, you may be nervous about being put on the spot to provide an unrehearsed response. Keep in mind that you do not have to answer every question, and if you cannot answer one, it is best to be honest and admit it. You can add that you will have to consider and research the question further. Also, remember that because they request clarification or additional information, people who ask questions are usually those most intrigued by your topic and have a sincere interest in the response to their questions.

SUMMARY

Informative speeches are an important part of public speaking. Although the essentials for giving any speech have been carefully detailed in preceding chapters, this chapter has highlighted aspects that are especially relevant to this form of communication.

This chapter began by discussing three different types of informative speeches: descriptive, demonstrative, and explanatory. The second section of this chapter presented ways to increase understanding including recognizing and adapting to audience knowledge, giving listeners the right amount of information, trying not to be too technical, and involving your listeners in your speech. Various ways to involve listeners in your speech were discussed, as were methods for emphasizing important points.

The final section recommended that you answer audience questions during informal speeches to small audiences but after formal speeches to large audiences. The key to handling questions effectively lies in being prepared for the unexpected and responding honestly if you don't know the answer. The point of giving informative speeches is to help listeners understand your subject. The advice in this chapter should improve your effectiveness in this endeavor.

Sample Speech

As you study this informative speech, notice how the speaker makes her topic interesting.[5] Pay special attention to how well the speech is organized, how the speaker selected strong supporting materials to bring her topic to life, how she clarified her ideas with effective language—especially her use of technical words—and how she established her credibility within her speech.

It's SAD—Seasonal Affective Disorder

The speaker shows two pictures—one bright and sunny, the other glum and overcast. She begins with a unique way to capture audience attention and interest. To increase involvement she asks specific questions of listeners as well.

Now the speaker reveals her subject. Notice how she not only mentions it but cites a reputable journal and provides a definition as well.

Notice here how the speaker previews the main points of her speech.

The speaker now begins her first main point.

Where would *you* rather spend time? (Show pictures.) Which picture makes you feel better? You may think you are reacting psychologically to these pictures, but it has been proven that changes in exposure to sunlight can cause physical changes as well. How many of you have had the "winter blues" or have heard of "cabin fever"? Did any of you realize that these are physical reactions to shorter days and less exposure to sunlight?

These physical reactions to exposure to light have been documented and studied, and they are called seasonal affective disorder (SAD). According to *American Health* magazine, seasonal affective disorder is defined as "a pattern of depression and sometimes mania that comes at one time of the year and evaporates in another,"[1] and there must be a pattern to it—it cannot be feeling depressed just one winter.[2] Today I want to look at SAD's history, a description of how it works, and methods of prevention.

The first scientist to observe SAD was Frederick Cook, an American naval officer, doctor, and polar explorer who was born in the 19th century.[3] His ship was

She has made history interesting by telling a short story, but she has kept it short to keep listeners interested.

Here the speaker refers once again to her very reputable source and brings the history of SAD into the modern day. She keeps her history brief.

Here the speaker cites her second source, gives another label to SAD, outlines the symptoms, and leads listeners to her second main point.

She has now firmly established her credibility on this subject.

This is her second main idea. After a brief history, she provides some description.

She wrote these statistics on the chalkboard because they were important to confirming her main point.

Notice the way she handles the use of this technical word. She does not assume listeners will understand it.

She uses her sources effectively, and she cites useful statistics to show the significance of her topic.

The speaker uses more highly reputable sources proving she has done her homework and adding to her already well-established credibility.

She uses a transition into her third main point, in which she describes causes.

Another technical term is used and quickly defined for listeners.

Here the speaker uses another visual aid, in addition to the chalkboard, which illustrates and labels this process. She is careful to talk to her listeners as she points to her chart.

Notice her use of technical language.

trapped in the ice, and his men saw no sun for 68 days. He noted that his men gradually became affected "body and soul," but when they were exposed to artificial light, their normal attitudes returned.

The first modern studies on recurrent melancholia, as it has often been called, began in 1980. According to *American Health* journal, the National Institute of Mental Health began studying the patterns after a client showed them records of the patterns of his mood cycles.[4]

According to *Consumer's Research Magazine* in an article called "Winter Blues," these mood cycles, or recurrent melancholia or SAD, have symptoms including changes in appetite (carbohydrate craving),[5] sleeping patterns, and reduced energy, libido, and cognition. The pattern of occurrence shows a distinct correlation with latitude and season.

Some description of SAD will help you understand it better. Studies have shown that it increases as latitude increases.

For example, in *USA Today* it says 2 percent of the population of Florida, 6 percent of the population of Maryland and New York, and 10 percent of the population of New Hampshire have severe symptoms.[6]

In this same copy of *USA Today* it says that approximately 19 percent of the population in a Fairbanks, Alaska, study were subsyndromal—which means they are bothered by some but not all symptoms.[7] But 50 percent of the population of Fairbanks, where it is dark longer than it is light, reported lack of energy, increased appetite, and trouble sleeping.[8]

According to the *American Journal of Nursing*, it is estimated that 450,000 people in the United States suffer from seasonal depression,[9] and according to *Sierra* magazine, an estimated 5 million Americans have seasonal depression.[10]

According to the *American Journal of Psychiatry* the ratio of women to men affected is four to one, and it seems to be more prevalent in those under 40, or people like you and me.[11]

These figures show how many people are affected by SAD, but what is causing this widespread problem?

The exact physical process that causes SAD is unknown, but it has to do with our circadian rhythms, which follow a 24-hour cycle and are our bodies responses to our environment.[12]

It is believed that light goes into the eye and triggers a nerve impulse in addition to the sight impulse. The path this impulse takes is a light meter that is delivered to the section of the brain that determines "all kinds of important behavior including mood, hunger, sleep, and libido."[13]

This information is then sent to the gland known as

She incorporates her sources easily and naturally into her speech.

Here she uses a transition into her final main idea.
She uses "you" to be more direct with her audience.

To keep her listeners involved, she pretends they are the patients.

Notice, once again, how she introduces technical words into her speech.

She ends this section on preventative measures by relating her material directly to her listeners.

the "interpreter," which produces a hormone called melatonin. Melatonin, the "sleeping hormone,"[14] has a sedating effect similar to Valium.[15] In animals, melatonin is high in the winter and low in the spring, so it has been labeled the "hibernation response."[16] According to *Prevention* magazine, it has been proven that sunlight causes the skin to produce vitamin D, which builds bone mass. There is loss in bone mass in the winter months when exposure to sunlight decreases.[17]

So what can be done to prevent these physical changes, thus preventing SAD?

There are several things you can do to decrease the symptoms of, or prevent the possibility of getting, SAD.

For those with the most serious cases of depression, according to the *American Journal of Nursing*, phototherapy or light therapy works wonders. You would sit in front of broad spectrum bulbs—just a special name for lightbulbs that give off special light—for one-half hour to three hours at a time, once or twice a day. You have your eyes open, and you are approximately three to five feet from the bulbs.[18] The symptoms decrease after three to seven days of this therapy, and they return after three to seven days away from this therapy.[19]

According to the *American Journal of Psychiatry*, the ultraviolet rays—or dangerous rays—which can damage your skin and eyes are screened out without any decrease in effectiveness.[20]

Much more research is being done on phototherapy—which is the name for this procedure—including differences in the effects of green, red, and white light.[21] The *Scandinavian Review* has reported that a professor at a psychiatric hospital has created a "white room" to help maintain melatonin balances.[22]

There are some side effects to light therapy, according to the *American Journal of Psychiatry*. These include eye irritation and redness, headaches, irritability, and hyperactivity. These, however, can be reduced or eliminated by reduction of exposure time and by moving farther away from the light source.[23]

In her article in *American Health*, "Solar Power," Winifred Gallagher, the writer, points out that some architects and designers have become aware of the effects of lighting and are now offering options that can reduce some depression.[24]

You can reduce depressive symptoms by getting outside—especially to exercise—increasing your exposure to sunlight while inside by opening window blinds and curtains, and utilizing the sunshine that comes indoors by rearranging furniture and desks to use areas in front of windows.

This is a transition from her last main idea into her conclusion, which follows.

Not only does this conclusion summarize the speaker's points effectively, but notice how she increased her credibility even more by referring to the interviews she had and by adding that these doctors asked her to prepare an article for them.

She ends the speech with a touch of humor that would be immediately relevant to members of her audience.

SAD is a problem for many people that can easily be reduced or eliminated by using these suggestions.

While there are physical and psychological effects to reduced exposure to sunlight, there are several solutions that can reduce symptoms and increase quality of life for those affected. Dr. Ann Salisbury and Milt Whitmer, counseling psychologists who practice in Perrysburg, Ohio, feel that SAD is a problem that can be controlled through education and awareness.[25] They asked me to prepare an article about SAD for the *Perrysburg Messenger-Journal* to be published under Dr. Salisbury's name. Although a tremendous number of people are affected by these depressive symptoms, you can make yourself feel better by just increasing your exposure to sunlight throughout the winter months. And you thought you were going to Florida during spring break just for the parties!

Speech Notes

1. Winifred Gallagher, "Solar Power," *American Health* (January 1991), p. 36.
2. "Light at End of Wintry Tunnel," *USA Today* (January 1992), p. 5.
3. Gallagher, p. 35.
4. Gallagher, p. 36.
5. Guy Murdoch, "Winter Blues," *Consumer's Research Magazine* (January 1993), p. 2.
6. "Light at End," p. 5.
7. "Light at End," p. 5.
8. "Light at End," p. 5.
9. Kathy Lee Dunham, "Seasonal Affective Disorder: Light Makes Right," *American Journal of Nursing* (December 1992), p. 45.
10. Michael Castleman, "Brighten Up, Lighten Up," *Sierra* (November 1991), p. 24.
11. John M. Booker, Ph.D., and Carla J. Hellekson, M.D., "Prevalence of Seasonal Affective Disorder in Alaska," *American Journal of Psychiatry* (September 1992), p. 1176.
12. Gallagher, p. 38.
13. Gallagher, p. 38.
14. Dunham, p. 45.
15. Michael Castleman, "Brighten Up, Lighten Up," *Sierra* (November 1991), p. 24.
16. Kim Naylor, "The White Room: Antidote to the Winter Blues," *Scandinavian Review* (Winter 1992), ProQuest abstract.
17. "Supplemental Sunshine," *Prevention* (February 1993), p. 15.
18. Dunham, p. 46.

19. Dunham, p. 46.
20. Dan A. Oren, M.D., et al., "Treatment of Seasonal Affective Disorder with Green Light and Red Light," *American Journal of Psychiatry* (April 1991), p. 510.
21. Oren et al., p. 509.
22. Naylor, ProQuest abstract.
23. Anthony J. Levitt, M.B.B.S., et al., "Side Effects of Light Therapy in Seasonal Affective Disorder," *American Journal of Psychiatry* (April 1993), p. 651.
24. Gallagher, p. 42.
25. Ann M. Salisbury, Ph.D., and Milt Whitmer, M.S.W., L.I.S.W., Interview, November 4, 1993.

Chapter Questions

1. What are the most important factors in the success of informative speakers?

2. How can speakers involve their listeners? Which methods do you feel most comfortable using?

3. If you had to emphasize important points in a speech, which methods would you most likely use?

4. How else might a speaker emphasize important ideas in a speech?

5. Think of some informative speeches you have heard. What made those speeches effective or ineffective? How would you improve on the informative speeches you have heard to make your own speeches more successful?

6. What additional suggestions do you have for speakers who must answer questions at the end of their speeches?

7. Critique the speech "It's SAD—Seasonal Affective Disorder." How effectively does it fulfill the criteria discussed in this chapter?

8. What would be the specific purpose and central idea for this speech? Write them out.

Further Reading

Joseph A. Devito, *The Elements of Public Speaking*, 5th ed. (New York: HarperCollins, 1994).

In this 500-page textbook Devito includes two chapters on informative speeches. One covers principles, description, definition, and demonstration; the second covers amplifying materials. His sample speech by a professional (with helpful annotations) offers a useful example.

Isa N. Engleberg, *The Principles of Public Presentation* (New York: Harper-Collins, 1994).

Engleberg has organized her book around the seven "P's," or principles, of effective speech making. The writing is clear, the examples are useful, and the information is sound.

Endnotes

1. Wendy Liebmann, "2001: A Retailing Odyssey: Confronting the Consumer of the 21st Century," *Vital Speeches of the Day* LXI (April 15, 1995), pp. 409–10.
2. See Charles F. Vick and Roy V. Wood, "Similarity of Past Experience and the Communication of Meaning," *Speech Monographs* 36 (June 1969), pp. 159–62.
3. See Ray Ehrensberger, "An Experimental Study of the Relative Effects of Certain Forms of Emphasis in Public Speaking," *Speech Monographs* 12 (1945), pp. 94–111.
4. See Alicia Fortinberry, "The Art of Piquing Art Questions," *Psychology Today* (April 1980), pp. 30–33.
5. The sample speech is reprinted here with the permission of Jane MacMillan. It was originally given in the basic speech communication course at Bowling Green State University on November 8, 1993.

Words in Action: VIDEO STUDY

The preceding chapters have provided you with information for analyzing any type of speech, and Chapter 13 discusses considerations specific to informative speaking. After watching the accompanying video, which presents a student example of an informative speech, critique the informative speech in detail. Considering the many elements that make up a speech, which aspects of this speech are effective? Which are ineffective?

14

Persuasive Speaking

After reading this chapter you will be able to:

- describe the specific considerations for influencing listener attitudes

- determine what persuasive impact you can realistically expect to have

- distinguish the three types (or purposes) of persuasive speaking

- compare and contrast propositions of fact, value, and policy

- compare and contrast four different persuasive organizational patterns

- use the Monroe motivated sequence

- follow three guidelines to make certain your persuasion is ethical

Stefanie is the local chairperson for a Red Cross blood drive. This position is a natural for her because she has been donating blood since she was first old enough to do so. Because of her position as chairperson, she is asked to speak before a number of community groups; her goal is to encourage members of those groups to donate blood.

Fernando is a 31-year-old student returning to school after a recent divorce. In preparing his final persuasive speech for his public speaking class, Fernando wants to choose a topic he knows something about. He has recently joined a support group for divorced and separated people. In addition, some years ago he benefited greatly from attending Alcoholics Anonymous meetings and was able to resolve and control his dependency problems. Finally, Fernando is a member of the Alzheimer's Association, an organization for caregivers of those with Alzheimer's disease. He receives support and assistance in caring for his mother from the group. When Fernando chooses as his persuasive topic, "Finding Help from Support Groups," his heartfelt message is to convince listeners to join support groups in times of need.

Stefanie and Fernando were involved in giving persuasive speeches. Although we most often associate persuasive speaking with politicians, advertisers, and religious leaders, most of the communication we engage in and listen to every day has an underlying persuasive intent.

The first section of this chapter addresses the process of influencing attitudes, and the second examines your potential persuasive impact. The third section differentiates three persuasive propositions; the fourth looks at several persuasive organizational patterns. The final section discusses the ethics of persuasion.

INFLUENCING ATTITUDES

Persuasion is the process of trying to get others to change their attitudes or behavior. Attitude change usually precedes behavior change, so the main purpose of persuasive speaking is to influence the attitudes of listeners. An *attitude* is a tendency or predisposition to behave in a certain way. For example, a student who has a negative attitude toward oral examinations may avoid all courses where oral examinations are required. You can start, stop, change, or reinforce attitudes. Doing so alters the psychological set (mental stance) of your listeners so they will act in a particular way—the way you want—in certain circumstances. For example, you may want to change students' attitude toward improving their writing skills. If you succeed, when they select courses for the following term your ideas might cause them to pick a course that includes writing projects.

How to discover listener attitudes

You can determine listener attitudes in two ways. First, you can *observe audience members and from their behavior ascribe or attribute attitudes.* For example, you might observe that people spend much time talking about and attending parties, which suggests that people's attitudes toward partying are highly favorable. Attitudes toward achieving success, finding adventure, and participating in sports can be discovered in the same manner. If you are the same age as your listeners, observations might also include some self-analysis. For example, you could ask yourself, "What do I like?" or "How do I feel?"

A second way to discover attitudes is to *ask listeners what their attitudes are*. For example, you can ask, "Do you think computer literacy should be required of high school students?" or "Do you think foreign languages should be taught in grade schools?" or "Do you think no-fault divorce should be instituted?"

The importance of listener attitudes

Once attitudes are determined, you can approach your listeners more precisely. When you know where people stand on an issue, it is easier to persuade them. You can show listeners how adopting or changing an attitude will help them structure their world or take charge of their lives. That is, you should try to show how accepting an attitude is really a logical extension of what listeners already know or feel. People try to rationally structure the world they live in. Knowing this, you might, for example, show

- how a de-emphasis on grades will raise the quality of education
- how better organization of time will result in more free time
- how more concern for eating habits will result in better health

How to use benefits or handicaps

If you can show listeners the benefits or handicaps of adopting certain attitudes you can help cause persuasion to occur. For example:

- Free speech allows you to say what you please about the government.
- Pass–fail grading allows you more freedom, more choices, and more variety with few of the restrictions of a graded system.
- Voting for these officers will bring you the changes you want, will help the organization grow, and will bring a fresh, new approach.

How to use ego defense

Our attitudes are formed at least in part by our desire to defend our egos. When something will make us look good or bad, we may alter our attitudes toward it accordingly. For example, Sandy is a college student who never thought much about clothes or cars until she became a businessperson in an area where clothes and cars are important to image. Sandy changed her attitude—valuing clothes and cars—because they became important to her image. People who rebel against authority, for example, may change their attitudes if they become administrators with control over others. If you can show your listeners how your topic will in some way affect their egos, there is a good possibility for persuasion to occur. For example:

- Learning to listen will win you more friends.

- Reading will make you a more interesting person.
- Greater self-confidence will cause others to respond more positively to you.

How to use attitude history

It is not just the attitude your audience has toward an issue that makes a difference. How they came by their attitude (its history) also may count. For example, if you have heard from friends that a movie is lousy, you might be inclined to believe it until you see the movie for yourself. Such an attitude is not strongly held and thus may be easily changed. Attitudes are not so easily changed when listeners have been brought up to believe them. Beliefs and attitudes about important issues such as abortion, premarital sex, drug use, and so on are likely to be deeply held and unlikely to be changed easily regardless of their validity or evidence presented in an attempt to discredit the attitude.

Attitudes may have been learned early from family or peers and then reinforced through rewards (praise) by family members or peers, or by example. Thus, *how* people learn to feel as they do (the history of their attitudes) becomes an important factor. Information about attitude history tells us (1) how strong the attitude is, (2) how likely the attitude is to be changed, and, perhaps, (3) how change can or should be approached (if change is desired).

YOUR POTENTIAL PERSUASIVE IMPACT

In an ideal world, listeners would respond to you in just the way you wanted. In the real world, however, many things affect your personal impact. How much information is available? What are the potential persuasive elements? What is the likely effect you, as one individual, can have? How does persuasion actually take place? These issues are discussed here to keep the persuasive process in proper perspective.

How much information is available?

You get information from many sources. Obvious sources are television, radio, magazines, newspapers, and other people. The amount of information you can share during a speech is likely to be minimal compared with the amount listeners get from other sources. Just think, for example, how you acquired the information you have. Much of it probably came from friends and from groups to which you belong. Add to these sources all the news media to which you are exposed and your own experiences. As a speaker, you can shape, narrow, and focus information, but you cannot hope to override or negate the base of information otherwise available. Seldom should speakers assume listeners have no information. It is more appropriate to assume that the base of information that listeners possess varies dramatically in both breadth and depth.

What are the potential persuasive elements?

A *persuasive element* is anything that contributes to an eventual change in attitude or behavior. As we just noted, people are persuaded by many factors. What causes change is usually not a single factor but rather a combination of elements. Think about how you were persuaded to change your major, your impression of another person, or your point of view on a public issue like health care. Often attitude change is a complex process that does not happen in a clear and distinct manner. Attitude change is subtle, often operating at a low awareness level. It also requires gathering together a number of different sources of information.

Many factors may contribute to attitude change. You read or hear about something from a doctor or lawyer. Or you might hear about something from several sources, first a friend, then a relative, and maybe a teacher as well. You might hear a piece of information on several news programs. You might change, too, simply because something that was once remote and didn't matter much begins to touch your life directly. One family that had little interest in and paid little attention to mental health issues became deeply involved when a family member was discovered to have a serious mental health problem. Changes in the environment, in our physical condition, in our capabilities, and even in our friends can bring about changes in our attitudes.

The point of this discussion is that your goals as a persuader are likely to be aided or hindered by the number or kind of persuasive elements already at work in listeners' lives. The degree to which you know this and can use this information in your speeches—even if it is just to acknowledge these factors—may determine your persuasive success.

What is the likely effect you can have?

Think first about the short amount of time you will be speaking. Second, think about who you are with reference to your listeners. Are you more experienced, more knowledgeable, more credible than they are? Are you older or younger? If you will be talking to people of approximately the same age and experience, how do you expect to stand out from them? Are you considered a source worth listening or responding to? Third, consider your power and ability to influence others. Are you generally effective as a persuader in everyday life? If by virtue of your personality and inherent characteristics you consider yourself shy, weak, or introverted, these same characteristics may affect any persuasive situation in which you find yourself. In short, numerous factors affect the outcome of persuasive situations, and you can (1) know what many of these factors are, (2) control them where possible, and (3) predict the probable effects of these factors on your listeners.

The mind-set of your listeners and their skepticism also influence your persuasive effect. Because we are constantly being persuaded, our senses become numbed or desensitized. Think, too, of the other speakers who have preceded you. Are your listeners ready for another speech? You may have to rise above listener expectations to succeed.

Listeners have a natural and healthy skepticism. Because our educational system encourages the asking of questions, they have learned to question rather than accept ideas when first hearing them. For example, all of us have been exposed to salespeople who hard-sell a lousy product, advertisers who do more to mislead than to inform, service station attendants who create a need to sell an unnecessary product, and politicians who speak out of both sides of their mouths. Listeners have every reason to question and doubt, even to be cynical. How are they to know that you are any different? You have some convincing to do.

How does persuasion actually take place?

Often we feel that speakers persuade listeners. This is not so. When persuasion takes place, listeners actually persuade themselves. People hold basic beliefs about many things. When they hear a subject discussed, they make associations between the subject and their own experiences. Persuaders simply provide the stimulus or trigger for listeners to think and react in certain ways. For example, if you can tie your listeners' love of little children to the need to contribute to a children's fund for disadvantaged youth, you increase the likelihood that you will persuade them to contribute.

Although listeners ultimately persuade themselves, as a speaker you must stir up the appropriate associations, the kind of associations that listeners make between their past knowledge and experiences and the knowledge and experiences that you are presenting. For example, Wendy connected her speech on how to prevent suicide and depression to a recent suicide that had occurred on campus. Akbar got students interested in his speech on environmental concerns by focusing on a toxic waste site recently discovered nearby. Most political speeches strive to involve, motivate, and persuade their listeners by using examples and metaphors to which the "common person" can relate. Once speakers allow listeners to relate to the topic, to believe they have something vested in the topic, they begin the influence or shaping process. If no associations occur, no persuasion takes place, and listeners go on acting or believing the way they did before.

The more accurately you can identify the associations listeners will make with your words and ideas, the more likely you will succeed in persuading your audience. Your speech is not an event or activity that stands alone in time: Everything you say fits into each listener's framework of previous experiences. Even if you do not acknowledge or recognize these ties, listeners will make these associations in their own minds. Unfortunately, listeners may make associations different from those you seek. For example, Joan set out to persuade her listeners to donate their bodies to medical science upon death, not knowing that one of the students had just lost a small child and thus this was a more sensitive topic than she anticipated. Although you cannot predict all the associations listeners will make, you should recognize those that can be assumed about your particular audience. The better you can direct the associations made, the more persuasive you will be.

TYPES OF PERSUASIVE SPEAKING

The three types of persuasive speeches are the following: (1) a speech that convinces (if speakers want listeners to agree with them), (2) a speech that actuates (if speakers want listeners to act on some matter), and (3) a speech that stimulates (if speakers know listeners agree but need reinforcement). Although a distinction is made here between three basic types of persuasive speeches, some persuasive speeches include two or even all three of these types.

How do you get listeners to agree with you?

If you want listeners to agree with you on these topics your goal is to *convince* and thus secure agreement.

- People do not get enough sleep.
- Lectures are an ineffective means for educating students.
- Violence depicted on television is detrimental.
- Excessive consumption of alcohol is a serious campus problem.

The best way you have for gaining agreement is to clearly explain the problem and use solid evidence to support its existence. In addition, if you can closely relate the problem to your listeners, there is a greater likelihood you will present your evidence to a receptive audience. Notice in the topics just listed that the speakers are not seeking action, so they do not present a plan of action. Instead, they are trying to get agreement that a problem exists, and they should present supporting evidence to do so.

How do you get listeners to act on some matter?

Now look at these ideas:

- College students should learn to manage their stress.
- People should learn to care for their environment.
- Students should join a club or organization.
- Students should learn to handle competition.

If you seek action from listeners on some matter, your purpose is to *actuate*. Sometimes audience members must be convinced before they can be moved to action. This is where there is some overlap—actually reinforcement—between persuasive speeches that seek to convince and to actuate. Actuating speeches are usually formulated around a proposition of policy; this concept will be discussed in the next section.

The actuating part of the listed speech topics could include having listeners attend a workshop, seminar, or lecture, having them talk informally about the topic, or trying some practical "how-to-do-it" advice. Actuation may involve signing a petition, writing letters to important people, or voting. Getting the audience to take some action is the goal. As discussed previously, if listeners are alerted to some benefit to themselves, they are more likely to be persuaded and to act.

How do you stimulate listeners?

Sometimes listeners already believe or feel the same as you do. What such listeners might need is reinforcement or rejuvenation—not convincing or actuating. Their feelings need to be heightened, sharpened, or just brought out. A speech designed to do this is a speech to *stimulate*. A church sermon is a good example of this type of speech. At pep rallies, speakers want to heighten present feelings. After-dinner speakers often wish to excite listeners on topics they already support. Commencement addresses also try to reinforce commonly accepted ideas and principles.

Although all three types of persuasive speeches—convincing, actuating, and stimulating—may be goals of speakers, generally only one purpose will constitute the final goal. For example, though we may all agree that we will benefit from a particular effort, such as physical exercise, we may not have all the facts. As a speaker, you may begin by stimulating us, reinforcing our knowledge, then convincing us of its importance by offering additional facts, and finally, actuating us by providing a simple series of exercises we can do every day.

PROPOSITIONS OF FACT, VALUE, AND POLICY

The propositions of fact, value, and policy are basic to persuasive speaking. Learning the distinctions between the three will help you make your persuasive speeches clearer and more distinct. You will also find it easier to focus and narrow topics.

How to use a proposition of fact

A proposition of fact suggests the existence of something. Using this kind of proposition, you try to prove or disprove a statement. For example:

- Marijuana is effective medicinally.
- Organ donation helps save lives.
- U.S. firearms kill more people between the ages of 15 and 24 than all natural causes combined.
- College is not the place for all students.
- Hypnosis can contribute to the improvement of personal skills.

Each of these statements can be disputed on a factual level. That is, each proposition alleges the existence of truth; it becomes your job to prove it is true. Whether propositions refer to the past, present, or future, your job is to amass strong factual evidence to convince listeners one way or the other.

A proposition of fact underlies every proposition of value or policy. It is important to understand the proposition of fact as an essential component, or building block, of the other types of propositions.

How to use a proposition of value

A proposition of value contains a value judgment as part of the proposition. When you use this kind of proposition, you maintain that something is good or bad, beneficial or detrimental, justified or unjustified, worthwhile or worthless, and so on. The proposition itself contains the value term, which is obvious, as you can see by the italicized words in the following propositions:

- Dictatorial education is *detrimental*.
- Soap operas are a *valuable* source of information on interpersonal relationships.
- Violence in professional sports is *unjustified*.
- The unharnessed accumulation of garbage is *harmful* to the environment.

To support propositions of value, it is necessary to first use facts to prove the importance or existence of the issue, event, or thing. This is why the proposition of fact is a basic building block. For example, each of the above examples contains at least one proposition of fact including:

- Some education is dictatorial.
- Soap operas provide information on interpersonal relationships.
- Violence exists in professional sports.
- The accumulation of garbage is unharnessed.

These are propositions of fact designed to buttress the propositions of value listed above.

In addition to facts, you should use expert opinion and testimony to support propositions of value. Legislators, doctors, lawyers, educators, and writers in the field must be used to strengthen the speech. Many speakers depend mostly on their own opinion. This is usually insufficient because your own opinions often do not reflect extensive background, experience, or credibility on the topic, and one experience is insufficient to establish credibility. These comments, however, should not lead you to assume that the *only* evidence possible with propositions of value is that of authority. It is usually the major form of evidence, but other forms such as facts, polls, studies, statistics, and examples also may be applicable.

How to use a proposition of policy

A proposition of policy proposes a course of action. Using this type of proposition you would argue that something should or should not be done. Within the proposition of policy, one of the following terms must appear: *should, ought to, have to,* or *must.* You might support any one of the following propositions of policy:

- Instructors should be more available to students.
- Sports at the college level ought to be abolished.
- Animals should not be used for product testing in scientific laboratories.
- People must follow a vegetarian diet.

Propositions of policy depend on propositions of both fact and value for their effectiveness. The first example above entails one proposition of fact: that instructors are not available to students. The proposition of value might be that instructor availability is good or beneficial. Only when these ideas are obvious, understood, or established can speakers go on to suggest a plan for solving the problem inherent in the proposition of policy.

Let's suggest some of the underlying propositions that Dominic used for his proposition of policy, "General education requirements (the language, math, science, and social science requirements that all students must take) must be eliminated":

General education requirements exist. (fact)

All students must take required general education classes. (fact)

General education requirements are worthless, detrimental, or unjustified. (value)

Therefore, general education requirements must be eliminated. (policy)

This example demonstrates that supporting propositions of policy requires some of the same support suggested for propositions of fact and value: Both facts and opinions are essential. In addition, one of the strongest forms of support for a proposition of policy is actual situations or examples where the policy has already been adopted or implemented. These enable a speaker to show where the policy has already been successful and where it has enjoyed effects such as positive feelings and attitudes.

ORGANIZING PERSUASIVE SPEECHES

This section introduces some organizational patterns unique to the persuasive situation. These patterns lend themselves especially well to situations where you want to change listener attitudes. Four patterns will be examined: inductive, deductive, causal, and the Monroe motivated sequence. The choice of which pattern to use depends on the topic, the speaker, and the audience, or, to put it more precisely, the topic–audience–speaker interaction.

Inductive patterns

You use *induction* when you move from the specific to the general. This might mean using specific data to build a case, then drawing it together with a general conclusion. When you feel your listeners may be hostile to your ideas, this approach is often wise. Stating the general conclusion first without explaining the evidence may turn listeners off so that they do not listen to you make your case. When Shenan wanted to assert that foreign languages should be required of all students, he knew the reaction would be negative, so he built his case first by describing the advantages of foreign language fluency in finding jobs, developing cultural understanding, understanding coworkers, and reducing business and training costs.

Deductive patterns

Deductive patterns are the reverse of inductive patterns and are far more common in speeches. In a deductive pattern the conclusion is stated first and then followed with specific supporting data or arguments (or both). Because the synthesizing comment, purpose, or conclusion is provided at the outset, listeners are given a clear picture of what is to come in your speech. This also enables listeners to better understand all that follows because they know the direction in which you are going with your speech.

Causal patterns

Using the *causal pattern* you can move either from the cause to the effect or from the effect to the cause; cause to effect order is more common. Using this pattern you might state specific causal behaviors:

We can boycott the dining hall.
We can speak to the dieticians.
We can speak out against the food we are served.

From these, you could then state the conclusion or effect:

If we do all of this, we *can* be successful in getting our meal selections changed.

In contrast, using an effect-to-cause pattern, you might begin with the conclusion: The tax supporting increased aid for education did not pass. You might follow this effect with the specific causes:

There was a strong campaign against it.
People did not believe it would accomplish much.
Many people thought there were more important things to spend their money on.
People did not want to be bothered.

In this case, the pattern of organization moves from a description of a present condition, or effect, to an analysis of the causes that seem to have produced it.

Monroe motivated sequence

A popular and workable problem-solving pattern in persuasive speaking was developed by Professor Alan H. Monroe in *Principles and Types of Speech Communication*. He called his pattern the "motivated sequence";[1] it is useful for two principal reasons:

• It provides a clear and definite pattern to follow for getting from the definition and analysis of a problem to its solution.
• It follows the normal process of human reasoning—the way people normally think.

Although his full pattern of five steps is designed for a problem-solving speech, the pattern can be adapted to other speeches as well. Our concern here is with the problem-solving persuasive speech alone.

To use the full pattern in a problem-solving speech, you would follow these steps:

1. *Attention*—you call attention to the topic or situation.

2. *Need*—you explain the audience needs being addressed. How does this topic relate to the needs of my listeners?

3. *Satisfaction*—you explain how audience needs will be satisfied. How will my topic or proposal solve the needs (problems) presented in step 2?

4. *Visualization*—you show how the solution will work. Once the solution (satisfaction step) is implemented, what changes will result? How will things be improved and changed? (This is probably the most important step because of its power to persuade.)

5. *Action*—you explain the action listeners should take. What kind of action by listeners is necessary to bring about this change? What is needed or required?

If this five-step sequence is committed to memory, it can serve as a handy organizational tool for any problem-solving situation. Because all the stages are important, each step will be examined in detail, and an example of each will be cited from a speech by Katerina Brennan titled "Effective Speech Communication Habits Should Be Practiced by Everyone."[2] The endnotes cited within the quoted portions of her speech are from Katerina's outline.

Attention step. Often this is thought of as the most important time to gain listener attention, but because attention duration is short and comes in spurts, holding listener attention must be a concern of speakers throughout their speeches. Introductions cannot be the only time for gaining and holding listener attention.

In the attention step you should let listeners know about the topic. Why are you speaking about it? Why is it important? Why should listeners be concerned? You must call attention to the topic and to the occasion (if appropriate) to make certain listener attention is focused on your speech.

For effect—to draw the attention of her audience and make a point—Katerina began her speech like this:

> "Ahh...Uhmm...Okay! Like...drugs in America have really presented...ahh...like...Oh, wait! I know this!...Give me a second. Could I start over? The drugs...crap!...Oh..." This is a prime example of how you do not want to present yourself in front of an audience. It is unfair to listeners and to yourself. Getting up in front of people and presenting a speech is a difficult task to accomplish, but it is one that is very necessary. That is one of the reasons why we are taking this class. I hope to demonstrate in the following speech why it is so important for everyone to practice effective speech communication habits....

Need step. This step can draw from and capitalize on a successful attention step. Now that listener attention is focused on the topic, *why* does it require listener attention and concern now? Involve listeners in this. Not only must you demonstrate the significance and magnitude of the problem, you must also show dramatically and forcefully how it touches the lives of listeners. Here Katerina presents her need step. She divides it into four parts: (A) statement of the problem, (B) explanation of the problem, (C) proof that the problem exists, and (D) relationship of the problem to the audience.

Statement of the problem. *Webster's New World Dictionary* describes speech as the act of speaking; expression or communication of thoughts and feelings by spoken words. According to this definition, anyone could give a speech. What all of us need to learn is how to give an *effective* speech. An effective speech is one composed of a strong message, delivered by a self-confident, knowledgeable speaker with conviction, organized well, and bolstered by facts and strong language.[3]

Explanation of the problem. The importance of giving speeches can be seen throughout history. If we step into the past we can see that Columbus gave one. Before he went to Spain he was advised by navigational experts from Portugal and Spain to sail westward to reach the Far East. This would have had him going in the wrong direction. Fortunately, Columbus understood the art of persuasion, and he tailored his message to his audience.[4] He knew how to put together an effective presentation to get what he wanted—which is exactly what he did.

Giving speeches and presentations to audiences will soon be part of our everyday lives, especially if we will be going into careers of communications, advertising, or teaching. The experience of communicating your ideas, having them understood, and having listeners respond to you in a positive way is the point I wish to accomplish.[5] Speaking to an audience does not come naturally. If it did, we would not have to take such a course as this. It is a skill that must be learned. Finding a great topic may be easy to all of us in this class, but communicating it effectively to listeners is the issue.

Proof that the problem exists. Many students, as we all know, are not effective public speakers. We have all watched speakers fumble through their speeches. During the last round, I gave one very similar to the example I used at the beginning. Maybe it wasn't to that extreme, but I did say "ahh" and "uhm" every other word. Notice how I am trying to control that this time?

Relationship of the problem to audience. Why is giving great speeches so important? When we graduate, we will be out in the real world competing for jobs. Most of our careers will demand that we give effective speeches, brief announcements, and captivating presentations. It may be as simple as providing an introduction, thanking someone publicly, making a toast, or accepting a gift.[6]

Satisfaction step. This step relates directly to the need step because here you must offer the solutions that will satisfy the need just established. Because you have researched the problem and thereby command a thorough knowledge of it, you are in a position to recommend a workable solution. A simple statement of the conclusion is necessary, but that is not all that is needed. You must also address the various reservations listeners may have regarding the solution:

1. Does the solution treat the causes of the problem?
2. Will the solution be practical?
   a. Will it cost too much money?
   b. Will it take too much time?
   c. Will it create new or more difficult problems?
3. Will the solution be acceptable?

You need to be as specific as possible at this point, showing listeners directly and forthrightly how adopting your solution will satisfy their reservations, objections, and concerns. In her speech Katerina again divided her satisfaction step into parts: (A) plan of action, (B) explanation of the plan, and (C) countering arguments against the plan. Here is the way she worded it:

> Learning effective speech communication habits is the main goal. No one should leave college without a good idea of how to go about giving great speeches and experiencing them, too. Knowing how to give them and practicing them are how all of us can accomplish effective speaking. Practice will be done not only in the classroom but outside the classroom as well.
>
> A. *Plan of action.* Though IPC 102 may be a required course for some of you, it really leads you in the right direction for effective speaking. This cannot be denied! Only practicing will make us truly effective speech communicators. In her book, *Fearless and Flawless Public Speaking*, Mary-Ellen Drummond says, "Preparation and practice are crucial to dynamic and powerful speaking."[7]
>
> B. *Explanation of the plan.* Whether your speech objective is to inform, persuade, inspire, motivate, or entertain, an effective one is made up of several important factors. I will briefly mention ideas, organization, and delivery.
>
>   1. You need to have worthwhile ideas. They need to be significant for, relevant to, and interesting for your listeners. But you don't need a whole lot of ideas. "You will be more effective," says Christina Stuart in *How to Be an Effective Speaker*, "if you choose one or two points, develop them, present supporting evidence, choose relevant illustrations, and recap and summarize frequently."[8]
>   2. Another part of an effective speech is being well organized. Joan Detz, in *How to Write and Give a Speech*, says "No matter what your speech is about, you must limit, focus, and organize your material."[9]
>   3. The final part of an effective speech is delivery. The teacher and coach John Davies advised his students to remember three specific actions when speaking: "Stand up so you'll be seen. Speak up so you'll be heard. And then sit down so you'll be appreciated."[10] [Here Katerina discusses voice, eye contact, posture, and vocalized pauses, and she gives specific suggestions to her listeners.]

C. *Countering arguments against the plan.* Some of you may argue that you already have effective speech habits. This may be true. But there is always room for improvement, no matter how experienced you may be.

Visualization step. This step may require the most time and attention in a problem-solving speech. In this step you *demonstrate* how the solution you have outlined satisfies the need. This step provides listeners with a clear relationship between the satisfaction step, your solution, and the need step. Listeners must have a chance to *see* the solution working for them and in their lives. What will it mean to them if they adopt the solution and put it into effect?

The visualization step is precisely what it sounds like: You create a mental picture for listeners of how things will look or be if your solution is put into action. You can do this positively by showing the many benefits of adoption, or you can do it negatively by illustrating vividly the dire consequences that will occur if your solution is not adopted. You can even do both.

In her speech Katerina included the following visualization step. In this case the visualization step was not subdivided.

> All of us will be listening to more speeches than we give. Won't we all be better off listening to speakers who are prepared, organized, and effective? None of us want our time wasted. None of us want to be in the presence of speakers who talk more to themselves than to their audience. None of us want to hear speakers ramble away from their subject, forget their objective, ignore the setting, ignore the clock, and conclude their speech inconclusively.[11] Then why should we put up with any of this in the speeches we give? Just imagine how effective speaking can affect all of us as both speakers and listeners.

Action step. In this final step you call for action or change. You ask listeners to adopt your conclusion. The action step must be specific, telling listeners *how* to act. If your recommended action is not concrete and specific, listeners are unlikely to do anything.

When you design your action step, you need to answer the question, "What do you want individuals in your audience to do?" You cannot have them sign petitions unless you either *have* the petitions for them to sign or tell them where they can go to sign them. You cannot get them to vote unless they know where and how to register and to vote. They will not contribute money unless they know who to give it to and where and when this person will be available. You cannot ask them to read an article or book unless they know the author and title and where it can be found. You should give your listeners detailed cost and availability information: What stores have it? What is the library call number? Answer all questions, and be as specific as you can.

Katerina ended her speech with the following action step:

> I urge all of you to do more research and experiment on your own. Not only is the library full of information that can help you

become an incredible speech communicator, but I have brought with me some of the sources I referred to in this speech that can help you, too. Practicing to become an effective speech communicator is an important and valuable goal. I have provided you with reasons to practice; I have given you some helpful hints on how to become more effective; now let me leave you with a statement from Norman Cousins, who wrote this in the preface to Steve Allen's book called *How to Make a Speech:*

> The area in which a poor education shows up first is in self-expression, oral or written. It makes little difference how many university courses or degrees a person may own. If he [or she] cannot use words to move an idea from one point to another, his [or her] education is incomplete.[12]

Don't let your education be incomplete. The rest is up to you.

The Heart of the Matter

Most often, persuasion involves using all the available means at your disposal to move others to belief or action (as Aristotle contended), but at the core of persuasion is responsibility. As a persuasive speaker, you have an enormous responsibility. Quintilian said persuasion involves "the good man [person] speaking well." It is true, but what of those who are not "good" or who have not lived "good" lives? We can ask for "good," but we may not get "good." It may be too much to ask. What we *can* get, however, is responsibility. We can ask that speakers treat listeners fairly, with respect, and to remain honest. We can ask the speaker to treat listeners as the speaker would want to be treated as a listener. No, we can ask even more. Speakers should treat listeners better than they expect to be treated by other speakers. Let's move one step above what might be expected!

PERSUASION AND ETHICS

If all speakers considered the feelings of audience members, adapted their message to the audience's frame of reference, and worked toward mutual understanding and benefit, a section on persuasion and ethics would be unnecessary. Unfortunately, unethical persuasion does occur. *Ethics* are principles of conduct. If you keep the following three guidelines in mind, your persuasion will probably remain ethical.

Be informed. When you choose to speak about a particular topic, you must prepare yourself as thoroughly as possible. Only in this way can listeners get the information necessary to make reasoned choices. And only in this way are you treating your listeners with dignity and respect.

Be truthful. Lying, of course, is unethical. You must attempt to give your listeners the truth as best as you understand it. Truthfulness also means presenting the facts without exaggeration or distortion. Many people believe that exaggeration and selective omission are the same as lying.

Keep audience interests in mind. If audience members listen to a speech, or if they are asked to change their attitudes or behavior, it should be for their ultimate benefit. That does not mean you cannot speak out of personal interest, as long as it doesn't deny audience interests—such as promoting a product or idea that could harm listeners or that would bring them no benefit but would cost them money.

Listeners, however, also have an ethical responsibility: They must give you a full hearing. Laying aside their biases and prejudices, they should try to see things as you do. Listeners have an obligation to give you open, honest feedback. You have a right to expect active listeners.

SUMMARY

This chapter opened with a section about influencing attitudes. It discussed how to discover listener attitudes and how to persuade by using benefits, handicaps, and ego defense. The influence of attitude history on persuasive attempts was also explored.

The second section addressed how to assess your potential persuasive impact and keep your persuasion effort in its proper perspective. It is unrealistic to think that your persuasive speech can make major changes in listener attitudes, but you can have a significant effect.

Next, the three types of persuasive speeches—convincing, actuating, and stimulating—were described. Propositions of fact, value, and policy were described, as were the persuasive organizational patterns: inductive, deductive, causal, and the Monroe motivated sequence. Finally, three ethical guidelines were given: Speakers need to be informed, remain truthful, and keep audience interests in mind.

Chapter Questions

1. What do you need to consider when you try to influence others' attitudes?

2. What is the point of discovering listener attitudes?

3. How much impact do you think the average persuasive speaker can have? The average classroom speaker?

4. If you were giving a speech to encourage listeners to donate to a charity, which type of persuasive speech would you give? What kind would you use to convince your classmates that class length should be shortened?

5. Describe the differences between propositions of fact, value, and policy. Using the topic of parking on campus, frame a proposition of fact, one of value, and one of policy.

6. Discuss the differences between the four persuasive organizational patterns. If you were trying to convince listeners to boycott class in favor of attending a local political rally, which pattern would you use?

7. Who do you feel has the greatest responsibility for maintaining ethical standards in speaking? Why? Should it be this way?

8. If you had to teach someone about his or her ethical responsibility in persuasive speaking, what principles would you teach?

9. Critique Katerina Brennan's speech, "Effective Speech Communication Habits Should Be Practiced by Everyone." Include in your evaluation specific suggestions that Katerina could use to improve.

Further Reading

Erwin P. Bettinghaus and Michael J. Cody, *Persuasive Communication*, 5th ed. (New York: Holt, Rinehart and Winston, 1994).

This well-written, well-documented book for the serious student includes discussion of ethics, attitudes and beliefs, and structuring messages.

Charles U. Larson, *Persuasion: Reception and Responsibility*, 7th ed. (Belmont, CA: Wadsworth, 1995).

Larson provides a comprehensive look at persuasion in society with chapters on ethics, propaganda, advertising, campaigns, and the mass media. His focus is primarily on the receiver or consumer of persuasion.

Tom Rusk, *The Power of Ethical Persuasion: From Conflict to Partnership at Work and in Private Life* (New York: Viking, 1993).

Rusk focuses on ethical principles and how readers can apply them in life's most important negotiations. The book is an insightful, practical guide to ethical behavior and explains how to express your viewpoint effectively.

Endnotes

1. Bruce E. Gronbeck, Raymie E. McKerrow, Douglas Ehninger, and Alan H. Monroe, *Principles and Types of Speech Communication*, 12th ed. (New York: HarperCollins, 1994), Chapter 8, "Adapting the Speech Structure to Audiences: The Motivated Sequence," pp. 193–223.
2. Katerina Brennan, "Effective Speech Communication Habits Should Be Practiced by Everyone." Speech given at Bowling Green State University in the basic speech communication course (IPC 102), December 8, 1993. The speech is used here with Katerina's permission.
3. Henry Ehrlich, *Writing Effective Speeches* (New York: Paragon House, 1992), p. 202.
4. Patricia Ward Brash, "Beyond Giving a Speech," *Vital Speeches of the Day* 59 (November 15, 1993), p. 83.

5. Saundra Hybels and Richard L. Weaver II, *Communicating Effectively* (New York: McGraw-Hill, 1992), p. 337.

6. C. W. Wright, *Better Speeches for All Occasions* (New York: Crown, 1960), p. 14.

7. Mary-Ellen Drummond, *Fearless and Flawless Public Speaking with Power, Polish, and Pizazz* (San Diego: Pfeiffer, 1993), p. 123.

8. Christina Stuart, *How to Be an Effective Speaker: The Essential Guide to Making the Most of Your Communication Skills* (Chicago: NTC, 1989 [1993 printing]), p. 22.

9. Joan Detz, *How to Write and Give a Speech* (New York: St. Martin's, 1992), p. 40.

10. As cited in Roger E. Axtell, *Do's and Taboos of Public Speaking: How to Get Those Butterflies Flying in Formation* (New York: Wiley, 1992), p. 66.

11. Ed Wohlmuth, *The Overnight Guide to Public Speaking* (New York: Signet, 1990), pp. 13–15.

12. Steve Allen, *How to Make a Speech* (New York: McGraw-Hill, 1986), p. xiii.

Words in Action: Video Study

Chapters 1 through 12 discussed the essential elements of any type of speech, and Chapter 14 discusses considerations specific to persuasive speaking. After watching the accompanying video of a student's persuasive speech, critique the speech in detail. Considering the many elements that make up a speech, which aspects of this speech are effective? Which are ineffective?

Speeches for Special Occasions

After reading this chapter you will be able to:

- communicate with others
- talk on the telephone confidently and courteously
- interview successfully
- participate effectively in small groups
- present toasts and introductory, acceptance, keynote, commencement, inaugural, farewell, and eulogy speeches
- appear comfortable, relaxed, and in control before a television camera

After Caroline graduated from college with a major in journalism, she went to work as part of a small public relations team for a furniture manufacturing firm. Her job included facilitating focus groups on furniture designs and aesthetics, and Caroline was able to use all her speech communication training to plan, organize, conduct, and evaluate these focus groups.

To help put himself through college, William worked for a telemarketing firm, a company subcontracted by other firms interested in determining customer satisfaction with products already purchased, such as automobiles and large appliances. Based on specific survey questions, William conducted brief telephone interviews. Because of his success rate, largely attributed to effective communication skills, William was quickly promoted to supervisor of his section, a job that included training new employees to do what he did so well.

Flavio had a business degree, and his first job out of college was working as a city employee for a rural town interested in enhancing its image and attracting more tourists. He worked one-on-one with local government and business representatives. He brought people who had common interests together into small groups such as the Kiwanis, Rotary, and the American Legion. And he made numerous presentations before local organizations, not just to introduce himself and his plans but also to solicit financial support.

Caroline, William, and Flavio found themselves in situations that required effective communication skills. Their applications were not easily categorized as informative or persuasive, and often they depended on skills beyond these two areas: talking one-on-one with others, using the telephone, organizing and leading groups, and giving a variety of speeches. In many cases they simply had to be prepared for any type of communication situation that arose.

This chapter provides tips about speaking in a variety of contexts. Because our lives are likely to introduce us to a wide array of potential applications of our communication skills, this chapter offers brief and applied suggestions for many of these contexts.

The chapters before this one have offered knowledge foundations; this chapter offers specifics to guide communication skills. Situations and possibilities are emphasized; the only cautions are these:

1. All situations are different; thus, some suggestions are likely to work better than others.

2. All of us will apply the suggestions and guidelines differently. No two applications are likely to be the same. All of us have different knowledge and abilities; thus, our successes are likely to differ as well.

3. Because our listeners are likely to have different backgrounds, how they accept or respond to the information we share is likely to vary.

This chapter will help you begin to think specifically about the contexts you are likely to face as a communicator. The suggestions will start you thinking and motivate you to do your best. You will always benefit when you approach new situations with a well-thought-out plan—even though the plan may change as you discover more about the situations.

Think of this chapter as similar to the ancient story of stone soup.

Even though the villagers thought that all they had were a few pebbles for soup to feed the citizens, when each was able to add just one ingredient to the boiling mixture, a delicious and complete soup was produced. When you tap into your vast potential, you will find that you possess all the ingredients for success.

In this chapter, the following contexts are examined: interpersonal (one person to another person); small group (groups of from four individuals to 15 or 20 members); public speaking (groups larger than 15 or 20); and television (general remarks concerning communication via television or video).

The Heart of the Matter

All communication begins with attentiveness to others. Effective communication is listener-centered, not self-centered. Others do not have to agree with you or support your ideas. To win cooperation, you need to offer something of value. And beginning with respect for and consideration of others will help in every communication context. A caring attitude will show your decency and sense of fairness. You will appear genuine, and this will increase your appeal to others and the likelihood that your communication with them will be successful in any context.

THE INTERPERSONAL CONTEXT

The kind of interpersonal communication discussed here is *purposive*—that is, it seeks to accomplish goals. Remember, for example, how much interpersonal communication Flavio found was involved in his job of increasing visibility and tourism for his city. Flavio used communication to show others that his goals and theirs were compatible. Attention to goals is essential for purposive interpersonal communication. Such communication is likely to create a compatible, positive friendship or working relationship because everyone involved will be rewarded by it. The accompanying box outlines the basic components of good interpersonal communication.

Some interpersonal techniques are distractions to effectiveness; these might be referred to as *barriers*. If you talk compulsively, if you have unpleasant vocal habits such as saying "uh," "Y'know," or "like, I mean," if you are perceived as self-centered, or if you are excessively argumentative, you may decrease your effectiveness. Enlist the help of a friend or teacher to assist you in ridding yourself of distracting elements; this effort will contribute to your success.

Talking on the telephone

William's job as a telemarketer was directly related to telephone effectiveness; Carolyn had to call focus group members to set up meeting times; and Flavio used the telephone to make contacts and to set up presentations and

The Components of Effective Interpersonal Performance

1. Have clearly defined goals.
2. Choose a time and place to meet where distractions will be minimal.
3. Listen carefully and provide feedback to show that you are actively observing the other person(s) and processing information.
4. Sensitively monitor the other person's feelings so that you can respond in a positive, concerned manner.
5. Always be courteous during conversations.
6. Be careful not to talk too much. Most people appreciate equality in the give-and-take of conversations.
7. Interpret the information you receive. Seek out necessary additional information for clarity and completeness or to resolve confusion.
8. Strive to appeal to others' needs, wants, and values. Most people desire safety, rewards to self-esteem, amusement, useful knowledge, and ways to advance toward personal goals; thus, when you know what they need, want, or value, you will be able to appeal specifically and directly.
9. Run regular conversation checks to make certain that both you and your listener(s) are processing information accurately. "Is that what you mean?" "Is that correct?" "Is that the way you understand it?" might be some examples of conversation checks.
10. Make plans for future contact if that is appropriate.

group meetings. Most of us use the telephone as a necessary and active part of our jobs. You may not realize the relationship between your telephone manners and your social acceptance and success. The more effective we are in communicating on the telephone, the more we can accomplish because of correct information being shared and proper directions being given.

Many of the interpersonal guidelines already mentioned apply to telephone usage as well because talking on the telephone is clearly a specific interpersonal context. Here are more specialized guidelines specific to helping you increase your telephone effectiveness.

1. Create a favorable impression on your listener. Besides a pleasant voice, use animation and enthusiasm. Act interested and involved in your listener and the conversation. How many telephone salespeople lose sales because of a bored, disinterested, or rehearsed-sounding presentation?
2. Always be polite.
3. Ask for others by their first and last names. Be sure to give your first and last names as well.
4. Check to make certain others have the time and are in the mood to talk with you.
5. Do not waste the time of others with idle talk. Public speakers are often advised to be brief, be to the point, and be seated, and similar advice should be given to those who talk on the telephone. Have a clear plan, follow the plan, and end the conversation when the plan has been completed.
6. If you do not have time to talk as long as others would like, be courteous in ending your call. You could say, when they pause for a breath of air, "Forgive me, Lou, I have a meeting in five minutes, and I must get my papers together."

The interview

Many of you will take part in an employment interview to secure a job. Periodically, you may have an appraisal interview where your progress is assessed. You may find it necessary to conduct information acquisition interviews to find data that will help you on your job, allow you to be fully informed about a project you are undertaking, or help you prepare for a presentation.

There are many skills related to effective interviewing, and many books cover the topic accurately and completely. If interviewing will be a substantial or important part of your job, reading a book on interviewing is highly recommended. Here are some general skills that apply to most kinds of interviews:

1. Prepare thoroughly. Know your information. Practice.
2. Orient the other person. Introduce yourself.
3. Communicate skillfully. Relax and smile. Maintain eye contact. Speak loudly enough. Avoid "you know," "like," "okay," and other unnecessary expressions.
4. Demonstrate a positive attitude. Show interest. Take the interview seriously.
5. Use effective questions and probes. Know them so you don't have to read them.
6. Stick to the topic.
7. Do not rely too heavily on notes and written questions.
8. Avoid looking at your watch.
9. Be businesslike.
10. Bring the interview to a natural close by summarizing, thanking the other person, and expressing hopes for future contact.

While many of the suggestions apply to both interviewer and interviewee, the following are intended for interviewers alone. When you are the interviewer, here are some specific guidelines that will help you:

1. Open the interview by establishing rapport. Maintain a friendly, warm, interpersonal atmosphere.
2. Make the interviewee feel comfortable.
3. Motivate the interviewee by indicating the importance and the relevance of the interview.
4. Structure the interview. Have a clear pattern in mind.
5. Be supportive of the interviewee even if things do not go as well as he or she might like.
6. Know your information and questions well.
7. Be alert and assertive as well as sensitive and responsive.
8. Close the interview by summarizing the main points.
9. Strive to leave the interviewee with a positive final impression.

There are important suggestions and guidelines for interviewees also:

1. Watch your appearance. Dress neatly and look healthy. Try to do nothing that will distract from your credibility. Strive to come across as someone who is well cared for.
2. Demonstrate enthusiasm.
3. Be prompt, attentive, and responsible.
4. Reveal positive personality attributes such as pleasantness, tact, animation, and a good outlook on life.
5. Demonstrate a good vocabulary, and use good grammar, diction, and pronunciation.
6. Contribute significantly to the overall quality of the interview.
7. Listen carefully to the interviewer's questions.
8. Keep to the subject being discussed. Try to avoid distractions.
9. Be brief and to the point. Avoid extensive elaboration of ideas unless specifically asked.
10. State your personal ideas when appropriate and when you are asked.

THE SMALL GROUP CONTEXT

Although you may not be asked to organize and conduct focus groups as Caroline was for her furniture manufacturing firm in the opening example of this chapter, it is likely that you will have to perform in a variety of group situations. To be a better communicator in the context of a small group, it will be helpful if you can talk, listen, and respond to other group members effectively. When this is not done, group meetings can degenerate into unpleasant, unproductive experiences.

Whether you are a group leader or a member, one key skill is preparation. The more information you have ready, the more control and power you have. If you are to lead a discussion, the following suggestions and guidelines may help you:

1. Introduce the topic.
2. Show the importance of the topic to the group.
3. Motivate group members to participate.
4. Make the topic interesting to group members.
5. Ask interesting questions for group members to discuss.
6. Summarize and synthesize group comments.
7. Provide concluding remarks that reemphasize the importance of the topic to the group.
8. Control the discussion and structure it clearly so that members can follow it.
9. Be prepared to evaluate and assess the results of the discussion.
10. Thank group members for participating.

Different skills are important for group participants. The likelihood that you will be a member of a group at some point in your life is strong, especially because a democracy is built upon its groups. Your goal in a small group is to be an effective communicator; thus, any or all of the following skills will be helpful in projecting positive credibility to others:

1. Ask questions. Do not sit by and say nothing.
2. Propose new ideas, activities, and procedures where appropriate.
3. Share your knowledge and expertise when you can. Cite examples and illustrations when needed.
4. Speak up when you feel strongly about something, but do not dominate the conversation. Keep your comments brief and to the point.
5. Try to synthesize ideas by drawing together the comments of other participants.
6. Understand the goals of the group, and try to keep the discussion moving toward them.
7. Question the practicality and logic of what is happening when appropriate. Try to keep everything in proper perspective.
8. Encourage fellow group members to do well. Be sensitive and responsive to their efforts.
9. Serve as a mediator and peacemaker when necessary. Although constructive conflict is often helpful, ill feelings are not.
10. Try to compromise on issues, or try to work out compromises when appropriate.
11. Encourage other group members to participate, and give everyone a fair chance to speak.
12. Encourage evaluation and assessment of the group's work.

Think of your small group communication as broken conversation rather than speech making. The group participants share bits and pieces of information rather than large chunks in unbroken chains. But you can apply many of the same public speaking skills to make your presentations—even short ones—effective. For example, effective listening is crucial. You must know who your audience is. Originality and focus will give your ideas sharpness and distinction. Your credibility will depend on both your information and your presentation. Careful language choices will help control the impression you make. And remember the need for animation, enthusiasm, and motivation as you deliver your ideas.

THE PUBLIC SPEAKING CONTEXT

Many public speaking contexts go beyond mere informative and persuasive speaking. For example, special-occasion speeches often are part information and part persuasion. Here are guidelines for giving toasts, introductions, acceptance speeches, keynote speeches, presentation speeches, inaugural addresses, farewell speeches, and eulogies.

Toasts

Toasts are given at weddings, at luncheons and dinners, and at many other special ceremonies. I include a section on toasts because I looked for information to help prepare me for my daughters' weddings, and I found nothing. Toasts have a number of characteristics in common:

1. They are upbeat and positive.
2. They acknowledge the recipient or the occasion.
3. They add an example or illustration to show the toaster's relationship to the toastee, or the relationship of the toaster to the occasion.
4. They are brief.

Because spontaneous remarks often are unorganized and hard to follow, when I offer toasts I prepare my remarks completely. I memorize my main points, but I allow the specific words to come to me as I express myself in front of the audience. In the case of each of my daughters' weddings, I spoke of my relationship to my daughter, I acknowledged the change that their marriage initiated, I welcomed the groom's family members into our family, and I gave them brief advice and counsel for a long and happy life.

A business toast might be as simple as "To the future health and prosperity of this organization and its members."

Introductions

These speeches, designed to introduce a speaker to an audience, are delivered by someone besides the person who is being introduced—often the program planner, the president of the organization, or a friend of the speaker. The introduction speech sets the stage for the main speaker.

The main purposes of the introduction speech are to gain audience attention and arouse interest in the speaker. The introduction speech is mainly an informative speech, and it follows the patterns established for such speeches. However, instead of examining a topic and its issues, it focuses on the speaker and what the speaker will talk about. In most situations listeners already know why they have gathered, and they know that a speech is forthcoming. Here are some guidelines for preparing an introductory speech:

1. Alert listeners to the significance of the speech, if this is not already known.
2. Establish the speaker's credibility. What are the speaker's accomplishments that he or she could not mention with modesty? Listeners are likely to be wondering what it is about this speaker that has earned the right (or privilege) to speak about this topic.
3. Connect the speaker to the topic and to the audience. Why should this audience listen to this speaker about this topic? Why is the speaker especially appropriate? Answers to these questions will arouse listeners' interest in the speaker.
4. Maintain consistency between the introduction speech and the main speech. A serious speech requires a serious introduction; a humorous or light speech can have an amusing introduction.

Watch out for easily avoided pitfalls: Do not, for example, cover the speaker's topic. If you think your material may duplicate something the speaker plans to say, check with the speaker first. Also, provide a reasonable introduction. Don't oversell either the speaker or the topic, which can leave listeners with an impression that is impossible for the main speaker to live up to. Finally, be brief. Often speakers provide their introducers with information or even a prepared introduction. For a speech of 15 to 20 minutes, a one- to two-minute introduction is appropriate; for a lengthier speech, the introduction can be a bit longer. Introducers need to remember, however, that listeners have come to hear the main speaker, not the introduction.

Keynote speeches

Conventions, conferences, and meetings often begin with a speech intended to highlight the importance of group deliberations. These addresses should make listeners feel that their presence is important and the meeting is worthwhile. The most well-known examples of keynote speeches are those that begin the presidential nominating conventions of the Democratic and Republican parties every four years. Often they are characterized by vivid language, emotional appeals, powerful examples, and an inspirational tone.

Even though most keynote speeches are given in less dramatic circumstances, their purpose should be the same:

1. Refer to the occasion and the special nature of the people present.
2. Choose your language carefully with the purpose of creating mental pictures.
3. Motivate listeners to participate, act, or believe in a specific manner.
4. Try to find examples and illustrations that will rivet attention to your main purpose.
5. Inspire enthusiasm.

Presentation speeches

Most organizations have ceremonies at which those in the organization who deserve awards are presented them. A presentation speech pays tribute to the man or woman being honored and has three functions:

1. Clarify the nature of the award or situation (including background and history if appropriate).
2. Mention the qualities that the award is intended to honor.
3. Discuss the qualities of the person chosen that make this award appropriate in this instance.

Acceptance speeches

Many organizations present awards, honors, or gifts to members. Oscar, Emmy, and Grammy award ceremonies are among the most public examples. Organizations honor those people who represent or symbolize the values of members of the group.

If you are selected to be honored, your acceptance speech should be dictated by audience expectations. Audience expectations can be determined by precedent—what has occurred previously—or simply by asking several people what the expectations are. There are a number of important guidelines for most acceptance speeches:

1. Be appreciative: "I am deeply honored" or "This is one of the happiest moments of my life."

2. Acknowledge others who helped. Be humble: "I couldn't have accomplished this without the help of a lot of people."

3. Be dedicated: "Ever since I first heard about this organization, I wanted to make it the focus of my time and energy." Put the award into personal perspective for your listeners—what it means to you now and will mean in the future.

4. Project personal qualities (those qualities the award is designed to honor): "This award means a great deal to me, and I will try to live up to the spirit, dedication, and honor that this award has come to symbolize." Anything you can say that will allow listeners personal insight into your character will be appreciated.

5. Express thanks. Be sure to thank the people responsible for sponsoring and awarding you the award. These may be students of an organization, fellow teammates, board members, or other special people.

Avoid being trite, vacuous, or inane. Platitudes and clichés often fill speeches of acceptance. Although you should keep your speech brief, you should try to reveal your personality, be sincere, and offer a creative approach. Brevity, however, is a key.

Inaugural addresses

When organizations elect new leadership, and when the new group president or chairperson assumes his or her office, often that new leader presents an inaugural address. This address is designed to symbolize the transfer of leadership.

The best-known inaugural addresses occur every four years at the presidential level. When an incoming or reelected president of the United States is sworn in, the accompanying events are a study in pageantry, formality, and organization.

Most inaugural addresses have specific guidelines:

1. Note the passage of leadership.
2. Praise past group values and achievements.
3. Identify the values of your administration.
4. Set the goals and challenges you perceive for the future.
5. Motivate listeners to commit themselves to these values as well—for their purposes, needs, and interests.

When you present an effective inaugural address, you will convince your audience of their wisdom in selecting you as their leader. You will rekindle their commitment to the values and goals of the organization, and you will calm any fears regarding this transfer of leadership; your goal will be to try to make this transition a calm and steady period of continued progress and stability—if these latter comments or issues are appropriate.

Inaugural speakers need to recognize that change is frightening for most people, and because they represent change, they need to calm any unwarranted fears or at least offer help and advice to deal with it.

Farewell speeches

In a highly mobile society the likelihood of having to leave a community with which you have come to identify is fairly good. The consequences of a mobile society include frequent goodbyes. Luncheons, receptions, and formal public ceremonies are arranged to accomplish these, and departing members are expected to give a farewell speech.

Although farewell speeches vary in their emotional flavor, seriousness, and length, most have several characteristics in common:

1. Comment on the quality of the experience shared with this group.
2. Try to recognize, by name, any individuals who have directly contributed to the high quality of your past experiences.
3. Describe the emotions experienced as you leave the group.
4. If possible, offer any hopes for future contact or influence.

The farewell speech permits speakers to leave some small portion of themselves behind. For this reason, it should allow your personality to shine through. Because your departure is the reason the ceremony is being given, you need to choose your words wisely.

Eulogies

Eulogies pay tribute to the lives of individuals and are frequently part of memorial services. By virtue of your friendship or association with someone, you may be asked to prepare a eulogy. When giving a eulogy, you can follow a fairly prescribed pattern:

1. Mourn the passing of the person being honored.
2. Provide brief glimpses (from examples or anecdotes) into the life of this person.
3. Find in the life of the departed values or lessons that can give strength and courage to those who remain.

When the eulogy is part of a funeral service, sensitivity must be revealed to the grief being experienced by those who knew and loved the deceased. This is not an occasion for humor or sarcasm. Extreme care, utter respect, and proper decorum must be exhibited.

Even when a eulogy is designed to praise the living, a similar pattern can be followed:

1. Praise the person.
2. Provide examples or anecdotes to offer a clear mental picture of the person in action.
3. Reveal the values or lessons to be learned from this person's life. Advise your listeners to use the person's life or experience as a model.

THE TELEVISION/VIDEOTAPE CONTEXT

Many of you will have the opportunity to present your ideas via television or on videotape. The more preparation you can do beforehand, the less likely the situation will terrify you. The lights, cameras, microphones, people involved, and even the exact timing that is required can have a jolting effect on those who are not prepared. If asked to appear before a television or video camera, consider these tips:

1. Watch what you wear. Men are advised to wear a shirt with some color. Women should wear something with both color and design. Do not wear black or white; these colors are not picked up well by the camera.

2. Avoid wearing glasses because they tend to reflect light. However, some are specially treated to not reflect light. Contact lenses are recommended, or go without your glasses temporarily.

3. Check yourself in a monitor before your appearance for unbecoming makeup, poorly arranged hair, or unflattering shadows. It pays to protect your image before appearing publicly. The camera picks up small details.

4. Be alert and attentive. Try to sit straight. Slumping on television looks like poor posture. If you are standing, remember to stand up straight.

5. Try to talk to the camera with the red light as if it were a person. Include it in your conversation just as you would another person.

6. Avoid reading your remarks. Instead, speak with your viewers eye-to-eye for greatest effectiveness. If you use a TelePrompTer™, try to speak naturally and comfortably so that it doesn't appear that you are reading.

7. Avoid looking at people off camera when the camera is on you. Try to pick up signals from the technical staff without revealing that you have received the signals.

8. Be natural, comfortable, and relaxed. Smile!

SUMMARY

My goal in this chapter has been to offer suggestions and guidelines to assist you when you have to apply your communication skills in specialized contexts. First, I suggest that being other-oriented and always informed are ways in which you can prepare yourself for any context. Interpersonal context guidelines were presented for interpersonal performance, talking on the telephone, and interviewing. For the small group context I offered guidelines for leaders and members of small groups. In the public speaking context I discussed a variety of different speeches: toasts, introductions, keynote addresses, presentations, acceptances, inaugural addresses, farewells, and eulogies. Television context guidelines were presented for appearing before the television or video camera.

If I were to offer overall guidelines for all occasions, I would suggest brevity first. Most listeners appreciate speakers who are brief. Second, strive to remain consistent with the occasion and listener expectations. This will both show respect and heighten your credibility. Third, whenever possible, try to connect with or involve your listeners in order to hold attention and arouse interest. Finally, remain humble, relaxed, comfortable, and in control. This, too, will heighten your credibility, and it will demonstrate your respect for yourself and your listeners. Strive to be yourself.

Chapter Questions

1. What situations are you likely to encounter where effective interpersonal communication skills will help you succeed?

2. If you were to assess your current communication skills, in what areas discussed in this chapter are you likely to need the most growth and development? In what areas do you feel your current skills are strong and effective?

3. If you were to make suggestions to friends about the most necessary skills for effective communication in any context, what would you suggest?

4. Think about having a public relations job for a large multinational firm. What are likely to be the different contexts in which you will need effective communication skills?

Further Reading

James E. Sayer and Lilburn P. Hoehn, *Interviewing: Skills and Applications* (Scottsdale, AZ: Gorsuch Scarisbrick, 1994).

> This thorough and well-written textbook covers interviewing skills in a variety of contexts. Numerous examples and suggestions guide readers toward effectiveness and success.

Richard L. Weaver II, *Understanding Interpersonal Communication*, 7th ed. (New York: HarperCollins, 1996).

> The value of this textbook is in its strong skills orientation. Each chapter ends with a section that provides suggestions and guidelines for skill development. Some of the areas include self-disclosure, listening, interpersonal persuasion, sharing feelings, assertiveness, conflict management, friendship, and intimacy.

John K. Brilhart and Gloria J. Galanes, *Effective Group Discussion*, 8th ed. (Dubuque, IA: Wm. C. Brown, 1995).

> This thorough examination of small groups offers readers a wide variety of skills to help them succeed in all group situations they may encounter. This is a well-written textbook full of examples and suggestions.

Appendix

SUGGESTED TOPICS FOR SPEECHES

The topics listed here are broad. Most will require considerable work to narrow, focus, and then adapt the topic to a specific audience. They are designed to spark interest—to get speakers started in their quest for the appropriate topic.

abortion
abortion pill
acne
addiction
adoption
adult entertainment
advertising
aggressiveness
AIDS
alcohol
alcoholism
animal experimentation
anorexia nervosa
apathy
art
arts education
assertiveness
assertiveness techniques
assisted suicide
astrology
athletic participation
athletic programs
attitude
beer
big business
biorhythms
birth order
blood donation
books
broadcasting
business
caffeine
caffeine addiction
cancer
capital punishment
censorship
centralized health care

cheating
child abuse
child care
child care providers
child support
classics
coffee
college sports
common sense
competition
compulsive gambling
condoms
corporal punishment
cost of living
coupons
courtesy
court system
CPR
credit
credit cards
cults
dangerous toys
date rape
daytime television
death
death penalty
decision making
defeating cancer
deforestation
Democrat
diabetes
dialects
dietary supplements
dieting
direct marketing
discrimination
disease

domestic violence
dreams
dress for success
drugs
eating disorders
eating healthfully
education
educational decay
elderly
elderly care
elderly couples
elderly drivers
electoral college
eliminate tenure
emergency rooms
emotions
empathy
endangered species
entrepreneurs
ethanol
ethics
euthanasia
exercise
fads
failure
fantasy
fat
FBI
films
financial aid
fishing
foreign language
foster care
foster parents
fountain of youth
free speech
freedom

gambling
gambling legislation
gangs
gender
gender equity
general education
   requirements
genes
genetic screening
getting involved
"good" music
GOP
government
government control
government waste
greed
Greek life
gun control
guns
habits
hazing
health
health care
health care providers
healthy students
hemophilia
highway speeds
homelessness
homophobia
homosexuality
hope
hunting
hype
hypnosis
immigration
income tax
independence

independent thinking
information
    superhighway
initiation rites
insurance
insurance fraud
internet
investment
investment
    opportunities
IRS
jobs
junk mail
leaders
literacy
living together
living wills
lotteries
love
mainstreaming
manners/etiquette
marijuana legalization
marriage
martial arts
materialism
media
media influence
media responsibility
medical ethics
medical insurance
medical malpractice
medicine
meditation
mental retardation
metaphors
migraine headaches
military service
modern witchcraft
money
money management
movies

multiculturalism
music
NAACP
NRA
nutrition
organ donation
overcoming failure
overpopulation
ozone depletion
part-time work
patriotism
performance
performing
persuasion
phenomenology
plagiarism
Planned Parenthood
politically correct
politics
pollution
pornography
positive thinking
power
prayer
pregnancy
premarital sex
procrastination
profanity
professional sports
propaganda
prostitution
Prozac
psychoanalysis
psychological
    counseling
public relations
Puritan work ethic
race
racial differences
racism
rain

rain forests
rape
recycling
relationships
religion
responsibility
romance
rumors
running your own
    business
safe sex
safety
second-class citizenship
serials
sex
sex education
sex in the movies/
    television
sexual diseases
sexual harassment
sexual permissiveness
shoplifting
shyness
siblings
single-parent
    households
slang
sleep
sleep deprivation
sleep disorders
sports
stars
staying healthy
steroids
stock exchange
stress
stress management
student government
study skills
success
suicide

suing
suits
superstitions
talent
tanning
tattooing
taxes
telephone scams
television
television violence
tenant rights
tenure
therapy
time management
trust
twins
underachievement
unemployment
using coupons
vacations
virtue
virus
virus control
vitamins
vitamin usage
voluntary organizations
volunteers
voting
voting rights
waste disposal
water
water pollution
welfare
welfare fraud
welfare system
welfare system reform
white-collar crime
white-collar jobs
witches
worship
zebra mussels

Index